RSNA

TH-
T

DISCOVERY

TURNING POINT SERIES

WITH-OUT DISCOVERY

A Native Response to Columbus

Edited by

Ray Gonzalez

Broken Moon Press · Seattle

The essays in this collection appear by special permission of the authors
and of the publishers of the following publications. Some of the essays were
written especially for this book. Others first appeared in periodicals,
anthologies, or books; to their editors and publishers, thanks are due.

"For Some, It's a Time of Mourning" by Wendy Rose first appeared in
The New World, Spring 1990, No.1 (Smithsonian Institution). "Some Thoughts
as We Approach the Five Hundredth Anniversary of the Discovery of the
Americas" by Victor Hernández Cruz first appeared in *Red Beans* (Coffee
House Press, 1991). "The New World Man" by Rudolfo Anaya first appeared
in *Before Columbus Review: A Quarterly Review of Multicultural Literature*,
Fall–Winter 1989, Volume 1, Nos. 2 & 3 (Before Columbus Foundation). "The
Columbus Quincentennial Is Nothing to Celebrate" by Robert Allen Warrior
first appeared in *Sojourners*, January 1991. "What 1992 Means to American
Indians" by José Barreiro first appeared in *Native Nations*, Volume 1, No. 3,
March–April 1991 (Solidarity Foundation). "Reclaiming Our Heritages"
by Carlos Muñoz, Jr., first appeared in *Crossroads: Contemporary Political
Analysis and Left Dialogue*, May 1991, No. 10 (Institute for Social & Economic
Studies). "We Have No Reason to Celebrate an Invasion" by Suzan Shown
Harjo and Barbara Miner first appeared in *Rethinking Columbus*, Fall 1991,
No. 1. "Moccasin Games: Christopher Columbus on Talk Radio" by Gerald
Vizenor first appeared in *Caliban*, No. 9. "An Open Letter to Chicanas: The
Power and Politics of Origin" by Inés Hernandez first appeared in *Changing
Our Power: An Introduction to Women's Studies* (Kendall-Hunt, 1991).
"Without Discovery" by Ray Gonzalez first appeared in *Blue Mesa Review*,
Spring 1992, No. 4.

Printed in the United States of America.

ISBN 0-913089-31-1
Library of Congress Catalog Card Number: 92-72435

Cover image, "Whitehouse Ruins," copyright © 1972 by Terry Eiler.
Used by permission of the photographer.

Text preparation: Bonnie Mackay
Copy editors: Cathy A. Johnson
                   and Lesley Link
Proofreader: Cathy A. Johnson

Broken Moon Press
Post Office Box 24585
Seattle, Washington 98124-0585 USA

PART ONE

PART TWO

PART THREE

PART FOUR

PART FIVE

Without Discovery: A Native Response to Columbus is a wonderful collection of essays, stories, poetry, and reflections on the meanings of history, race and culture, life and conflict and survival, the struggle for identity, for truth and meaning, the struggle for a rich and fulfilled life. There is much anger here, a lot of understanding, a powerful ebb and flow of emotion, pride, curiosity. Many voices speak with love of the investigation of origins: Victor Hernández Cruz in Puerto Rico; Rudolfo Anaya in Albuquerque, New Mexico; Ray Gonzalez in El Paso. Benjamin Alire Sáenz's essay on being a Chicano poet is a beautiful testimonial, not only to his own roots, but also to the magic of being a writer and giving meaning and power to all of us. Diane Glancy's epic "Sugar Woman" poem is a fiercely energetic disquisition on history, genocide, survival. Alicia Gaspar de Alba's story of a Mexican slave girl is a heartbreaking chronicle of despair and extraordinary courage in the face of oppression. Many voices are represented, and there is no single clichéd version of Columbus or his impact on the Americas. Linda Hogan's clear, quiet essay about post-Columbian madness ends as a powerful statement that we are all unified in history, responsible for the future; it is impossible for that responsibility to be separate. Suzan Shown Harjo's brief statement on the teaching of history ought to be required reading in all elementary classes in America today.

There is much pain in these reflections by indigenous, mixed-blood, complex, and very rich writers; there is also a lot of hope, the uplifting courage of beautiful survivors, and a message that, ultimately, is universal, and applies to all of us. In the end, we all have similar origins. Certainly, we are all going to share the same future, and probably more equally than ever before. The voices in this collection, so rich in lore and history, will help to show the way.

This is a special and important anthology of radical, and loving, and compassionate writers, speaking from the heart.

—John Nichols

Without Discovery: A Native Response to Columbus gathers Chicano, Puerto Rican, and Native American writers who have written about the impact of the five hundredth anniversary of Christopher Columbus's voyage to the Americas.

As poets, fiction writers, essayists, and political activists, their voices have been heard before, but what they offer in this collection is a response to a time in our history when writers of all cultures are reflecting on historical events that shaped the way each of them matured as artists. These individuals share their insight on the collective artistic and political development of their people, a clash of American cultures familiar to many of us, but also a personal history which takes greater significance during the Quincentennial focus of 1992.

Asking writers for their points of view during a time when Columbus is being reevaluated, attacked, or defended and exploited in the media, gives us a different vision of past and present history.

These writers carry the historical weight of racism and genocide through their art, but go beyond familiar calls for justice to show how literary merit is one measure of triumphant cultures. Listening to their voices reveals how writers must be placed alongside historians when it comes to fully understanding how the "Old World" changed the "New World" forever.

Chicanos, Puerto Ricans, and Native Americans reflect on five hundred years of history and will be heard, not because they wish to change history, or cry that we have all been oppressed, but because the story of the Americas is too complex for official history books to record. This history has been too bloody for parades on October 12 to carry every flag or tribal banner that has fallen over five centuries. Even revisionist historians cannot gather all the tales, myths, and tragedies that followed the conquest of the western hemisphere.

Blasting Columbus's past legacy as a "discoverer" is not enough. Asking countries like Spain and the United States to acknowledge the native point of view will not turn things around.

It is too late for that.

Five hundred years have passed, and these writers know it. Five hundred years of native and foreign languages have already created voices of mixed cultures, the true sound of the Americas, as its artists and writers mark history with honest visions of what it means to be citizens of the Americas, not American citizens.

Native writers can speak about their own families, customs, and political necessities without relying on what they were taught in school. Too much has happened in contemporary America in the last thirty years for us not to know native people are going to react differently as they look back at 1492, and ponder what that means in 1992. Official versions about the glory of the *Niña, Pinta*, and *Santa María* we got in the fifth grade have been out-of-print for a long time.

What native writers have to say in this book resonates with the political and social progress of their cultures, but is also a diverse meditation on what has lain hidden under the mainstream version of events.

Contributors to *Without Discovery* realize this is a time of great political and literary power. As native writer Vine Deloria, Jr., says, "The celebration of the Quincentennial contains the potential for great reconciliation or immense misunderstanding."

These writings express many points of view, while attempting to reach as many listeners as possible to show that understanding is the goal of their words, the aim of giving this much time to the year 1492 and its consequences. By speaking out, even through anger, these writers move toward their own kind of reconciliation, creating a stage where American history is transformed into native history— personal experiences, grief, and the determination to preserve traditional values influenced by the path set when Europeans conquered the Americas. These writers will be heard because a look at the past five hundred years means more Americans will have a say on the next five hundred.

Native writers do not have the exclusive right to speak about the impact of Columbus, but by the end of 1992, after the media overkill has died down, there will be more to think about, because these pieces come from writers who have been speaking for a long time. Their messages are going forth during a time of opportunity, which means their significance and impact will be greater. There will be more issues to debate at the end of this long-awaited anniversary than most people expect.

Without Discovery can serve as one starting point in a year when millions of people want time and space to be heard, but this book also contains writing that does not waste time. It has been created in the final years of the twentieth century, when the voices behind the words are reaching crossroads in their literary and political development.

A great deal has already been gained by native people before 1992. Having them represented by one group of writers who have been in the thick of rapid cultural and political change means this book is vibrant with energy that spills beyond public anniversaries to prove the true mark of history comes from individuals living and writing their own stories.

—Ray Gonzalez

PART ONE

Wendy Rose

For Some, It's a Time of Mourning

Great Spirit and All Unseen, this day we pray and ask you for guidance.... We ask you to be seen in an image of love and peace. Let us be seen in beauty, the colors of the rainbow. We respect our Mother, the planet Earth, with our loving care, for from her breast we receive our nourishment. Let us not listen to the voices of the two-hearted, the destroyers of mind, the haters and self-made leaders, whose lust for power and wealth will lead us into confusion and darkness. Seek visions always of world beauty, not violence or battlefield. It is our duty to pray always for harmony between human and earth so that the earth will bloom once more.... Pray for the great leaders of nations in the House of Mica[1] who in their own quiet ways help the earth in balance.... Let us sing for strength of wisdom with all nations for the good of all people. Our hope is not yet lost; purification must be to restore the health of our Mother Earth for lasting peace and happiness.

From "Hopi Prayer for Peace"
by James Kootshangsie

As I walk upon my Mother Earth, I listen for the voices. All of my relations whisper to me: the pines and buckeyes, the finches and hawks, the delicate down of spring mountain grass, the tiny spiders and red ants, the enormous vermillion evening sun, Hopi and Me-wuk ancestors whose songs are not finished. My flesh is in contact with the granite bones of my Mother, and Her strong pulse moves softly beneath my feet. These are not the only voices. There, too, is Joseph, who joined the colonial army in Canada after losing the Irish estate that his ancestors had stolen five hundred years earlier, and Henrietta, his wife, descended from the native Picts and mystic Celts of the Scottish Highlands, great-great-grandmother who followed her husband to the California goldfields. But there is a difference.

Is it the pitch of the voices? the volume? the clarity? In all of the voices, I find my life. This is especially true on mornings like this one, cool and deeply dramatic with impending rain and swirling wind. My morning commute takes me through the Mother Lode's southern foot, from my home in Coarsegold (not far from

3

the place where Joseph and Henrietta settled) to the foggy floor of the Great Central Valley where the native people of the Sierra Nevada were imprisoned when miners wanted their land and treaties were signed in disappearing ink.

I am a modern consumer, a new voice with little substance. I wonder if the generations to come will hear mine among the many, will hear any human voice within the increasing wail of the injured earth. Every blow to the flesh of my Mother drives the colonial knife in deeper; this indigenous world, the real world, is crying.

I must remember that all of this death was for money. The very beginning of this episode, five hundred years ago, was the legacy of losing the Crusades to a stronger market, a sharper sword. Within one generation, the "discoverer's" son had destroyed all native human life on the island his father had claimed for the "new" world piled high with Spanish *reales*. I do not believe that the physical shape of my Mother was ever the question; even then it must have been obvious that, like me, She was round, asymmetrical, large.

I must remember that exploration and genocide have always been just business as usual. Neither scientific nor strictly political, those brave trekkers whose names frost the pages of every American child's schoolbooks carried their banners not for kings, but for companies, for traders, for miners, for every kind of coinage, for the freedom, not to worship or walk or speak or elect, but the freedom to profit beyond the reach of the king. Was there even a single explorer whose concern was the fresh-fallen snow of new knowledge or friendly contact with the citizens of previously unknown (to him) nations? Did any traveler experience awe at the Creator's diverse and supremely logical creations? Was exploration merely endured for the sake of economic expansion, or was there, perhaps, one who might have gloried in the difference between what was familiar and what was remarkably new, in the equally ancient places of his travels?

When the United States inherited the status of "discovering nation" from England, it quickly forgot the promises of the Northwest Ordinance to seek peace with the native people and to protect the sanctity of their borders; in utmost bad faith, George Washington did not merely father a new country but surveyed and coveted

4

western Indian lands, becoming, more accurately, a rapist. When the colonists revolted against the king, I must remember that the king had wanted to protect Indian land from men like Washington. Every American schoolchild learns of George's hatchet and cherry tree as if it were true, but when are they told the truth of his punitive raids into Iroquois country to burn crops and houses, slaughter innocent people? When are the children told the story of these starving and murdered Indians, the very people from whom Benjamin Franklin gained the knowledge of governmental balances of power, centralized federal administration over autonomous states, and the revolutionary idea that power flows up from people rather than down from the ruler? It did not take long for America to forget—so that "manifest destiny" could be invented in order to justify the continuing theft of land. America is accountable today; there is no choice, for that same "manifest destiny" has turned on her with sterile burning eyes and radioactive teeth.

The voices remind me that there are other things I must remember. The natural people of the earth have survived with their aboriginal wisdom intact. Even if they have lost individuals to the lure of Wasi'chu/Pahana[2] from time to time, the Center has survived. Much more so than the vast destruction, I am in awe of my Elders' strength. I have learned that the traditional people are not protected from the continuing colonization of their nations by a cadre of college-educated Indians; rather, the reverse is true. I derive my strength and my survival from them. As long as they live, there is a place for me, and if they do not live, all of us will go with them. Though some of us may pretend that we are not still tied to the Elders, I am certain that those ties remain strong.

The voices live in my very bones and shiver in them with rage and with prayer. I cannot acknowledge defeat even though my people and my land have been obstacles to the maximization of profit for five hundred years. I will not give up my ancestors' dust, nor their songs, for the complacent and deadly half-life offered by Wasi'chu/Pahana to those Indian people who begin to believe they have been defeated. I hear many voices, but of them all, the most enduring ones, the ones with the strongest and sweetest songs, are native. More than that I am irrevocably linked to the two-legged, four-legged, flying and swimming of earth, to the vanished Taino who first felt the heavy hand of colonization, to the frozen huddled walkers on the Trail of Tears, to the buffalo skull mountains piled high near prairie railroad tracks, to Bikini Islanders left with invisible brooms for cleaning their devastated sacred land, to the napalmed and betrayed people of Vietnam/Laos/Cambodia, to the misled boys who carried corporate rifles into clouds of Agent Orange, to the shadows of evaporated men on the sidewalks of Nagasaki, to the weeping Elders who pray on Big Mountain and keep safe the graves of their grandparents, to the brave new poet-diplomats of Nicaragua, to all who wait for Purification and stand ready within our Mother's heart, to all who remember their origin and have traveled the great circle to return home, to the choice that we made and the promise that we gave to be thankful for each new sunrise, each drop of rain. You know, nothing of the past five hundred years was inevitable. Every raised fist and brandished weapon was a choice someone made. The decision to become a nation of thieves and liars was a choice. The decision to censor the native truth was a choice. The decision to manipulate the knowledge of American history was a choice. My immediate choice is to celebrate or to mourn. With my relations around me, I go into mourning—but I go angry, alive, listening, learning, remembering. I do not go quietly. I do not vanish. I do not forget. I will not let you forget.

Notes

1. House of Mica: Hopi prophecies expressed publicly during the 1930s referred to the leaders of nations making profoundly important decisions in a House of Mica on the east coast of the North American continent. Today we realize that this was a foresight of the United Nations Headquarters in New York.
2. Wasi'chu/Pahana: "Wasi'chu" is a Lakota word meaning "fat grabber," one who is greedy. The term was applied to the white people during the nineteenth century. Today it is used to refer to systems, such as the military-industrial complex of the United States, rather than to a race. However, it must also be noted that those who control such systems are almost always white and male. "Pahana" is a term for Hopi prophecies of centuries ago in which the lost white brother would return with gifts and knowledge to help complete the Hopi

ceremonial cycle. As I understand the term, today it is used much like "Wasi'chu," perhaps with an ironic twist because of the many ways in which it is obvious that white people do not represent the return of the lost white brother.

Victor Hernández Cruz

Some Thoughts as We Approach the Five Hundredth Anniversary of the Discovery of the Americas

Puerto Rico: an isle in the Caribbean where I was born in a wooden house which is now a popular cafetin (a small combination bar and grocery store) with a loud jukebox featuring the bolero music of Felipe Rodriguez, Trio Los Panchos, and more Salsa than you can throw on fish. Ruled by Spain for four hundred years, we became a possession of the United States as a result of the Spanish-American War. Goddamn Spaniards lost, tyrants that they were with our indigenous population.

Understanding that the history of this small planet is migration and expansion as one group of people with their culture and language move in on another. It makes me wonder about Spain and how unprepared they were for expansion in 1492. It was the same year that they were fighting the Arabs in Granada to regain Castilian territory. It was one of Europe's most divided nations, a land conquered and reconquered. It had no linguistic unity to speak of. Within its borders people spoke Basque, Catalan, Castilian, Aragónese, Hebrew, Arabic, and then there were the Gypsies with their universal speech stew. I must then believe in a sacred motion of history, a hidden power moving the strings of events. Regardless of all of those obstacles, off they went, and their thirst was such that they made it all the way to Guam and the Philippines.

Who were the deckhands sailing on the first trips? Could they have been Moors and Jews who had to vacate anyway—after all, it was the Spanish Inquisition that was coming, and those priests would not even forgive their own mothers. Life aboard the caravels must've been mind-exploding. It is well documented that Spanish authorities emptied many prisons and gave the prisoners

9

an offer they couldn't refuse. Either you go off with this Genovese racketeer to wherever or you stay in that cell. Try and picture life within a medieval Spanish prison. To be booked upon a sailing circus, even if it was going to hell, was indeed a blessing. On board it was a great bazaar. Some of the men were speaking Spanish, Columbus was speaking Italian, others were yapping in Arabic, another group was spouting Ladino.

The Spanish language had been freshly hatched out of a Latin chicken. Here they come, three boats on the horizon. Swarthy bearded men singing coplas and smoking hashish, playing Arabian la'uds or the emerging Spanish guitar. With such a band how could they not get lost. The myth of the earth being flat was for popular consumption. Columbus knew he was going somewhere. Had he not read Plato, who knew that there was a bright sun shining upon a garden in the West? Had not Marco Polo been up earlier taking a stroll; he should have detected a curvature upon the earth's crust on such a long venture. All of that because his palate was unsatisfied with the local cuisine. It's a long way to go for the gourmet section of a supermarket. He found the spaghetti, Columbus found the tomato sauce. The Spaniards also ran into chile, which must've awakened the Andalusian gift of blasphemy, they are the world's greatest cursers. We could pretend that the real reason for the Spanish voyages of exploration was an unconscious urge for guayaba; but lo and behold, their mouths were not as opened as Marco Polo's. When a group of Tainos (Caribbean natives) bestowed some juicy pineapples upon their unexpected visitors, they immediately went into facial contortions, running into the bushes to vomit. It was one of the first encounters of the native fruit with the Iberian tongue. That alone should have been adequate warning of the massacres to come.

The colonization proceeded on a massive scale. The island of Santo Domingo saw one of the first cities of the Spaniards go up. Its principal street was named Calle de las Damas. Old San Juan came up after; in the chambers of El Morro, the old Spanish fortress built to protect the city from coastal invasion, one can still hear the cries of the Tainos jailed and slaughtered within. After 1500 the main thrust of Spanish colonization went toward Mexico City. It was in Mexico where the Spanish language was hindered the most; it had to confront the Mayan and Aztec tongues, which were rich and abundant. Unlike in the Caribbean, the native populations of Mexico and other parts of Central and South America were not extinguished. The battle and fusion in the Antilles was between the African and Spanish, with the indigenous population disappearing but still leaving a strong racial and cultural influence, making us Caribbeans the true harmonizers of world civilizations, the true *Raza Cósmica* that Mexican educator José Vasconcelos wrote about.

In Puerto Rico the gold was emptied from the rivers by the newcomers, who gave it a value much more than its symbolism for the sun. Occasionally I venture out on the edges of El Río Mula, close to my Aguas Buenas home, hoping that perhaps they missed a nugget or two.

As we approach the five hundredth anniversary of the discovery of the Americas by Columbus, Puerto Rico still remains in a colonial situation, controlled economically and militarily by the U.S. but not culturally or spiritually. After over ninety years of U.S. presence we remain speakers of Spanish, a culture rich in folkloric traditions of song, music, and dance. We have also witnessed the U.S. invasion of Panama as 23,000 men were sent to capture a single individual. It could be a sign that the Good Neighbor Policy of the past is coming back in style for the nineties. If you have any doubts about the colonial status of Puerto Rico, just note that eighteen days after Hurricane Hugo brushed through our island, President Bush sent Dan Quayle's wife to inspect the damage, which she did within two and a half hours. Her visit to the island was managed in such a way that the governor of the island, Hernández Colón, was notified two hours before her plane was to arrive. When the first lady of Puerto Rico, the governor's wife, rushed out to the airport to greet the visitor, she was informed by a spokeswoman for Mrs. Quayle that the vice president's wife would not ride in the same limousine with her into San Juan. Proud Puerto Rican lady that she is, she left faster than a lizard's head can pop.

If plans to invade Panama were at hand for over six months, as the U.S. media indicated, there was some consideration for the Sugar Ray–Roberto Duran fight. Think of all the millions that would have been lost internationally if the U.S. Marines had invaded three days before the fight. No, capitalism knows better, the fight must go on.

Spain had its golden period during the Arabian occupation, which commenced in A.D. 711 and lasted some eight hundred years. The Arabs encouraged the study of science and the development of the arts. Public libraries were established in the large cities. Religious tolerance allowed Jews as well as Christians to practice their manner of worship and to communicate one with the other. Men of learning such as Averroës, Avicenna, ibn ʿArabi began to translate and comment upon dormant Greek classics, contributing to the reawakening of Europe. It was a place of great architecture, great centers of medicine, and beautiful paths that led to gardens where fountains were flowing with water. The Moors gave the Visigoths much to improve and enhance their civilization. There was much intermarriage, and many Christians abandoned their religion for that of their conquerors.

It is clear and recognizable that much of what came upon those boats from Spain across the Atlantic contained this Islamic Dynamism. The Spanish is full of Arabian words as well as indigenous words; add to that the inclusion of Africa to our world, and you get a picture of the rich universal vocabulary that we are coming down the mountains and streets with. As a Hispanic of the Americas I look back upon our history of turbulence, of conquests and migrations. The extinction of the indigenous peoples of the Caribbean is one of mankind's great tragedies. Despite this anthropological knowledge, there are moments in my hometown of Aguas Buenas when the sentiment and appearance of the Tainos swell all of my senses and the small streets of my childhood become ageless.

It is difficult to conceive of Spain as merely a European country, especially its southern region, Andalusia (Al Andaluz), rich in Moorish and Gypsy blood. Perhaps a new category is needed, something that would place it between Europe and the East. Spain is the one country in the world where the notorious wandering Gypsies have established traditions of song and dance and have settled into community. The Gypsies and the Moors are the soulful base of the rich musical traditions of Iberia. Puerto Rico inherited one of the great classical musicians and composers of the twentieth century from Spain in the figure of the cellist Pablo Casals, who made this tropical isle his home. He lived and produced great music here and has left an enduring love for classical music in a sizable portion of our population.

Franco (who was not French)—a modern-day arrogant Cortés patriarchal pig do-as-I-say tyrannical nut, the kind we know of very well in Latin America, both in terms of political power and family relations—had his men hunt down and assassinate the country's greatest living poet, Federico García Lorca, during the Spanish Civil War. One of Lorca's biographers points out that the firing squad took off the gold ring and watch Lorca was wearing but failed to detect a belt buckle of high-quality gold. Since the whereabouts of his grave remains a mystery, I feel that somewhere in Spain there is a golden light emanating out of the earth. The message was clear. Miguel Hernández, another passionately brilliant poet, died in one of Franco's jails. Spanish writers, intellectuals, and painters began to abandon their homeland in fear of what was obviously coming.

Once again Spaniards migrated to the Americas. The poet and scholar Pedro Salinas landed on the shores of San Juan and was able to write and continue to develop. He recognized the richness of Puerto Rican Spanish, a language of strong expressiveness full of proverbs and folktales which poured down from the campesino mountains. It is the campesinos who keep particular vernaculars alive and pumping worldwide. Language seems to stagnate in the cities, where it is cut off from agriculture and thus from rhythm; in the cities people sing less. Peasants are nowadays an endangered species being replaced by individuals who are products of the industrial-technological processing age. Ecology-minded radicals should take up their cause, for of what good is it to have a good green earth if a bunch of jerks are going to be the ones to live in it? You can see the human rootlessness in the form of the Yuppies who now fill most large North American cities. Career freaks who opinionate nothing but go out and pay $6.00 for an avocado sandwich. In Puerto Rican terms that is a financial disgrace and enough sin to have the Gods recycle you into the same kind of nerd. Pedro Salinas defended the importance of tradition in life as well as literature, for without it there is no real freedom.

The Nobel Laureate Juan Ramón Jiménez also made Puerto Rico his home for a period of his life. Unlike their ancestors, these men came with their pens and not with their swords. All of them were embraced by the thriving University of Puerto Rico at Río Piedras; there they were given opportunities to teach, and a generation of Puerto Rican students were blessed by their presence.

San Juan of the mid-forties offered a rich cultural life to both exiles and natives. The music and lecture halls were always full. Old San Juan, the second city of the Hispanic Americas, had its art galleries and bohemian cafés, as it still does today, where conversation and creativity soared to great heights as Europe slaughtered itself across the Atlantic.

María Teresa Babin, one of Puerto Rico's prominent poets and educators, had front row seats on the whole drama of Spanish exiles as well as the meaning of the great adventure and experiment that was unleashed at the encounter of Spanish culture with the indigenous civilizations of the so-called New World. She believed strongly upon native ground: *"Somos criollos del Caribe y no españoles; somos puertoriqueños y no otra cosa."* María Teresa Babin died in 1989, the same year that I came back to Puerto Rico. She once told me that "we can't live in the nineteenth century," meaning that she knew that the Jíbaro folkloric culture would have to go through transformations. Teresa Babin will live in all the centuries to come as each singing bird chirps the letters of her verses.

Now about this business of the five hundredth anniversary of the discovery of the Americas by Columbus (over here it's Colón and it has more pitfalls). It seems that everybody and their mother has discovered the Americas. Very true it all is, for it is well documented that the Chinese were in Mexico. Sinaloa for everybody. Central American pre-Colon(ization) art is abundant in Buddhist symbols and figures of Tibetan priests. Phoenician and Egyptian hieroglyphs have been found in Peru—and I mean to the letter— and there it is, the thing itself. There's that gigantic Olmec sculpture with African features. Ah, no that the Vikings...that the...the...I discovered America in El Guanabano of Aguas Buenas on a Sunday morning of February 1949 in Colmado-Cafetin El Poema, where a group of *pueblanos* make rum evaporate as I walk by and hear Felipe Rodriguez singing the songs of his memories.

The truth of the matter is that only artists discover, for they discover things that are not of this world.

Robert Allen Warrior

The Columbus Quincentennial Is Nothing to Celebrate

But five hundred years of native people's resistance is

In the summer of 1990, I was one of approximately 350 Indian people—including Yanomanis, Mapuches, Kunas, Quechuas, Caribs, Navajos, Hopis, Lummis, Lumbees, Osages, Inuits, Crees, and Seminoles—from North, South, and Central America and the Caribbean who met in Ecuador for the first-ever intercontinental *encuentro* of American Indians. The theme was "Five Hundred Years of Indigenous Resistance."

We heard a lot of speeches, wrote a lot of statements and manifestos, and drove a couple dozen translators to exhaustion. In our final statement, "The Declaration of Quito," we committed ourselves to international indigenous solidarity in confronting the Quincentenary.

Our coming together was a fulfillment of prophecy. The Runa people of Mexico believe that the indigenous people of the Americas were divided long ago into two groups—people of the Eagle (those from the North) and people of the Condor (those from the South). When the Eagle and the Condor rejoin their tears, the Runa story goes, a new era of life and spirit will begin for American Indian people.

In Quito, and in a North American follow-up meeting over the 1990 Columbus Day holiday weekend in Minneapolis, we committed ourselves to two things. First, whatever else happens, we want 1992 primarily to be an opportunity to mobilize American Indian communities for long-range, constructive political action.

For instance, Native American activist and writer Winona LaDuke told us at the Minneapolis meeting how Anishinabe organizers at White Earth in Minnesota are raising funds, pursuing legal strategies, and employing media in their campaign to recover

15

tribal land that federal, state, and county governments now hold. The year 1992, she said, is an opportunity for them to bring increased public attention to their efforts and make land recovery a major state issue. Others discussed plans to organize in local communities around issues of religious freedom, protection of sacred sites, and economic development.

We also discussed events and protests that will draw attention to American Indian issues. The International Indian Treaty Council will have its annual gathering in the Black Hills of South Dakota in June 1992. Indian organizations in San Francisco, New York, and Minneapolis will coordinate responses to major Quincentenary celebrations.

In the United States and Canada, many groups see the Quincentenary as an opportunity to create new movement toward fundamental social change. In South and Central America, the various popular movements are planning to stage major disruptions of government celebrations.

The second commitment made in Quito and Minneapolis was to resist non-Indian groups that attempt to exploit the cause of Indian people in 1992. In Latin America, Indian people have historically been a major factor in political movements. They have laid down their lives on the front lines of revolutionary struggles but have benefited least when revolutions were successful. Their demands for self-determination and land rights have been dismissed, ignored, or forgotten.

Since the sixteenth century, Indian people have been surrounded by paternalistic mythology, getting lost in someone else's political agenda. Within a few years of the invasion, Indians were a hot topic in Europe. People on one side described Indian people as savage brutes who deserved to be exploited, tortured, and exterminated. People on the other side described Indian people in glowing utopian terms and held Spain in contempt for its cruelty and injustice.

But these battles were always about Europe. The English published accounts of Spanish cruelty and injustice to fuel their anti-Spain propaganda machine. The church in Rome used evangelism of Indian peoples as a way to divert attention away from its crumbling European authority. Protestants and reformers, on the other hand, pointed to the conquest as evidence of papist evil and decadence.

The same kind of moral battles about Indians have continued ever since—in Puritan New England, the winning of the West, Hollywood westerns, the environmental movement, and New Age spirituality. Indian people are forever being discovered and re-discovered, being surrounded by thicker and thicker layers of mythology. And every new generation predicts our inevitable and tragic disappearance.

After five centuries, Indian people are still here, resisting and surviving in whatever ways we can. The year 1992 can be a time for all of us—Indian and non-Indian—to begin learning how to be in solidarity with each other, mutually empowering our struggles for justice and peace. If we can stand together in defiance of the self-congratulatory celebrations, perhaps we will see the way toward standing together in constructive praxis, respect, and hope for all humanity.

When the *encuentro* meeting in Quito was over, Indian people at a nearby village called Huaycopungo feasted our coming to-gether. From paper bags, we ate a dinner of goat, roasted corn, po-tatoes, and salsa. We laughed across languages. We gathered on a public field for speeches, our numbers having grown to 3,000 or so, raising our fists and yelling "Viva!" whenever it was appropriate and sometimes when it wasn't.

All night long we danced. Terengo bands from around the con-tinent played songs of love and heartbreak. Even when I awoke the next morning, frozen to the bone at 6 A.M., three bands were still playing and people were still dancing.

In the midst of the speeches and the dancing, some of us from North America borrowed a drum and got permission to sing. We stood on the crowded stage of orators and musicians, waiting for our turn. Someone lit some sage to bless the drum and our singing. We passed the burning sage around, clearing our minds in its cloud.

Soon, we stepped forward to sing. The drummers began the slow, persistent beat of a Plains honor song that I did not know. Eugene Hasgood, a Diné (Navajo) man who lives on Big Mountain in Arizona, stretched his throat, tilted his head, and sang the first phrase, alone, in a face-contorting high pitch. *"Way yah hey way yah hi yah."* Two more men joined him at his pitch, and then all of us joined them in whatever octave was comfortable.

When the beginning of the song came around again, I tilted my head, stretched my throat, and added my voice after Eugene's first phrase. We sang through the song more times than I can remember, each time gaining power and strength.

Before 1492 and every year since, Indian people have been singing songs and burning sage and sweetgrass, whether people hear their voices or not. After the Quincentenary, Indian people will still be singing songs and burning sage and sweetgrass.

As 1992 approaches, clouds of sage smoke will be visible wherever people gather to crash the colonial party. The sweetgrass will not be so easy to find. The sweetgrass is what will linger after the countercelebrations and protests are over.

And if you listen closely, you will hear that music—the slow, patient drumbeat and the stretched-neck strains. When you do, join the circle, listen to the sounds, and smell the smells. And if someone invites you to add your voice, by all means sing.

Rudolfo Anaya

The New World Man

My wife and I first traveled to Spain in the fall of 1980. We took an overnight train from Paris to Barcelona, journeyed through Andalusia and then on to Madrid. We returned home with wonderful memories of the Alhambra, Toledo, Madrid, El Escorial, and many other places we visited. At the famous El Prado museum I fell under the spell of the genius of Goya, and the images of his prophetic vision are with me still. In 1988 when we returned to Spain, my trip was in part a pilgrimage to meditate again in the presence of Goya's work and to visit and contemplate the genius of Gaudí's inspiring church, La Sagrada Família, in Barcelona.

That return was made possible by my invitation to Barcelona to discuss my work at the Third International Conference on Hispanic Cultures of the United States; after that conference I attended a small gathering of Spanish scholars and professors from the University of New Mexico at La Fundación Xavier de Salas in Trujillo.

Spain was preparing for the celebration of its 1492–1992 quincentennial, and the conference was the beginning of a series intended to rekindle the relationship of Spain with Hispanic America. We *Nuevomexicanos* are part of that history: we speak the Spanish language. I prefer the term *Nuevomexicano* to describe my cultural heritage. My parents and my grandparents of the Puerto de Luna valley of New Mexico spoke only Spanish, and as I honor my ancestors, I keep up their language and folkways. *Hispano* to me means using the Spanish language of my ancestors. I use it because it also connects me to other Spanish-speaking groups in this country.

The great majority of the *Mexicanos* of the Southwest are *Indo-hispanos*, part of *La Raza* of the New World, the fruit of the Spanish father and the Indian mother. We take pride in our His-

19

panic heritage; that is, we know the history of the Spanish father, his language, and his character. We also know that in this country it has been more seductive to identify with one's white, European ancestry. But that identification with that which is Spanish has often caused us to neglect our indigenous Native American roots, and thus we have not known and honored the heritage of our mother, the Indian mothers of Mexico and the Southwest.

In world mythology there are few archetypal searches for the mother, perhaps because the mother is always in evidence, she is always there; in early religions she was the goddess of the earth, the provider. We forget that it is the mother who cultivates and in many ways creates our nature, both in an individual and communal sense. For the Mexicanos of the Southwest the mother is Malinche, the first Indian woman of Mexico to bear children fathered by a Spaniard. But the mother figure is more real than the symbolic Malinche; our mothers embody the archetype of the indigenous Indian mother of the Americas. If we are to truly know ourselves, it is her nature we must know. Why have we neglected her? In other words, why have we neglected that part of our history that was shaped by indigenous America?

I was born and raised in New Mexico, heir to the land of my Nuevomexicano ancestors, son of those Spanish and Mexicano colonists who settled the fertile Río Grande Valley of New Mexico. My ancestors settled in the Atrisco land grant, across the river from present-day Albuquerque. I trace my family back a few generations because the land grant has created a sense of communal belonging for the Anayas. But how do we relate to that Hispanic legacy that left the peninsula in 1492 to implant itself in the New World? How do we relate to the peninsular consciousness of the people who crossed the Atlantic five hundred years ago to deposit their seed on the earth of the New World?

Located at the heart of what is now the southwest United States, the people of Nuevo Mexico have retained the essence of what it means to be Hispano, having preserved the Spanish language, the Catholic religion, and the folktales and folkways which came from Spain. Our ancestors imbued the history of Nuevo Mexico with their particular world view. For more than four centuries our Mexicano ancestors have lived in the isolated frontier of northernmost New Spain. But they did not survive and multiply in a vacuum; they survived and evolved because they intermarried and adopted many of the ways of the Pueblos. The Spanish character underwent change as it encountered the Native Americans of the Southwest, and from that interaction and intermarriage a unique American mestizo was born.

We need to describe the totality of that world view that was formed in what we now call the Southwest, understanding that we are heirs not only of the Spanish character but of our Native American nature as well. The Spanish character may be the aggressive, conquest-oriented part of our identity; the Native American nature is the more harmonious, earth-oriented side. We need to know both sides of our identity in order to know ourselves. We need to know the unique characteristics that have evolved from this union. To pay attention only to one side of our nature is to be less knowledgeable of self. If we are to fulfill our potential, it is important that we know the indigenous side of our history.

As I review my writings, I understand that it is the indigenous American perspective, or New World view, that is at the core of my search. I have explored the nature of my mother, not only the symbolic Indian mother, but the real Indian mothers of the Americas. The blood that whispers my feelings about the essence of the earth and people of the Americas is the soul of my mother; it reveals the symbols and mythology of the New World, and that comprises the substratum of my writings.

During the Columbus quincentennial, a discourse will take place between Spain and its former colonies in the Americas. I wish to add a definition of my New World view to that discourse, hoping not only to share some of the findings of my personal literary quest but also to encourage my community of *raza* to pay more attention to our multicultural and multiethnic history. We must know more of the synthesis of our Spanish and Indian nature, and know more of the multiple heritages of the Americas.

The Americas represent a wonderful experiment in the synthesis of divergent world views, and each one of us is a representative of that process. The illuminations of self that are revealed as we explore and understand our true natures can be one of the most rewarding experiences of our lives, for so much of the sensitive part of life is a search and understanding of the inner self. To define ourselves as we really are and not as others wish us to be allows us to become authentic, and that definition carries with it the potential of our humanism.

In the mid-sixteenth century, our Hispano and Mexicano ancestors began to settle along the Río Grande of Nuevo Mexico, bringing to the land a new language. They gave names to the land and its features. It is in the naming that one engages in the sacred; that is, by naming one creates a *sacred sense of time*, a historic sense of time. By engaging in naming, our ancestors imposed themselves on history and gave definition to history. The language used in that naming ceremony is our birthright.

I live in Albuquerque, a name that invokes some of the history of the Iberian peninsula. In Spain, I spoke my Nuevomexicano Spanish, a dialect that was preserved by my ancestors and which evolved in the mountains and valleys of New Mexico. But language changes with the passage of time and the vicissitudes of survival, and so I returned to Spain more proficient in English than in Spanish. All my novels and stories are written in English. While my parents' generation still communicated only in Spanish, my generation converses almost completely in English, a function of survival in the Anglo-American society. We struggle to retain the Spanish language, not only because it was the language of our ancestors, but also because it connects us to our brethren in Mexico and Latin America.

I returned to Spain to share with Spaniards the nature of my New World consciousness. At times I felt uncomfortable, believing I had to conform to the Spanish character, but the truth is that we who return to Spain no longer need to feel constrained to conform to the Spanish character. My generation of Hispanos, or Mexican Americans, liberated ourselves from that constraint by naming ourselves *Chicanos*. For us, using the word *Chicano* was our declaration of independence, the first step toward our true identity. By creating a Chicano consciousness we created a process by which we rediscovered our history.

By naming ourselves Chicanos we stamped an era with our communal identity, we reaffirmed our humanity by exploring and understanding the nature of our mothers, the indigenous American women. We took the word *Chicano* from *Mexicano,* dropping the first syllable and keeping the *Xicano.* We are proud of that heritage even though we are not Mexican citizens, and although we are citizens of the United States we are not Anglo-Americans. We have our own history rooted in this land. The word *Chicano* defined our *space in time*, that is, our history and our identity. *Chicano* embraces our Native American heritage, an important element of our history.

Our first declaration of independence was from Anglo-America; that is, we insisted on the right to our Indo-hispano heritage. Now I believe the declaration has to go further. We have to insist on being the *señores of our own time*, to borrow a phrase from Miguel Leon Portilla. To be the *señores and señoras of our own time* is to continue to create our definition and sense of destiny; it is a process of synthesis that embraces the many roots of *la raza*.

This essay is a declaration of independence from a narrow view that has defined us as Hispanos with only a Spanish heritage. The definition of our identity must be a New World definition. Such a definition should encompass the multiple roots and histories of the Americas; it should encompass the nature of the mothers whose soul provides the unique aesthetic and humanistic sensibility that defines us.

Language is at the essence of a culture, and we must remember that in Nuevo Mexico, as in the rest of the New World, there existed pre-Columbian languages. The indigenous Indians had named their tribes, the rivers, the mountains, and the flora and fauna. They were the *señores of their own time*. The New World did not live in silence, awaiting the sound of European languages; it had its languages and it had participated in the sacred ceremony of naming thousands of years before 1492. This is a fact we must accept when we discuss our ethnicity, for not only was the Mexico of our indigenous ancestors peopled with Indians, but the Río Grande Valley, which became the home of our Hispano/Mexicano ancestors, was also thriving with many great Indian pueblos.

Language follows the urge of the blood, it moves with the adventurer to take root and be nourished by the colonist who tills the new soil. Languages mix, as does the blood, and so my gene pool is both Indian and peninsular. In reality, it has deeper and more interesting roots; roots I will never know. Knowing this allows me to honor *las madres de Las Americas*. My journey has been that of a writer, and in my first novel it was the *curandera* Ultima, the indigenous woman who came to speak to me and share her secrets. She reflects the nature of *La Virgen de Guadalupe*, the indigenous mother born of the synthesis of Spanish Virgin and Indian goddess. It is through Ultima that I began to discover myself. In my writings I have sought the true nature of the New World man, that person who is authentic to the New World view. I had only myself to encounter in the journey; I am the New World man I sought. I am an indigenous man taking his essence and perspective from the earth and people of the New World, from the earth that is my mother.

One of the most interesting questions we ask ourselves as human beings is that of identity. Who am I? We seek to know our roots, to know ourselves. When we encounter the tap roots of our history we feel authentic and able to identify self, family, and community. Finding self should also mean finding humanity; declaring personal independence also means declaring that independence for all individuals.

How did I begin this journey of self-knowledge? I listened to the *cuentos* of the old people, the stories of their history, and in retelling those stories and starting my own odyssey, I had to turn within. I had to know myself. Everyone does. The spiritual beliefs and mysticism of the Catholic Church and the love of the earth were elements of my childhood, so I used those sources in my stories. The folkways of my community became the web of the fictions I create, for the elements of drama exist within the stories of the folk. Even today, when I feel I have outgrown some of the themes I explored as a young writer, I know my best writing still comes when I return to the essence of my Nuevomexicano culture.

But in all writing the depth of the universal element is that which allows us to communicate across national or ethnic boundaries, and so for me the most meaningful and revealing area to enter in search of the New World person was mythology. It is in myth that we find the truth in the heart, the truth of "our place in time." Everyone can enter and explore his or her memory, and discover there the symbols that speak to the personal and collective history. It is in this search that I found the legend of the Golden Carp and the other mythological symbols that permeate *Bless Me Ultima* and my later work. I found universal archetypal symbols, but these symbols were colored with a Native American hue. The earth, the elements, the sacred directions, the tree, the owl of the old *curandera* Ultima, the golden carp, the shaman as mentor or guide—all of these elements spoke to me of my New World nature. And it was Ultima, my Native American mother, who led the way and taught me to see.

My search continued. In *Heart of Aztlán* I reworked the myth of Aztlán, a legend that describes the place of origin of the Aztecs. I attempted to make legend meaningful in a contemporary context by exploring its possibilities as a Chicano homeland. In *Tortuga* I continued the search into the earth and totem animals, the search into the healing process of water and earth as well as the art of writing itself. The writer may well be the new shaman for the old, displaced tribes of the Americas. In the novel *Tortuga* I returned to the important revelations available to us in the nature of the mother, whether the mother was viewed as earth goddess or the feminine presence of the young girl who loves Tortuga.

I understand that many of my *manitos*, my Nuevomexicanos, often praise our Hispanic identity and shun the indigenous roots that have also nurtured our history. The young Chicano artists have changed part of that, and now I declare my independence of consciousness from the Iberian peninsula. I have found that the symbolic content that best describes my nature comes from the people and earth of the Americas. So I declare, as an important step in the process of knowing myself, my independence. I see myself as a New World man, and I feel that definition is liberating and full of potential.

During this time of the Columbus quincentennial, it is important to look at the evolution of the consciousness of the Americas and to discern the unique world views which that evolution created. It is important for us and for Spain to look at the Americas and find, not an image of the Spanish character, but an image of our unique New World nature.

When I first traveled in Spain in 1980 I went into Andalusia. There in those wide expanses and mountains that reminded me of New Mexico, I felt at home. But people need more than the landscape to feel connected; we need the deeper connection to the communal body.

The broad, political history of the independence of the Spanish colonies in the Americas is well known; now we must turn to an exploration of our personal and communal identity. That is what

Chicano writers and artists have been doing since the cultural movement of the 1960s. The definition of Chicano culture must come from a multicultural perspective. Many streams of history define us and will continue to define us, for we are the synthesis that is the Americas.

Christ and Quetzalcoatl are not opposing spiritual figures; they fulfill the humanistic yearning toward harmonious resolution. Harmony within, harmony with neighbors, harmony with the cosmos. The Virgin of Spanish Catholicism and the Aztec Tonantzin culminate in the powerful and all-loving Virgen de Guadalupe. And *los santos* of the Catholic Church, and those more personal saints of my mother's altar, merge with and share the sacred space of the Kachinas of the Indian pueblos.

This metaphor, *Los santos son las kachinas,* the saints are the kachinas, has become a guiding metaphor of synthesis for me. The Old World and the New World have become one in me. Perhaps it is this syncretic sensibility of harmony that is the ideal of New World character. The New World cultures accepted the spiritual manifestations of Catholicism; Christ and the saints entered the religious cosmology of Indian America. A new age of cultural and spiritual blending came to unite humanity's course in the Americas. It was an age born in suffering, but the very act of birth created the children who were heirs to a new world view.

The New World view is syncretic and encompassing. It is one of the most humanistic views in the world, and yet it is a view not well known in the world. The pressure of political realities and negative views of the mestizo populations of the Americas have constrained the flowering of our nature. Still, that view of self-knowledge and harmony is carried in the heart of the New World person.

What is important to me as a writer is to find the words by which to describe myself and my relationship to others. I now can speak of my history and position myself at the center of that history. There I stand poised at the center of power, the knowing of myself, the heart and soul of the New World man alive in me.

This is a time of reflection for those of us who are the mestizos of the New World, and I believe the reflections in my writings and my attention to the myths and legends of Mesoamerica and of the Río Grande help expand the definition of our Indo-hispano heritage.

From Spain I brought back memories of the Alhambra, where I felt my soul stir to Moorish rhythm, and in the paintings of Goya's dark period I saw his apocryphal vision of an era ending. At La Sagrada Família of Gaudí I bowed to genius, in the Valle de los Caídos I reflected on the Civil War…and even on the wide expanses of Andalusia I thought of home. In all these places my memory stirred, and still I yearned for my home in Nuevo Mexico, the mountains I know, the sacred places of my way of life. In that yearning the message whispered its secret, it was time for me to state my declaration of independence, time to center myself in the consciousness of the New World.

I was the New World man I had sought, with one foot in the glorious *mestisaje* of Mexico and the other in the earth of the Indohispanos of Nuevo Mexico; my dreams are woven of New World earth and history. I could walk anywhere in the world and feel I was a citizen of the world, but it was Nuevo Mexico that centered me; it was the indigenous soul of the Americas that held my secret.

It is important to know that the search for identity is not an esoteric search and not a divisive process. It is a way to reaffirm our humanity. We are all on this search, we all advocate justice, basic human rights, and the right of all to declare their independence of consciousness. We hope the spirit generated in Spain during the 1992 celebration addresses and encourages these basic rights.

History and the collective memory are vast. One delves into these powerful forces and finds that one is part of every other human being. I am proud of my New World heritage, but I know the tree of mankind is one, and I share my roots with every other person. It seems appropriate to end on the archetype of the tree. The tree, or the tree of life, is also a dominant symbol of the Americas, and its syncretic image combines the tree of Quetzalcoatl and the cross of Christ. My ancestors nourished the tree of life; now it is up to me to care for all it symbolizes.

Francisco X. Alarcón

Reclaiming Ourselves,
Reclaiming America

Like many others, I went on in life without ever looking at mirrors. I always found ways to avoid most cameras. Friends and relatives came to expect this from me, another trait of my peculiar nature. Photographs of me were simply unacceptable and ruled out. The dark stranger in them just couldn't be me. I was always ethereal, elusive, "ideal." For a long time, I was a person without an image, without a shadow. How could I possibly identify or associate myself with this body of mine when almost everything around negated me. I was nobody, and nowhere was I to find my reflection, my image, my self. I was an alien at home and everywhere, and more important, a stranger to myself.

This sense of alienation and shame is shared by countless persons that are product of the violent expansion of Europe since the fifteenth century. Whole peoples were forced to perceive themselves as the defective copies of idealized realities. Vast territories of this continent were to be projections of imposed models from the "Old World," first "New Spain," and later, other European cultural models like the French and British as well as the newer Anglo-American ones.

And yet, this image in the mirror is me, and I am a *Mestizo*.[1] I am the physical proof of the violent transformation suffered by Native peoples on this continent in the last five hundred years. My face, my body, my soul are in constant turmoil. They don't seem to fit any European profile. Yes, there are elements in me that come from Europe, the Mediterranean Sea, and Africa, but there are other aspects of me that can come only from this continent. One of the most explosive consequences of the contradictory sociopolitical movement known as the Mexican Revolution that began in 1910, was the long overdue recognition that Mexicans were not faulty copies of Europeans but an original amalgamation of cul-

29

tures and ethnicities with deep roots in their Mesoamerican past. The Chicano Movement of the past two decades has had a similar effect on Mexican-Americans, Chicanos, and Mexicans living in the United States.

Behind the seeming monoliths erected by "official history," there are some forgotten cracks and gaps that sometimes hold the real story. This is the suppressed and mostly unspoken history of the Native peoples of this continent and of their descendants. In spite of the obsession of Spanish colonial authorities to eradicate any trace of this history, obsession later shared by their spiritual and temporal successors, markers of this time and history endure all around us. Their stories need to be told and retold.

Isla Mujeres:
The Bellybutton
of the Nightmare

Three years ago, I stumbled rather unexpectedly into one of those significant markers that locate the beginning of an important cycle in human history. On August 13, 1989, I found myself walking toward the eastern tip of Isla Mujeres, a small five-mile-long by half-mile-wide island set in the turquoise waters of the Caribbean Sea eight miles across from the new Mexican resort mecca of Cancún, on the Yucatán peninsula. *"Allá no hay nada,"* I had been told by a passing taxicab driver dispensing free advice on the dirt road I was tracking. But nothing or no one could dissuade me from visiting the easternmost point of Mexico, where Francisco Hernández de Córdoba had first arrived on March 1, 1517, thus beginning the process of exploration, conquest, and colonization of Mesoamerica.

The Spanish chronicler of the Conquest of Mexico, Bernal Díaz de Castillo, who was a member of this expedition wrote in his *Historia Verdadera de la Conquista de la Nueva España*, "On February 8, 1517, we sailed from Havana…twenty-one days after we had left port, we sighted land which made us happy and for which we gave thanks to God. This land had never been discovered nor was there any knowledge of it till then."[2]

Some one hundred yards from a whitewash stucco lighthouse and next to a cliff where the island meets the Caribbean Sea, I ran into an open wound made of stone and rubble, the half-buried memories of the temple of Ixchel, the Mother Goddess in the Mayan tradition. There was no need for a historic marker, nor any use for the official visitor's guide—which didn't even list the site. Somehow I just knew what I knew. Whatever pretention the limestones once had of being an erect construction had been blown away by the fury of hurricane Gilbert a year before in September 1988. And yet, on that place, I knew I was in front of an ancient oracle. I felt the ominous presence of Ixchel, the Great Mother, the Protector. She was there for reasons that might have been forgotten, trampled on, and simply discarded, but for me, she was more real and alive than all the modern reality and life embodied by the flashy new hotels of nearby Cancún. That humble pile of rubble stood for the state of abandonment and denial of a past that keeps haunting us. It was a testament of the fate of Mesoamerica. We have deserted our Mother and sold out for mere trinkets. Standing on a cliff at the edge of the island, all of a sudden I was once again looking, for the first time, at the mysterious mountains moving out in the sea and also squinting my eyes aboard one of the approaching Spanish ships.

In his *Relación de las cosas de Yucatán* written in 1566, Fray Diego de Landa explains the arrival of the Spaniards in this manner: "In the year 1517, during Lent, Francisco Hernández de Córdoba left Cuba with three ships to trade for slaves for the mines, as the population on Cuba was much diminished. Others say he sailed to discover [new] land and that he took Alaminos with him as pilot and they reached the Isla de las Mujeres, and that it was he who gave it this name because of the idols which he discovered there to the goddesses Ixchel, Ixchebeliax, Ixhunic, Ixhunieta; these were dressed from the waist down and had their breasts uncovered in the Indian manner. The building was of stone, which astonished them, and there they found some gold objects, which they took away with them."[3] Antón de Alaminos had been Columbus's pilot on the latter's final voyage in 1502. Alaminos had also sailed with Ponce de León to Florida in 1513, and later was a member of the expeditions of Juan de Grijalva in 1518 and Hernán Cortés in 1519 to Yucatán and the Gulf of Mexico.[4]

Francisco Hernández de Córdoba is the first to continue in Mesoamerica this colonial practice of renaming locations already well known by the natives with brand new Spanish toponyms. Even today some of our own names are a prolongation of this practice. Yes, my given name is also Francisco, but my *tonal* ("sign") in the Nahuatl tradition is *coatl* ("serpent"). I am ruled by *Chal-chiuhcueye*, the Goddess of Water. I am also a son of *Yemayá* in the *Yoruba* tradition via Cuba.

In order to understand history and be able to exorcise the past, we need to relive in flesh and spirit this history. We need to reenact all the misunderstandings, confrontations and contradictions, all the suffering and havoc brought about by the so-called discovery of this continent by Europeans. I spent the rest of that day among the ruins of the temple of Ixchel in wonder and in an altered state of consciousness. I was also overwhelmed by a sense of inner sadness and voiceless rage, mourning, anger, and despair. I walked back to my hotel in almost total darkness, in anguish. The dead I had invoked were as numerous as the stars in the sky. One day I would like to go back to Isla Mujeres and meet eye-to-eye Francisco Hernández de Córdoba, as one meets one's own murderous father for the first and last time: the synchronic nature of poetry and ritual can certainly make this possible.

This first European contact with the Native peoples of Mesoamerica took place less than twenty-five years after the October 12, 1492, "discovery" of another island by one Christopher Columbus. A quarter of a century was enough time for the *encomenderos*, governors, missionaries, and miners to wipe out entire populations of Native people from the Caribbean islands. On August 13, 1521, only four years after the first landing of Spaniards at Isla Mujeres, Hernán Cortés took prisoner Cuauhtemoc, the last *tlatoani* ("the reverend speaker") of Mexico-Tenochtitlan, who along with his people had valiantly resisted a long and terrible siege. The "Discovery of America" and the newly invented phrase the "Encounter of Two Cultures" are mere euphemisms for genocide, ethnocide, and ecocide that were the direct result of the invasion and conquest of the Indies.

America was not "discovered" by Christopher Columbus, nor by Viking seafarers, but by the first people who came to this continent from Asia at least 60,000 years ago. We would begin to understand the scope of the nightmare and holocaust that the arrival of the Europeans meant to the Native peoples of this continent, if only we could feel within ourselves the sorrow and despair of a Native population of 20 million in Mesoamerica at the time of the coming of the Europeans, reduced to less than two million one hundred years later. No account is possible. Words are useless. They dissolve in front of this haunting fact. We are forced to experience this knowledge outside language. We must feel again all the new fatal diseases that decimated our peoples. We need to bring back the deceased in order to continue living. We have to reclaim our suppressed tongues and spirits, our burned homes and fields, our slaughtered mothers and fathers, our enslaved sisters and brothers. By reclaiming ourselves, we will be reclaiming America.

I say "America" not in the chauvinistic way in the tradition of "God bless America," or "America, right or wrong." America is a continent and cannot be monopolized by a single country like the United States. America has no borders. It actually runs from Alaska to the Patagonia. "America" and "American" are terms that for too long have been misused to dominate, exclude, suppress, and eradicate the historical consciousness of the Native peoples of this continent. America did not begin five hundred years ago. America has fantastic and very deep cultural roots that go back many thousand years of continuous history. "Americans" are all the various peoples that once lived in any given part of this hemisphere. For America to be America, it needs to remember its long and painful past with the same energy and dedication it devotes to its present and its future.

1492: Prelude of the Conquest by Sword, Cross, and Grammar One can ascertain that plain greed played an important role as a main motive of Columbus's endeavor. On his famous letters to his patroness Queen Isabella describing his explorations, our navigator wrote the word "gold" eighty times with the same insistence of an avid prospector searching for any clue of this excrement-of-the-gods, as some Natives called this metal. But other important historical facts have been generally overshadowed by Columbus's deed of October 12, 1492. Columbus's voyage had been made possible by the successful military campaign of "the Catholic Kings," Isabella of Castile and Ferdinand of Aragón, against the last Islamic kingdom, Granada, in southern Spain. A new unified Spanish state had emerged, and in the same year of 1492, the state decreed some terribly harsh measures, such as the expulsion of the Jews from Spain and the forced conversion to Christianity of those who remained. A policy of religious intolerance and ethnic prejudice replaced the more humane practice of religious coexistence of Moslems, Christians, and Jews under more than seven hundred years of Arabic rule in Iberia.

Similar oppressive colonial institutions and practices were later transplanted to the Americas by imperial Spain. Religion was to be used as an expeditious weapon of the state. The spiritual conquest of the Americas was as bloody and ruthless as the military conquest itself. The pleads and denunciations of the Spanish *conquistadores* by Fray Bartolomé de Las Casas are an eloquent testimony of a Christian missionary deeply troubled by the terrible excesses and abuses of his Christian countrymen. But the missionaries themselves never really questioned the terrifying human price their own evangelization policies demanded from the Natives.

If religious and cultural homogeneity was to be obtained at all costs in the newly unified Spain, this goal also included a policy for linguistic uniformity imposed on the Arab-speaking communities claimed by Castile. With that in mind, in that fateful year of 1492, the royal chronicler Antonio de Nebrija completed the very first grammar of any Romance language. This grammar of Castilian was later used as a very effective instrument for the suppression of the ancestral indigenous languages in the territories occupied by Spain in the Americas. If Catholicism provided the cross, the Spanish language supplied the nails for the crucifixion of Native culture in Mesoamerica.

But no Christian holy sacrament or Spanish grammar rule could wipe out the deeply rooted ancestral Mesoamerican culture. Maybe there were just too many Natives in Mesoamerica to contend with. In reality, the dominant culture was never able to eradicate all pockets of resistance. And the same language, culture, and writing system brought over by the oppressors became at times agents for cultural survival and spiritual liberation, as Cuban intellectual Roberto Fernández Retamar eloquently stated in his 1971 essay "Calibán: Notes Toward a Discussion of Culture in Our America."[5]

For many of us, our America has been taken away from us. Our America has been invaded, occupied, whitewashed, gagged, suppressed, sanitized, and at best, ignored. But against all odds, the cultural tradition of Mesoamerica has survived and is alive, well, and all around us. It cannot be reduced to just museum artifacts, bones and stones, but can be found in the flesh and spirit of many contemporay Native and Mestizo peoples. Our mere existence is a testimony of our ancestors' will to live. The realization of this basic fact is both simple and complex. Mesoamerica as a civilization permeates all aspects of our daily lives, from the food we eat, the colors we prefer, to the ways we behave, worship, and even dream. Our nightmares and our visions are anchored in the psychodynamics of a Mesoamerican world view. The syncretic nature of La Virgen de Guadalupe is a case in point—ancient Mesoamerican goddess worship continues under a Catholic disguise.[6]

Mestizos/as have been actively engaged in a profound cultural revolution during the span of this century throughout this hemisphere. The universalist notion of *La Raza Cósmica* proposed in the 1920s by Mexican philosopher José Vasconcelos as the fulfillment of a Western humanistic utopia in which all human races intermingle to form an all-inclusive cosmic progeny has now been molded into the "new Mestiza consciousness" being advanced by contemporary Chicana writer Gloria Anzaldúa in her moving *Borderlands/La Frontera: The New Mestiza*:

> The new *Mestiza* copes by developing a tolerance for contradictions, a tolerance for ambiguity. She learns to be an Indian in Mexican culture, to be Mexican from an Anglo point of view. She learns to juggle cultures. She has a plural personality, she operates in a pluralistic mode—nothing is thrust out, the good, the bad and the ugly, nothing rejected, nothing abandoned. Not only does she sustain contradictions, she turns the ambivalence into something else.[7]

This new consciousness has been shaped by the present realities that we as Mestizos and Mestizas must face in our daily lives in the United States. It also implies a common struggle against the racism, classism, sexism, homophobia, and other forms of oppression still common in our complex society. But Anzaldúa warns, "Awareness of our situation must come before inner changes, which in turn come before changes in society. Nothing happens in the 'real' world unless it first happens in the images in our heads."[8] One of the most pressing changes that need to happen is our recognition and celebration of a cultural face of ours that has been suppressed and denied for so long: our living Mesoamerican heritage.

For me, this has been a very painful process that started the moment I was taunted as *el Indio* by relatives when I was a five-year-old boy in Wilmington, a Mexican barrio in Los Angeles where my family lived. I take after my father and happen to be much darker in complexion than my brothers. These relatives, originally from Jalisco as my father was, held some pernicious racist notions about skin color and Amerindian features. It wasn't until a family visit to Guadalajara, Mexico, in my childhood, that I got to meet my grandmother on my father's side, Doña Elvirita, *una prietita*, who immediately took me under her guidance and protection which endured even after her death when I was eighteen years old. Time has strengthened my memories of her. She was a shining example of a sound Mestizo way of life in unison with the Mesoamerican world view. This awareness has become sharper and more defined with years of study and reflection, and has helped me to take a real good look at myself. Gone are the shame and fear of before. I have come to see myself as part of a cultural continuum. Lots of things are beginning to make more and more sense.

Dialectics of *Mesticismo*   This awareness of our Mesoamerican past should be projected into our present and our future in radically new ways. Not in the nostalgic or romantic modes à la Rousseau, but as the liberating praxis of a new *Mestizo/a* consciousness. I have called this praxis *mesticismo*, which purposely combines *Mestizo* and *misticismo* ("mysticism"), in order to differentiate it from *mestizaje*. *Mesticismo* comes out of the experiences that the dominant cultures have confined to the realm of "other" and the "marginal," those condemned to live dangerously in psychological and cultural borderlands. *El mesticismo le da vuelta a la tortilla*, and sets out a fluid ontology in which any notion of "self" must include the "others," equally trespassing neat demarcations like subject/object, human/nature, us/them, and other similar dichotomies common to Western thought.

Old Mesoamerican paradigms are beginning to be studied and understood within their own systematic world views. Mesoamerican myth and wisdom, religion and science have often been dismissed out of ignorance and petulance.[9] Most missionaries and modern scholars have failed to recognize this Mesoamerican world as another human totality. As a cultural universe in itself, Mesoamerica has always been a constellation of different peoples, a historic area full of contradictions and riddled by conflict and ambiguities. But until now its sheer originality has been glanced over by missionaries, archeologists, anthropologists, and museographers. It's about time for contemporary artists, poets, and writers to interpret this reality in their own terms.

America must be able to see, hear, touch, taste, and smell this America. This may well lead us to new ways of "seeing," "reading," "feeling," "thinking," "creating," and "living." Why not envision, for example, a new eco-poetics grounded in a heritage thousands of years old that upholds that everything in the universe is sacred? Ancient Native paradigms could possibly offer some viable alternatives to modern dilemmas. Old keys could open new doors. But the ultimate irony of today is that five hundred years after the first landing of Columbus, America remains as mysterious as ever and a huge *terra incognita* for many who act and live as if they had just jumped ashore from one of first Spanish ships from afar, *La Pinta*, *La Niña*, and *Santa María*.

Notes

1. *Mestizo* is a Spanish word that identifies a person of mixed racial/ethnic background; it does not have the negative connotations of its English equivalents, "half-breed," "half-caste"; it has been increasingly accepted as a self-identity term by Latinos both in Latin America and in the United States.

2. Henry Wagner, *The Discovery of Yucatán by Francisco Hernández de Córdoba* (Berkeley, CA: The Cortes Society, 1942), p. 59.

3. *The Maya: Diego de Landa's Account of the Affairs of Yucatán*, edited and translated by A. R. Pagden (Chicago: J. Philip O'Hara, 1975), pp. 33–34.

4. Ibid., p. 168.

5. Roberto Fernández Retamar, *Calibán and Other Essays*, translated by Edward Baker, foreword by Fredric Jameson (Minneapolis: University of Minnesota Press, 1989).

6. According to tradition the Virgen de Guadalupe appeared and spoke in Nahuatl to Indian Juan Diego in Tepeyac, a hill in the outskirts of Mexico City, where Tonantzin, "Our Mother Goddess," was worshipped. Her image has been espoused to several social movements and causes both in Mexico and the U.S. Southwest. For example, her image appeared on the first Mexican flag of Father Miguel Hidalgo's Indian army fighting for independence from Spain in 1810, on the banner of the Mestizo popular armies of Emiliano Zapata in the Mexican Revolution of 1910, and also appeared in California along picket signs in the 1965 Delano grape strike organized by Chicano union leader César Chávez.

7. Gloria Anzaldúa, *Borderlands/La Frontera: The New Mestiza* (San Francisco: Spinsters/Aunt Lute, 1987), p. 79.

8. Ibid., p. 87.

9. A classical example of this is the colonial treatise on Nahuatl magic and curing practices titled *Tratado de las supersticiones y costumbres gentílicas que hoy viven entre los naturales desta Nueva España, 1629* (Treatise on the Superstitions and Heathen Customs That Today Live Among the Indians Native to This New Spain, 1629) by Hernando Ruiz de Alarcón, a Catholic priest who oftentimes missed (by large) the deep cultural insight of his captive Native informants. Using this same manuscript, I have intended to set the record straight with my own *Snake Poems* (San Francisco: Chronicle Books, 1992).

PART TWO

Diane Glancy

Sugar Woman

My heart is red & sweet.

—SITTING BULL

1.

What does Columbus have to do with America? He
came for gold. He wanted to find India and trade
spices. He had almost nothing to do with the
principles on which America is founded. That was
mainly England. And the Pilgrims nearly two hundred years
later.

But Columbus thought the world was round, and if he
sailed west, he'd come to India. He just didn't
realize there were a couple of continents in
the way. But he called us Indian anyway. He didn't
listen, but went ahead. That strong-headed, red-
blood gusto, that movement toward a goal despite
obstacles, is part of America. Putting a big foot
onto the world. Forging ahead. Even before
Copernicus & Galileo somewhere on a rooftop above
the night-blue streets of Poland or Italy looked up
into the skies and thought there was a good chance
we were the ones who moved. Didn't those kind of
people burn at the stake? Yet they insisted the
world was not flat. Columbus sailed because of it.

So in celebrating Christopher Columbus, America
celebrates someone who, five hundred years ago, stumbled
onto our land, or a little south of it, to be
exact. Nonetheless, after Columbus, the steady
flow of traffic from the east did not let up.

41

WITHOUT DISCOVERY

There had been the Vikings. Who knows who else.
But they left and not much changed. It was
different with Christopher Columbus. His arrival
marked the end of one time, and the opening of
another. After Columbus, the white man would keep
coming and forever change the life of the Native
American.

Thus, our 1992 quincentennial.

Part of them who came, by the way, were among my
ancestors, so I speak as an American, Native.

2.

So what of discovery?
Well, like the story of maple sugar
things would get harder.
At one time, you know
according to tradition
it used to rain syrup under the maple trees.
All you had to do was stick out your tongue.
And you know how the Indian loves sugar.

But the Trickster decided that was too easy.
He said the Indian would get lazy.
The Trickster said the Indian should work
for his sugar.
An offering of tobacco had to be made.
Fires built.
It should take a little patience & worry.
A little sweat.

So the Trickster taught the Indian
how to stick a hollow twig
into a maple tree
so the sap would run out.
He taught us to collect the sap
into birchbark buckets.
He showed the Indian how to cut & gather wood.
He taught us to make a rack
& light a fire underneath.

42

He taught us how to keep the fire burning
and to boil the sap for a long time.
This kept us from being idle.

1.

For one hundred-fifty-six years, from 1620 to 1776, our country
gradually developed a sense of law and self-
government. The Magna Carta. England's
Parliament. A lot of things. Certainly some ideas
of government also came from the Iroquois. Wasn't
it Ben Franklin who said that if self-government
could work for the savages, it could work for them?

There were some Visionaries. Real Human Beings, if
you want. Some in Philosophy. The Enlightenment.
The Individual going Somewhere.
A contract with government for that going.

Most of our Visionaries were in Politics. George
Washington. Thomas Jefferson. Madison. Hamilton.
Whoever else wrote the Declaration. The Constitution. The Removal Act. The opposite joint
of Democracy & Capitalism.

There should be said something about the English
Language.

Christianity.

But that is enough for now.

2.

So the life of the Native American moved west. No
longer would our ancestors be from the great salt-
waters toward the rising sun. Now we faced the
other direction.

To escape the new people that came.

To be removed to land west of the Mississippi where
we could be safe and reestablish ourselves as corn-
farmers.

WITHOUT DISCOVERY

The migratory Tribes moved also to follow the ever-
diminishing herds across the plains.

Hunger, disease, disheartedness, landlessness,
starvation, assimilation, annihilation.

1.

But the new America moving forward had Economists &
Moral Philosophers. Adam Smith said to be selfish
by working of the invisible hand produces good for
the whole country. That's why Capitalism. But it
has to be law enforced.

Morals between people to do right. The invisible
bonds which basically do by other people what
you do yourself.

The wealth of nations if people in the industrial
age making hayforks then the best hayfork at the
least price will sell. So it works. A good
hayfork at a reasonable price and the seller sells
with most saying what & who it is that sells.

2.

But without discovery would not have happened what
happened. The colluvium of two worlds. The running
amuck. Discovery had to be. What would we have
been without it? The coming sooner or later
wherever the land is vast & rich in grass and
leaves and clouds. The underneath workings. The
crackings. Blood flushing the Native American.
The American, Native. Fucking us up & down.
TaKING the land. Folding up our winter counts.
Giving us the dark ages.
It was going to be one of them.

Why not England with its brussels sprouts?

1.

But thc problern still The Bible says not one man
righteous. You know the godJesus whom they brought
too? And said they had the God we didn't know
and our blood was spilled because we didn't reckon
his.

Yes, it takes a Christian Conscience for Capitalism
to work. And the Equality of Democracy.
A Citizen has to judge his own actions the same way
he judges Others.

Pursuing one's own economic self-interest for the
good of the group.

But what when there is wrong? And The Bible says
there is.

So Capitalism only works with people being civil.
Having conscicnce respecting the law the others.
It doesn't work by itself alone.

So what do you do with the evil human nature?

2.

Despite the good of the Native American. The
American, Native. The knowledge of nature and
spirit. The sharing. Is it us too? With the evil
hand?

There in Vacation Bibleschool where my mother sent
me. Did not Jesus love the Sheep? If out of
animal transformations came the Shepherd. What out
of the Shepherd who gave Himself for his Sheep?
Called himself Lambie. The one-legged Christ on
the cross. Two-legged-nailed-to-one. I saw his
hobbling cross-walk when our legs tied together in
a sackrace. The sugarmaple Christ who called
himself Word. Who washed the evil hand. Is worth
a case of soda pop & all the sugared toast'ems you
can eat.

WITHOUT DISCOVERY

1.

Eminent Domain. Manifest Destiny.

It was going to happen. What other nation would
you rather have? Russia with its colossal economic
failure and disregard of human dignity?
Japan with its lack of individuality?

Communism is economic failure because the law of
supply & demand is put in reverse. Ideology & the
state decide what is made where and for whom the
broom.

The Japanese identify with their nation's central
planners for the good of the country and for
centuries doused the freedom. Brutal to the
individual.

If America has to be, then let it have its big
foot. Let it step unasked into the world.
Democracy & Capitalism & Christianity.
Let the American Work Ethic & Human Rightists
speak.

2.

So I, American, Native, a maple tree with a stick
stuck in my bark. The sap running out. Whee choo.
The collocation of my vocabulary. So what? Who
doesn't run with history. My sap gathered in the
birchbark bucket. Boiled until it turns syrup.
The syrup boiled until it's granulated. Until it's
maple sugar. Until I'm sweet roses & solid
as the icing's cake. I feel the rough tongues. Am I not
licked? My elbows & ears. Between my fingers.
Without discovery would I have had?

The tellings of the stories which have disappeared.
All that lighting extinguished.
It is enuf.
How long have I spoke of what I live without?

The trip from lodgepoles & canoes
to gravyboats & civilizedation.

The English & Amsterdamnthem.
Their lace curtains behind which the sap boils.
Am I not sweet?
Does not everyone stick out their tongue when I pass?

Against the cold
the new furnace heat.
No more framework of saplings, cattails & birchbark,
pineneedles & bullrushes, pinepitch & sprucegum.
Good-bye is what I had.

You know when Spring comes we move to maple trees
Build firerack for the iron kettles we traded
For birchbark buckets.
Ten skins beaver for one kettle.
You know the hot under the pot
The gathered-up-sap from trees
I now boiling sap
All kettles on fire
You see the white mans bring the heat
Yez they due
Their words danze in the iron kettle
The heats run up our legs
Into belly
Up into the hollows of our lungs
Out our mouth in hot words
I sing to godJesus save me
Whay deedo
Sometimes little holes
Pour some syrup into there
It holds-hard into candy
& granulated into maple sugar
Just boil long enough.

WITHOUT DISCOVERY

1.

But the truth has been stood on its nose if the
invisible hand means you can do anything you want
and everyone will profit. Human nature which is
the central self sucks in with all its lungs and
takes what is KING. Even the Indian would you
know.

So now they are in trouble and we can watch their
Wounded Knee.

We have lost our conscience.
As The Bible says we do.

Now American is the economic war.
What you put on others is what you get you see.

2.

The anger that rises. That's what I wouldn't have
without discovery. Possibly wholeness. Possibly
land. I may have even inVENTED something. But who
would have left the land alone? Come on. What am
I griping about? Just because I lost my hide-
scraper?

But it was more than that.

I feel outside the world that runs its separator
among us. The wings pulled out feather by feather
until there's only a scrawny wingbone flapping its
flying mov't. But going nowhere is a going into
finally somewhere. Did not our fathers speak
their vast world? What is vocabulary for? The
stickiness of maplesugar roses on a quincentennial
cake. Eat them and be glad.

Wehoda.

In Vacation Bibleschool

I saw the tobacco offerings in the smoke of the
tabernacle fire.
Making maplesugar.

I saw many strings of lives ago.
This knowledge of the godJesus.
Then burn off my hair like old brush in a field.
Clean a space for this New
coming horribly in ships & wagons & Cherokee
chiefs.

The English words are also Beings in themselves.
The bodies & spirit-transformations of them.
I speak the new language now.
My heart is jeep-red & sweet.

They suck me don't they?
I feel a lot of tongues.

Ed Chávez

The Minority Within

Los Reyes Catolicos decreed that by August 2, 1492, all Jews must leave Spain. There is speculation that Christopher Columbus did not coincidentally start his navigation on that date since some of his crew are believed to have been Sephardic Jews. And, because of the vagueness of what is known about his own beginnings, there is a persistent theory that Columbus himself may have been a *marrano*.

The departure date for his epic journey marks the time when the "Old" and the "New" Worlds, heretofore in mutual oblivion, were joined by a common identity as halves of the same world. Two distinct civilizations merged to spawn a third culture. And, as in any durable marriage, it has harrowed and hallowed, for better or for worse, these five hundred years.

In his endless exodus, the wandering Jew left Spain. Many fled to other parts of Europe rather than endure the Inquisition. For survival, some Sephardim denied their genesis and went through the motions of non-Jewish behavior in Spain by attending Mass, baptizing their young, and even eating ham. "Marranos," they called these pork-eating Jews. A lot of these *marranos* made their way to the New World.

But the Inquisition persisted even in this new Promised Land. Guilty until proven innocent, many careers and names were ruined merely by being accused of having sympathy for the Jew.

More flight. Oñate's assurance of property was as desirable as was the prospect of distance in his exploration. Distance from the Inquisition. North and further north they pushed settling at last in the mountains of the present upper New Mexico and lower Colorado.

Still the Inquisition prevailed. The *marranos* endured only by hiding. Of course, some telltale signs to the observant were there: work and frivolous activity stopped at sundown on Friday when

51

ancient menorahs were brought out only to be quickly snuffed when an unscheduled visitor called. Prayers from the *Pentateuch* were recited. But some were bold enough to mark the gravestones of their deceased with the Star of David. You can still find some of these markers in the very old cemeteries of northern New Mexico.

In time the Sephardim were absorbed and assimilated by the Catholic community, with only a stubborn faithful few passing down their Jewish practice at great risk through the generations. It is only a recent phenomenon that some of these Sephardic Jews are coming out. A few, but not all of them because of the historical recriminations. We hear of some of them expressing their shock, and later pride, upon learning what their *abuelita* or *tío viejo* had to reveal: *"Somos judíos."*

As a native New Mexican, my exposure to Jewry was practically nonexistent in my formative years. Jews were people who lived in New York. Or way over there across the sea where Hitler tried to destroy them. Only broader contact as an adult has made me more aware.

My first job with civil service was in a branch to the Watts Social Security office in Los Angeles. I was one of only three non-African Americans on the staff. I remember a disability beneficiary, Five Star Bradley, always came in at the beginning of the month to complain we spelled his first name wrong. He would explain it should not be spelled out but should be represented by five asterisks. Each month I would have to again explain the payee's name has to be spelled out on government checks to keep it negotiable.

Being the new kid on the block, this diversionary interview was routinely assigned to me. It took time but it freed up the more experienced representatives to complete applications. The interview was always a learning experience I welcomed because I was able to develop skills in listening and communication.

One particularly busy Monday morning, while filling out a difficult application in Spanish with a claimant who had a speech impairment, I heard Five Star up front complaining to the receptionist. Eyeing my two other appointment slips I had to do by noon, my groan leaked down to a sigh when the field representative volunteered to take the "quickies."

"Five Star Bradley," the African-American field rep called.

"I doan wanna talk to you, man," Five Star wagged his head.

"But I can help you right now." The field rep wasn't easily put off.

"Nosiree! I wanna talk to that Jew boy back there," Five Star said, pointing to me.

While I felt successful in achieving a rapport with Five Star, I was bemused he would misclassify my minority status. Oh, it wasn't the first time that happened to me. While in the Air Force I put up with the usual racial epithets, but two of those times were because I was mistaken for a Jew. I still don't know which stereotypical features I share with the Jew, but I can only guess it is my nose and my complexion.

So it has been with avid interest I have read about the hidden Jew in the Hispanic community. The Scotch-Irish lineage on my mother's side had already been traced by my grandfather, while my paternal Hispanic roots were taken for granted and accepted by oral tradition. However, I couldn't help thinking I am a descendant of the Sephardim, a member of the lost tribe of Israel, an exile of the *Reyes Catolicos*. The notion excited me, and I tracked my father's line with that in mind.

In my research I learned most Spanish names ending in *-es* or *-ez* may be Sephardic. Shimon Peres came to mind. Perez! I was on to something. However, I learned such discussions among my relatives, both sides, only caused alarm. Jewish blood!? My Hispanic relatives didn't see any celebrity in identifying myself—them!—with Jews. My search was debunked as silly, and I was advised to let well enough alone.

I was not so much surprised as disappointed when I perceived a latent bias against the Jew among my own kin. The Jew with whom we had little or no contact. A prejudice by we who had to put up with marginal acceptance.

Fra Angelico Chávez had already made an exhaustive study of the family name. It is only a coincidence my surname ends with *-ez*. My patronymic, it seems, comes from the name of a town in Spain not at all associated with the Sephardim. And another explanation holds that the name is a mispronunciation of the five keys on the family crest (that is, *llaves* = *chaves*). Other leads dried up or smacked into dead ends. I couldn't make any connection to the Sephardim.

So much for my link to the *Pinta*.

Still, this tangible lineage is not necessary for me to beam by the knowledge that my heritage is identifiable in this five-century chain. All Hispanic Americans for some reason escaped the Old for the promise of the New. It is debatable any *criollos* can trace their line back that far on American soil. But the *mestizo, mulatto,* and *genizaro* abound. These mixtures are unavoidable for most Hispanic Americans.

There is a uniqueness to this blend. No European or native American can point to the date they came to be. Nor by no means can the dominant European American lay claim to an American heritage on this soil for as far back as the Hispano can.

Yet…And yet there's that European-American side to me. Normally a *coyote* (mixed Hispanic and Anglo) grows up in one predominant culture. The Hispanic community usually welcomes *coyotes* affectionately as a curious unblemished "half breed." A strange misnomer since some explaining needs to be made if one is to claim he is a "pure Chicano."

But sometimes the *coyote* is reared in the Anglo community. If his surname is not Hispanic, and "racial purity" is important to his family, then his Hispanic strain can be conveniently overlooked and best left in the closet with the other Sephardic skeletons. But if the *coyote* has a Hispanic surname, then an anglicized pronunciation is in order if not a complete name change.

Then there are some of us *coyotes* who grow up in both the Hispanic and Anglo communities. While both sides are often loving, they're not all that forgiving. Funny little taboos encroach. On the Hispanic side, suspicions that you're not quite with them and, if you could (some perceive), you would deny or drain your Latin blood. On the other hand, the Anglo side in varying degrees doesn't entirely forgive the *coyote's* sanguine flaw. A *coyote*, after all, is impure.

That, at least, is the circumstance I grew up in. Neither fish nor fowl nor good red herring. Not one hundred percent accepted nor completely rejected by either side. Just a qualified acknowledgment, a bastard to chuckle over. At the risk of sounding whinish I mention this because I have discussed this with other *coyotes* and I can't dismiss it as a quirky paranoia. It's there and it's real.

So? So, the point is nothing has changed. We each have a little hidden *marrano* inside us. This is very much a part of the human condition. Look at the Iberian. He's very proud of his flamenco music and dance, but if he is of *pura sangre* (and I know of no Spaniard who will claim anything less), he disdains anyone of Gypsy descent. And, even five hundred years after the expulsion of the Moor, in spite of the grand architectural and scientific heritage, the subjugation can still rankle the Spaniard. The Sephardi, of course, had to go because he was a reminder of that past and avowed a faith no self-righteous Christian could abide.

Then Spain set up in the New World a system that penalized not only the Native American and the *mestizo*, but his own blood! The purebred *criollo* could not hold title since he was not *born* in Iberia. To matter in a Spanish colony, it was not enough to be an *hidalgo;* he had to have been born in Spain.

Mixed blood further diluted any claim he might have. The "purer" the blood, the more land and rights could he claim. It was imperative, then, to deny the *indio* in his lineage. Naturally, the Sephardi was anathema.

Small wonder then the Hispanic still feels oppressed in America. It's an imposed historical psychology of self-hatred perpetuated by modern attitudes. In spite of civil rights violations, if one man can dominate another, he will. And it's a natural tendency made easier for the predator by one who doubts his worth.

Man's perfectibility notwithstanding, if his pursuit of happiness is to be had at *any* cost, then that, too, is part of the human condition. A condition which dictates it's okay to tread on those who will let you, on those who missed out, and know it, merely because of the accident of their birth.

Which is too bad because it doesn't have to be. Such thinking ignores Benito Juárez's injunction for tolerance: *"El respeto al derecho ajeno es la paz."* There is no peace without mutual respect. This is an *indio's* timeless warning against irresponsible right. "Might is right" is what Juárez reasoned against.

To overturn the oppressor just for revenge doesn't work. It doesn't work not only because it's impractical but because it's plain wrong. It only perpetuates the cycle of hatred. A cycle in which there will never be peace.

But we are what we are. Good ol' Cristóbal Colón's voyage gave us all a chance to set the human condition right, and after five hundred years, we still haven't blown it. Yet. Even though the past half millennium spans boggling achievements in human discovery, man is still stymied by the way he treats himself.

People can't change people by wishing it or by even willing it; each has to change himself. Only with resolution and self-discipline can we turn this myopic scrutiny around in the next five hundred years. We have to. We've repeatedly come so close to undoing it all.

The New Testament offers a remedy. It tells us to love our neighbor as ourselves. Only, how can we respect anyone if we don't respect ourselves?

Indeed, we're still in the Promised Land. But we have to stop behaving like *marranos*. We have to step forward, not out of defiance, but with dignity. Until we achieve acceptance, acceptance of ourselves and acceptance of others, every man will remain a minority, every man a wandering Jew.

José Barreiro

What 1992 Means to American Indians

The Quincentenary events that will culminate in 1992 mark a decisive moment in the history of the American Indian peoples— the "other" eyes looking out from the "New World" shores on the eve of contact. A survey, initiated by Gabriela Tayac, a Piscataway student, asks the minds behind those eyes, at long last, for their viewpoints on the Quincentenary.

The rationale for the survey was not to seek cultural self-definition in one particular event, even one as momentous as the Quincentenary, but to delineate fundamental attitudes in Indian communities toward the event. Among the topics covered were cultural survival, cultural continuity, and strategies for culture-sensitive, ecologically sustainable development.

The principal message and concern of Indian respondents to the survey is that the five hundredth anniversary of contact between European and American cultures, which falls in 1992, will provide a rare hemispheric opportunity to review the history, as well as the contemporary social conditions, of the American Indian peoples. The majority of respondents believe that October 12, 1992, is a date signifying five hundred years of Native resistance. Those who voiced their attitudes concerning the Quincentenary conveyed expressions of rage and reconciliation, grief and hope, fear and endurance. "We have resisted assimilation and genocide," wrote Henri Mann Morton, director of Native American Studies at the University of Montana. Lorraine E. White, president of the Quechan Indian Tribe in Yuma, Arizona, wrote, "We as Natives still retain our individuality as a group in spite of continuous efforts to mold us into the mainstream of the white man's society." LaDonna Harris, Cherokee and director of Americans for Indian Opportunity, stated, "After five hundred years, we still exist—and not only exist, but contribute."

One widespread fear about the Quincentenary is that Indian perspectives will be drowned out. Tim Coulter, Potawatomi and executive director of the Indian Law Resource Center in Washington, D.C., voiced such a concern: "My fear is that the Quincentenary will become a kind of racist festival without meaning—that it will merely celebrate the European domination of Native Americans." In a similar vein, the Native American Ministry to the 1989 Annual Conference of the United Methodist Church noted, "Many immigrant peoples will be inclined toward a celebration of the Columbus Quincentenary...The potential exists for an uncritical self-affirmation during this time [which would only serve to] perpetuate an illusion of [the] continuing superiority of Euro-American culture and values."

Although respondents expressed a range of opinions, most agreed that "celebrating" the event was unacceptable. The Assembly of First Nations, a national Canadian Indian organization, issued a formal resolution stating: "For the First Nations to celebrate the near destruction of our culture and our identity would be insane."

That such feelings are not confined to the United States and Canada is seen in a number of responses from Central and South America. Margarito Crespin Esquino of the National Association of Salvadorean Indians, replied "Columbus landed in El Salvador on September 15. For us it's the day of the thieves, when they came to steal our land." "To celebrate," said Augusto Cana Mamani of the Tupac Amaru Inka Regional Council of Cusco, Peru, "would be like the Jews rendering homage to Hitler every few years or the Japanese revering Truman for Nagasaki and Hiroshima."

When asked the multiple-item question: "In what way would you characterize the Quincentenary?" seventy percent described it either as "five hundred years of Native people's resistance to colonization," or as the "anniversary of a holocaust." Twenty percent categorized it as a "commemoration of a cultural encounter," while only six percent considered it a "celebration of discovery."

Sixty-four percent considered the Quincentenary a "unique historical event," seventy-four percent even seeing it as some sort of "opportunity." Fifteen percent, on the other hand, said they would prefer to "ignore it" completely. As to the most appropriate activities for commemorating the event, seventy-eight percent favored educational conferences and festivals, while only nineteen percent preferred the idea of organizing protests and legal actions.

Finally, respondents indicated a desire to personally participate in the attainment of various goals: public education about Native issues attracted forty-three percent; advancing legislation to protect Native rights, twenty-seven percent; increasing communication networks, twenty percent; and demands of public apologies from Western states and churches, only seven percent.

The overarching mandate drawn from the responses was best articulated by Dianne Longboat, coordinator of Indian Health Careers Program at the Six Nations Reserve in Ontario: "We owe it to our ancestors to tell their story," she wrote. Beatriz Painquco, Mapuche from Chile, gave a similar response "[the Quincentenary] is an opportunity to publicly expose our vision and to put our voices together."

Kiowa author and Pulitzer Prize winner N. Scott Momaday, while admitting to "very mixed feelings about celebrating this event," insisted that "Indians have just as much right to celebrate the occasion as anyone else. If Indians exclude themselves from it, that's a negative thing. If they can find a way to celebrate it on a real basis, that's positive—they stand to teach the rest of the world something."

Based on these responses it would seem that Indians should initiate as many conferences and symposia as possible and take on the responsibility of drawing media attention to the alternative and independently valid "view from the shore." Efforts to coordinate the seasoned Indian and Indian-connected voices from across tribal nations and academic disciplines would be particularly fruitful.

Foundations should be challenged to search out the Indian grassroot organizations, small as well as large, and to make a special effort to identify Indian projects in this Quincentenary season. There is a critical need to fund tribal representatives and to sponsor their participation in conferences and seminars. Multiethnic views on the Quincentenary need to emerge.

Special programs directed at young people will be of particular value. There is an urgent need to provide programs that will challenge youth to formulate a contemporary sense of themselves and their cultural identity. Requiring special consideration are the efforts of tribal archives and museums to retain the knowledge base of traditional elders. It is important to encourage young people to spend time with their elders, and to encourage language retenetion. Another strategic area is land-based community development, particularly in agriculture, following both the traditional and the modern commercial models. Yet another is media development within Indian communities. Women's and community health groups need support as well, and in the area of law there are several strategic agendas dealing with Indian rights. Such programming can be diverse but in its own way still be relevant to the Quincentenary.

Some of the most important work being done on behalf of indigenous peoples over the past two decades is in the area of human rights and cultural genocide. In the United Nations this task is now being carried out by the Working Group on Indigenous Populations, a subcommittee within the Commission on Human Rights.

Less known, but just as important, are the efforts, goals, and achievements of the indigenous communities themselves. Many are now faced with the need to revitalize and rebuild their communities in a manner that will permit them to compete successfully with the world at large. In their struggles they are as concerned with modernization, economic markets, technologies, and networks as is the dominant society. For the Quincentenary to acquire legitimacy among indigenous peoples, the event must be an affirmation of such efforts. Then the indigenous peoples of the Americas might indeed see something there to celebrate.

Carlos Muñoz, Jr.

Reclaiming Our Heritages

Every year during the month of May, Mexican Americans celebrate a holiday called "Cinco de Mayo." The holiday as celebrated in Mexico commemorates a battle in the city of Puebla on May 5, 1862, between a poorly armed Mexican peasant army and a superior French military force sent by emperor Napoléon III to occupy Mexico. The Mexicans fought heroically and defeated Napoléon's army but eventually lost the war. Napoléon appointed Archduke Maximilian of Austria the emperor of Mexico. His reign lasted until 1867 when he was defeated by the army of previously ousted Mexican president Benito Juárez. Mexicans are proud of the Cinco de Mayo battle because it was won against overwhelming odds against a superior European imperialist power. But it is one of the least celebrated holidays in Mexico.

The Cinco de Mayo became a Mexican-American holiday because of the Chicano student movement during the late 1960s. Movement activists had actually preferred to celebrate the sixteenth of September, the most significant Mexican holiday, which commemorates the revolution of 1810 and the date Mexico won its independence from Spain. But that holiday occurred prior to the beginning of the fall quarter at most campuses. The fifth of May, in contrast, fit nicely into the spring quarter, allowing ample time for organization of festivities. The student movement therefore made Cinco de Mayo its annual major event to promote pride in Mexican culture and identity. The holiday came to symbolize a history of Mexican and Chicano struggles not widely known among Mexican-American youth and the society at large. It came to represent much more than simply the commemoration of a battle somewhere in Mexico over a hundred years ago. To Chicano movement activists, and to thousands if not millions of Mexican Americans, Cinco de Mayo came to represent their continuing struggle for jus-

61

tice in a racist, capitalist, and patriarchal society.

Lost Purpose   During the last twenty years,
however, Cinco de Mayo has lost much of its original purpose.
Cinco de Mayo concerts, fiestas, and parades have become commonplace on college campuses and in Mexican-American and Latino communities throughout the U.S. With very few exceptions,
the emphasis of all the events is on entertainment. Chicano musicians, movie stars, mainstream politicians, and other celebrities
have replaced the radical speakers from the leadership ranks of a
once vibrant Chicano movement and other Mexican-American
radical struggles. Discussions of issues facing Chicanos and Latinos as a whole, and serious dialogue emphasizing political struggle, is for the most part missing from the agendas at most celebrations. Cinco de Mayo has become simply a celebration of culture in
isolation from the political realities confronting our people in this
dark hour of the "New World Order."

Cinco de Mayo has sadly become an "American" commercial
holiday. It has been co-opted by U.S. multinational corporations,
especially in the food and beverage business. Television commercials featuring Latino actors during prime time become commonplace during late April and throughout the month of May. Taco
Bell and other fast food corporations spend millions of dollars
promoting their "Mexican" products. Budweiser, Coors, and other
liquor producers make big profits off Latinos while simulta-
neously contributing to the tragic high rates of alcoholism in our
communities. Apparel products are sold with Mexican motif. One
year Macy's sold a women's shoe style called "La Chicana."

More tragically, the message implicit in the television commercials is that "Hispanics" are a happy-go-lucky people with few
worries who are making it into the mainstream of society. They
can afford to buy not only the "best beer" but the hottest looking
cars and popular fashion as well. In addition, for the most part the
actors in these commercials are light-skinned Latinos, thus pro-
jecting our image as a white ethnic minority in conformity with
the Hispanic identity that has been promoted since the decline of
the Chicano movement. Cinco de Mayo has in fact become a His-
panic-American holiday promoting a politics of assimilation and
accommodation for Latinos. The politics of identity and culture

have shifted from the definition of Chicanos as a people of color rooted in the indigenous peoples of the Americas.

Between now and next year, Mexican Americans need to reclaim the original purpose of Cinco de Mayo and reject the Hispanic identity that undermines the racial and cultural realities of our people. Latinos as a whole are being prepared to be central to the forthcoming commemoration of the five hundredth anniversary of Christopher Columbus's "discovery" of America in 1492. The National Endowment for the Humanities, for example, has been funding research projects since 1984 on the "Columbian Quincentenary." Much is being said and will be said by scholars and politicians about the virtues of Spanish culture and civilization imposed on our indigenous ancestors. As Latinos we must prepare a critical response to the forthcoming events. We cannot and should not deny the historical reality that indeed Spanish culture and language are part of us. But collectively we must remember where the vast majority of us come from in terms of our indigenous racial and cultural origins.

An important response to the Columbian Quincentenary is to reject the Hispanic identity label that was imposed on us in the 1970s by Latino and white *burrocrats* (bureaucrats) in the corridors of power in Washington, D.C. It is an identity promoted by those committed to a politics of assimilation and accommodation. A politics of Latino bilingualism, biculturalism, self-determination, and change has not been in evidence since the late 1960s and early 1970s when the Chicano and Boricua movements existed.

Many Latinos have also accepted the Hispanic identity label as a means of protection from racism that comes when one is identified as non-white. Others truly believe they are indeed white and not people of color. Government, educational, and private agencies identify us as "Hispanic white." In California, for example, Mexican-American newborn babies are automatically identified as "white" on their birth certificates. The 1990 census included Latinos as part of the white population. Most Latinos, therefore, do not see much common ground with African, Asian, or Native Americans.

Hispanic identity is rooted in the old melting pot theory of assimilation that was first applied to white European ethnics. It underscores the white European culture of Spain at the expense of

63

the non-white cultures that have profoundly shaped the experiences of all Latinos. According to the dictionary meaning, Hispanics are "lovers of Spain or Spanish culture." *Hispaña* was the term given to the Iberian peninsula, which came to be known as Spain. No mention is made of the non-white indigenous cultures of the Americas, Africa, and Asia, which historically have produced the multicultural and multiracial peoples in all of the Americas.

It is argued by politicians, and others more well-meaning, that the Hispanic identity underscores our common denominator of the Spanish language, serves to unite us, and promotes our collective political clout. But the reality is that, due to a racist educational system and the process of assimilation that we are forced to undergo, most of us are unfortunately monolingual. Spanish is spoken largely only by those who are recent immigrants or who have consciously resisted white cultural hegemony. In addition, we are a multitude of different cultural groups, each with its own unique history, and each deserving its place in the sun. Furthermore, Latinos do not share the same extent of inequality. Consequently, there are different political agendas that are not conducive to political unity simply on the basis of Hispanic identity.

What we should do in 1992, instead of celebrating a Hispanic Cinco de Mayo and the "Columbian Quincentenary" commemorating the conquest of our indigenous ancestors, is to strengthen our respective Mexican, Puerto Rican, Cuban, Central and Latin American identities and limit the use of Hispanic to those who care not to acknowledge their indigenous cultural ancestry and those who in fact come from Spain. We should celebrate our respective unique cultures and strive for political unity with other people of color on the common ground of racial, gender, and class inequality.

Interview with *Suzan Shown Harjo*

We Have No Reason to Celebrate an Invasion

Suzan Shown Harjo is president and director of the Morning Star Foundation in Washington, D.C. The foundation sponsors the 1992 Alliance, formed to provide an indigenous peoples' response to the Columbus Quincentenary. Harjo, a 45-year-old Cheyenne-Creek, agreed to answer questions about why some people are not celebrating the Quincentenary. She was interviewed by Barbara Miner of Rethinking Schools.

Why aren't you joining in the celebrations of the Columbus Quincentenary?

As Native American peoples in this red quarter of Mother Earth, we have no reason to celebrate an invasion that caused the demise of so many of our people and is still causing destruction today. The Europeans stole our land and killed our people.

But because the Quincentenary is a cause célèbre, it provides an opportunity to put forth Native American perspectives on the next five hundred years.

Columbus was just "a man of his times." Why are you so critical of him? Why not look at the positive aspects of his legacy?

For people who are in survival mode, it's very difficult to look at the positive aspects of death and destruction, especially when it is carried through to our present. There is a reason we are the poorest people in America. There is a reason we have the highest teen suicide rate. There is a reason why our people are ill-housed and in poor health, and we do not live as long as the majority population.

That reason has to do with the fact that we were in the way of Western civilization and we were in the way of westward expansion. We suffered the "excesses" of civilization such as murder, pillage, rape, destruction of the major waterways, destruction of land, the destruction and pollution of the air.

What are those "positive" aspects of the Columbus legacy? If we're talking about the horse, yeah, that's good. We like the horse.

65

Indians raised the use of the horse to high military art, especially among the Cheyenne people and the tribes of the plains states.

Was that a good result of that invasion? Yes. Is it something we would have traded for the many Indian peoples who are no longer here because of that invasion? No.

We also like the beads that came from Europe, and again we raised their use to a high art. Would we have traded those beads for the massacres of our people, such as the Sand Creek massacre (in which U.S. soldiers massacred hundreds of Native American men, women, and children at Sand Creek, Colorado in 1864)? No.

Why do we focus on Columbus rather than any number of U.S. presidents who were also responsible for the death and destruction of Indian people? Because it's his five hundred years; it's his quincentenary.

Isn't criticism of Columbus a form of picking on the Spaniards? Were they any worse than other Europeans who came to America? In my estimation, the Spaniards were no worse than any number of other Europeans. The economy of slavery and serfdom that existed in northern Europe—how do you measure that in cruelty and in long-term effects against the Spanish Inquisition?

I view the issue more as the oppressive nature and arrogance of the Christian religions. And that continues today.

Our Indian religions are not missionary religions. We are taught to respect other religions. It was a shock when we were met with proselytizing zealots, especially those who thought that if your soul can't be saved, you're better off dead—or if your soul can be saved, you should be dead so you can go to heaven. And that's the history of that original encounter.

How does that arrogance and ignorance manifest itself today? How? Well, for example, the Catholic Church has said that 1992 is a time to enter into a period of grace and healing and to celebrate the evangelization of the Americas. My word, how can you be graceful and healing about the tens of thousands of native people who were killed because they would not convert to a religion they didn't understand, or because they didn't understand the language of those making the request?

It's difficult to take seriously an apology that is not coupled with atonement. It's as if they're saying, "I'm sorry, oops, and we'll be better in the next hemisphere." That doesn't cut it. We've had empty platitudes before.

The combination of arrogance and ignorance also results in making mascots of Indian people, of dehumanizing and stereotyping them—in the sports world, in advertising, and in society at large. The Washington Redskins football team is an excellent example.

There is no more derogatory name in English for Indian people than the name "Redskins." And "Redskins" is a prominent image right here in the nation's capital that goes by unnoticed. Because we are an invisible population, the racism against us is also invisible for the most part.

You don't see sports teams called the White Trash, the Black Chicks, the Jew Boys, or the Jack Mormons. And if we did see that, it wouldn't be for long, you can be sure of that.

Why can't we use the Columbus quincentenary to celebrate American diversity and the contributions of all, Europeans and Native Americans alike? There will be lots of people who will be putting forth the perspective of "rah rah Columbus, rah rah Western Civilization." Our perspective is putting forth native peoples' views on our past and present. We also want to get into the public consciousness the notion that we actually have a future on this planet. This is something missed by even what is hailed as the most progressive of American movies, *Dances with Wolves.*

We're more interested in the five hundred years before Columbus and what will go on in the next five hundred years. The truth of the intervening five hundred years is really known in the hearts of people worldwide, even though the particulars have been obscured by a cotton-candy version of history.

Aren't some of the criticisms of Columbus just substituting Native-centrism for Eurocentrism? Oppressed people need to be centered within themselves. Racism and centrism become a problem if you are in the dominant society and are subjugating other people as a result of your centrism. I don't accept the question. I think it's an empty argument.

Aren't criticisms of Columbus just another form of ensuring "political correctness"? The Eurocentric view, having been exposed for its underlying falsehood, now wishes to oppose any other view as either equally false or simply the flip side of reality: a secondary or dual reality.

Feelings are usually dual realities; perspectives are dual realities. But there are some things that don't have a dual reality. For example, if we look at who has polluted all of our water, causing a whole lot of death and a whole lot of illness in this country alone, then we have a bit of a clue where the problem might rest. We have a clue whose reality might expose the truth and whose reality might obscure the truth.

It's about time for the people who are the true historic revisionists, who are on the far right side of this whole political correctness debate, to stop lying to themselves, to their readership and to their students. They must stop their silly ivory tower kinds of debates about whether multiculturalism should be used, and so forth.

What is the true history? Just start dealing with some undisputable realities. The world is a mess. This country is a mess. The people who fare the worst in this country are poor, non-white children and poor, non-white old people. Societies who do not care for their young people and old people are decadent, decaying societies.

I think there are a lot of good minds that are reflecting that decadence and decay when they choose to spend their time on these kinds of ivory tower debates. There are things about which they can do much, and they are doing nothing.

What should be the goal and perspective of teachers when telling their elementary and high school students about Columbus? First, that no one knows the truth about Columbus. His story is a very complex history in and of itself. Too often, this history is posed as romantic myth, and the uncomfortable facts about Columbus are eliminated.

Explaining the unpleasant truths about Columbus does not

take away from the fact that he was able to lurch over to these shores in three little boats. In fact, it gives the story of Columbus more dimension. It also makes it easier for kids in school to accept not only Columbus but other things.

Teachers need to respect the truth. What happens if I'm sitting in a classroom and teachers are telling me that Thomas Jefferson was one of the greatest men in the world, and I also know that he owned slaves, but they don't tell me that? What am I going to do when I'm told, "Don't use or abuse drugs or alcohol"? Will I think there may be another side to that too? What else am I being told that isn't true?

Kids are smart. And they have not experienced enough setbacks to know that they have to be sheep. But that's what they're taught in the public schools—how to exercise not personal discipline, but top-down discipline. It's the "do as you're told" approach to the world, rather than trying to help kids understand their place in the world.

We have to inject more truth in the classroom generally. And that only comes from discussion. I guess I'm a fan of the Socratic method.

What are the key struggles that native people face today?
We need, in the first instance, basic human rights such as religious freedom. Or how about life, liberty, and the pursuit of happiness, and other things that many people in the United States view as standard fare but are out of reach for Indian people?

There is also the issue of land and treaty rights. We have property that we don't own and we should, and we have property that we own that we don't control and we should.

We have treaties with the United States that are characterized in the U.S. Constitution as the supreme law of the land. Yet every one, without exception, of nearly four hundred treaties signed between native peoples and the U.S. government has been broken. Every one of them.

A good place to start would be for the United States to live up to every treaty agreement. It's also the way you get at resolving some of the problems of poverty, alcoholism, unemployment, and poor health.

If we don't handle the big things, we can't get to the manifestations of the problem. We have to go to the basic human rights issues, the basic treaty rights issues.

If we don't resolve these issues, then all people in this country are going to be complicit in the continuing effort to wipe out our Indian people. It's as simple as that.

PART THREE

Gerald Vizenor

Moccasin Games
Christopher Columbus
on Talk Radio

The Heirs of Columbus

I never said he was a "genetic fascist," but newspapers had their way with our investigative report to the select committee on the insurrection of the Heirs of Columbus. Point Roberts, Washington, on October 12, 1992, became the tribal republic of Assinika. My report said he was a "political shaman with the mind of a genetic tribalist."

Stone Wabanish was the central figure in my investigation. He could be a tribal shaman; he is a dreamer with an interior vision, to be sure, and an adventurer who practices silence, but he is more secular than sacred, more public than private, and closer to cash flow than to ecstatic journeys and symbolic death. Shaman, or not, he and his band of mutant warriors invaded Point Roberts, once a military reservation detached from the international border, and declared a new nation in the name of tribal stones.

I was hired by two military intelligence agencies to report on the insurrection and to investigate the genetic research, genome regeneration, and potential for biological weapons in Assinika.

Stone told the world on talk radio that he had isolated the ultimate tribal power of his ancestors. No one paid much attention at first, tribal leaders are never serious about dreamers, but then there were reliable reports that mutants and tribal children with birth defects were being healed by a sacred tribal gene.

The Ghost Dance Gene heals diseases, regenerates bodies, and much more; parthenogenetic conceptions, for instance, the birth of tribal children with no sex or sin, have been reported at the new nation. So, you can imagine, when other countries and international corporations responded to this new tribal state, the military wanted more information.

I was hired as an investigator because of my previous assignments in military intelligence. I knew many of the warriors from the reservation where we lived and hunted as kids. Most of us were more religious than radical, more humorous than criminal, but we were serious at our stories and play, we had to be to survive.

Stone had always been ahead of the pack, nothing held him down, not the weather, not the government, not even night. He made the best use of his dreams, a practice he said was natural, "imaginative territories that came with the signature genes." So, he was always the source of good stories, and no one on the reservation was surprised that he made a fortune on a floating casino. But most people thought he had been touched by evil when he started his gene code talks on late night radio.

Stone wore a gold mask the first time he invited me to the Headwaters Tavern for the annual stories by the Heirs of Columbus. I knew he had real soul power, but the genetic theories he told on radio were too much for most people to believe. He had gone beyond the world of dreamers and play on the reservation. He was out there, way out there, and then we discovered how far out he had gone with molecular biologists.

Stone claims that Jesus Christ and Christopher Columbus are both Mayan Indians. Now, most people can laugh at that much, trickster stories you would assume, but our gene man insists that these two adventurers inherited a sacred genetic code that heals tribal souls, mortal racial wounds, and mutations caused by nuclear waste and chemical pollution. Stone has named his code, or signature, this ultimate tribal power, the Ghost Dance Gene.

The Natural Casino   The Christopher Columbus Casino opened on international waters and turned the weather out of season; winters were never the same on the reservation. Two Tone, for instance, the old man who lies that he is more than a hundred, taught his mongrels how to howl *"wingo, wingo, wingo,"* when someone won at bingo.

The tribal elders renounced satellite television to hear the wild sound of bingo numbers. For the few who won, there were trickster summers in the spring; even the losers returned with their best stories.

Stone Wabanish, a native son from the reservation, owned the casino and made a fortune in four seasons on games of chance; not in the winter with trickster stories, as his envious critics now contend, but in the heart of summer when white tourists gambled on vacation in northern Minnesota.

The Columbus Casino opened on a houseboat and then moved to an enormous barge near an island on Lake of the Woods. Stone, who was the grandson of a man who collected boxes on the reservation, convinced the federal people that a casino on international waters could be declared a new reservation area outside of state jurisdiction and exempt from tax laws; new, indeed, the casino was a word, water, and chance reservation.

The water casino was a natural sensation the instant it opened that summer; network television aired tumid series on the lost tribes, and three romantic feature stories on the unusual genetic theories of the crossblood founder who had traced his descent from the great adventurer Christopher Columbus.

"The red bloods returned to this continent more than a century before the blue bloods arrived the first time," he told a reporter for the *New York Times*. "Understand that some tribes trace their blood to the *Santa María*, not the late *Mayflower*."

Stone posed on television but he never spoke to a camera; he agreed, however, to be heard on national radio talk shows. He was raised on radio late at night; the discussions and arguments he listened to as a child earned his admiration and stimulated his imagination. Those late night talks were the sources of conversations on the reservation.

Stone trusted the radio, and he understood the voices he heard late at night; the mythic fears in the woodland, the sarcastic humor, and the bold patriotism that he heard on radio talk shows, he imagined in cold rooms and in the back seats of abandoned cars on the reservation. He was no trickster landlubber; he was a natural on a casino reservation in the water.

Big Bin Wabanish, his grandfather, insisted that his grandson was a genius because he could "reason much better than the radio." The old man convinced a few listeners that he was a shaman; he cocked an ear, listened to his box collection as a diviner might, and then told the histories of what the cardboard once contained. Whatever he said about the world seemed believable because he was the son of a shaman who could regenerate body parts by imagination.

Stone was heard on the radio by millions of people late at night in the summer. The crossblood of the northern air told stories that would soon transform memories, the origin of the tribes, and the genetic state of the nation. As he spoke from the bridge of his barge, thousands of people circled the casino in canoes, power boats, and float planes from the cities. The people came to gamble on a floating reservation; they were white and on vacation, urban adventurers who waited on the water to lose at lotto, cards, and slot machines.

"Admiral White is on the air, your late night host on Carp Radio." The radio was heard in four directions on enormous loudspeakers over the mast. "Stone is back to answer your questions and mine. Here we are once more in the dark, so, do you expect our listeners to buy the story that your brother is a stone, a common rock?"

"Stone is my name, not my brother, and we are not common," said Stone. His voice was rich and wild, a primal sound late at night that boomed over the lake. "The stone is my totem, my nation, there are stones in my tribal families, and the brother of the first trickster who created the earth was a stone."

"Really, but how can you be a stone, a real stone?" she asked and then paused for a commercial. The talks from the casino two or three times a week had attracted new listeners and pleased the advertisers.

"Stones hold our tribal origins and our words in silence, in the same way that we listen to stories and hold our past in silence," said Stone.

"Stone, listen, our listeners know you were born on a reservation, and we understand how proud you are to be an Indian, so how can you claim to be a direct descendant of a stone and Christopher Columbus?"

"Columbus was Mayan," said Stone.

"You must be stoned," she said and laughed. Her voice bounced on the water, and the boats rocked with laughter near the casino. "Really, you must be stoned on that reservation boat; Columbus was Italian not Mayan."

"Columbus was here on the great river, he was an adventurer in the blood, and he returned to his homeland," he said from the bridge of the casino.

"His homeland, now wait a minute, this is serious."

"Stories are always serious," he shouted.

"Mayan genes, are you serious or what?" asked the Admiral.

"The truth is in my genes; we are the tribal heirs of the great explorer, and he was here with us looking for gold and tribal women," said Stone.

"So, what did he find?"

"Dorado, the golden tribal woman."

"Now we get the real story."

"Dorado is a sister to the fish," said Stone.

"Stone, wait a minute, you leap from stones, to genes, to gold fish, and back again, so take your time and spell it out in your own words to our listeners," said the Admiral.

"There was a stone shaman sailing near the islands."

"Was she the Mayan?"

"The Mayans were much earlier," said Stone. "About five hundred years ago the stone shaman encountered three ships and many strange men from the sky."

"White men from the sky?"

"The white men from the sky were searching for gold, and my stone relatives told them how to find it," he said. Gamblers on the boats shouted, "Show us how, show us how to find the gold." Stone waved to them from the bridge. "Wait your turn and come aboard to take a chance," he told them over the radio. The mongrels howled, *"wingo, wingo, wingo."*

"So, what did the stone say?"

"Search for gold at the source of the great river."

"What river?"

"The Mississippi River."

"Fool's gold, that must be the punch line?"

"Columbus listened to our stone stories, and then he dreamed the river, he dreamed tribal women, and he dreamed that his heirs would wear gold masks," said Stone.

"But you said stones were silent," warned the Admiral.

"Stones are silent, stones speak with their hands."

"Now we have the hands of the Mayans?"

"Some of them; you see, the first tribal people to encounter the great explorer, could not hear—they were deaf, a silent tribe of wanderers who spoke with their hands," explained Stone. "Because they were silent, they could tell stories with their hands in the summer."

"Hand over hand, is there more?"

"The trickster does not understand hand talk."

"Stone, you lost me there, some sleight of hand," she said and then paused for a commercial. "Carp Radio is back to take calls, questions, and comments from our listeners. Columbus was a Mayan, what about that?"

"Columbus and Jesus Christ were both Mayans," said Stone. "Mayans were the great explorers, and they settled in the Middle East." His voice was slow, close to the water, and moved like brume in the cattails. "Jesus was a tribal dreamer, and a shaman, and he traveled out of his body. Christopher Columbus was a dreamer, too, and he searched and found his homeland."

"Albuquerque, what's on your mind tonight?"

"Mayans, man you must be crazy."

"Saint Louis, go ahead with your question," said the Admiral.

"How can you tell when you got the right genes?"

"Columbus genes are a signature, and we got the chemical code that proves that we are the first descendants of the great explorer; we got the secret in the stone," said Stone.

"You told me, so how can it be a secret?"

"The Ghost Dance Genes are the secret, the seventeen-gene signature is the tribal secret, and that secret is mine, held in stone, but soon you might hear about the power of our healer genes," said Stone.

"Admiral White has the last word, and the last word tonight is in the stone," she announced. "Carp Radio ran the wire once more. Hear you real soon on those late night voices of the truth."

The Columbus Casino was decorated with spirals of colored lights and a huge square sail that tossed in the wind; two tribal women danced in a crow's nest above the mast. Four tribal medicine poles and an enormous spirit catcher loomed over the bow of the barge to protect the new reservation from natural demons and disasters. The catcher seemed to hold the night, the water wisps, the boats that passed in the mist.

Stone wore a scarlet tunic and steered his casino in wide circles on the lake; each turn, he calculated, was worth more than a thousand dollars. He saved millions of dollars in four summers on the casino. In the cold winter, tribal elders were bused from the reservation to the barge at the island dock; they praised the ornate interior, the solid birch tables in the casino, ate a free lunch, and lost at bingo, but not at stories.

At the end of the fourth summer the casino was struck by lightning in a wild thunderstorm; the catcher surged, the sail burned, the rusted bow burst, and the barge sank in shallow water on the international border near Northwest Angle.

Stone continued his stories on talk radio from the remains of the casino. He lived on the barge for several years; his investments, bonds and notes, matured and carried him more than an estimated hundred million dollars. The tribal adventurer was in a position then to create a new tribal nation; when he established the genetic research laboratories he became the subject of international surveillance. The Ghost Dance Genes had a republic and instant political significance.

Gold at the Headwaters   The Headwaters Tavern was chartered by the Heirs of Christopher Columbus in 1868, the same year that the White Earth Reservation was established in northern Minnesota. Susan B. Anthony founded a suffragette newspaper, *The Revolution*, in that year, and the Fourteenth Amendment to the Constitution was adopted; at the same time the McIlhenny Tobasco Company was established at Avery Island, Louisiana.

The Heirs of Columbus gathered each year in the autumn to tell their best stories about the time the great explorer reached the headwaters of the Mississippi River.

Columbus, it seems, had been lured to the woodland by the silent hand talkers, that wandering tribe of deaf crossbloods, in search of women and gold. He discovered both, and more, at the source of the great river; the woman was golden and she was related to the fish. The adventurer had combined his two great passions, gold and women, and in the pursuit of both he lost an arm, an eye, and in some stories he lost his head over a woman who counted her sisters in cold water. Gold, cold, or not, he had his way with tribal women at the headwaters.

Truman Wabanish, the original founder of the Heirs, told stories that Columbus was Mayan, and that his tribal blood inspired him to search for his homeland in the New World. The Heirs of

Columbus, their ancestors, sons, daughters, and their children, continue the stories in his name once a year at the Headwaters Tavern at Lake Itasca.

"Columbus showed us that we are never equal in our genes, but with his genetic signature, we are the best survivors on the tribal run," said Stone.

"Truman, my grandfather, was like my grandson—he could reason even better than those hosts on talk show radio," said Big Bin. "When someone frowned, or groaned, or pulled an ear in silent dissent, the old shaman would say, 'Your doubts are the truth, your questions are my very answers.'"

"So, how does he come down so smart when he loses his head over a woman?" asked a young woman on her first autumn night with the Heirs at the Headwaters.

"When you lose your head, count it gone, but when he lost his he got a new one," said Stone. "Truman would say, 'Losing came with the white man who lost his imagination.'"

"Count me gone," she said and smiled.

"We called on the head shaman to mend the sky man, and he had the right genes to answer and imagine his own new head," said Big Bin.

"Columbus the phantom head, dead in the water," said the woman.

"Truman has the old head and bones in his medicine bundle, and that proves the stories that the explorer was here at the headwaters," said Big Bin. "Columbus talks in that bundle; listen he talks strange about gold and women."

Truman boasts that he holds selected skeletal remains of the great explorer: his original head, a femur, tibia, radius, and right hand. Indeed, the shamans imagined a new head and regenerated the other parts of his body, but the man was frozen in a cave by the ice woman.

Columbus died with his new shaman parts, most historians believe, on Ascension Day, May 20, 1506, in Valladolid, Spain, but they were deceived by the appearance of a trickster. The Admiral is frozen in a cave near the headwaters of the river with his new head; he was never buried in Spain, or at the Cathedral of Santo Domingo, or in Havana, Cuba.

Mikwam the ice woman lured the adventurer to her cave that

summer on the island; she promised that he could touch her golden pouch, but when he got there, she blew a cold wind down his neck. Then she laughed over his head and froze him solid. The shamans cracked his head and arms with their medicine sticks, but they had never been able to regenerate the bodies possessed by the ice woman. More than once the old men tried to rouse the frozen adventurer with stories about the sexual encounters of the trickster, but he was frozen solid and never responded.

"Best not to boast about our ancestors," said Big Bin. "The ice woman loves men with power, the terminal creeders, and she freezes the ones she loves the most."

"Columbus is frozen solid out there in a cave, dressed in his scarlet tunic, and one day, come the great tribal thaw, he's sure to tell our stories at one autumn," said Stone.

Big Bin hears the stories of the bones, the old stories, and from the remains of the great explorer the tribal heirs establish their genetic signatures, and their descent as imaginative survivors. Columbus lost his head at the headwaters of the great river, but the code of his genes has survived in a tribal medicine pouch. The Admiral of the Ocean Sea became the genetic signature of a new tribal republic.

Dorado Genomes   Jesus Christ and Christopher Columbus were Mayans and carried that sapient genetic strain of healers, adventurers, and tribal survivors. Doctor Pir Cantrip, the exobiologist turned genetic engineer, and other scientists at the new tribal nation, had isolated the chemical code of tribal survivance, the signature of seventeen mitochondrial genes that cured cancer, reversed human mutations, promoted imagination and regeneration, everted terminal creeds, and incited parthenogenesis, or the monopolitics of reproduction without men.

Teet Maleno, the certified tribal manicurist, protested that she had too many admirers on the reservation; she had the most handsome hands and feet in the woodland, as lean as a raccoon, but her huge head, twisted chin, and wild ears frightened children. She was golden, a sacred genome, more than hands and a tender voice; she hummed and cleaned, hummed and trimmed, hummed and healed between bingo games, and she was trusted to hear more secrets than anyone else on the reservation.

Stone invited her to the barge to treat hands and nails, and in the course of the manicures he discovered a sensible way to gather genetic material and genealogical information on tribal members.

Teet was inspired by the promise that her head would be regenerated by the Ghost Dance Gene. Stone proposed that she would be the first to receive a genetic implant. She collected and identified thousands of secret bits of skin and nails from the hands she manicured in preparation for a retral transformation; at the same time, she gathered information about tribal families on the reservation. The samples and histories provided molecular biologists with the scientific information they needed to isolate that genetic signature of survivance borne by the Heirs of Columbus.

Teet tested the molecules she collected from time to time; wild humor, and ecstatic motions in the brush, she wondered, might turn the night into a golden creation. She trusted humor and mirrors over memories of a mutant head, over the critical stares of strangers.

Stone held the mirrors as she returned to the fish and the animals in their memories; a return to the trickster stories, their relatives in the stone, the fires in the eye and hand roused from the cold water. The wind and the breath of bears were moments of dangerous conception that night.

Pleasures at the Panic Holes   Chaine Sevens and Lapel Browne, two private detectives who were born on the same reservation, were hired to investigate the political and biological activities in Assinika.

Lapel is a law school graduate who lives in San Francisco; she was hired by several tribal governments to probe the possible violations of child protection laws at the new nation. There were reports that hundreds of disabled and diseased tribal children were treated with genetic implants at the clinics in Assinika.

Chaine, on the other hand, is a retired warrant officer who lives on a remote lake near the reservation; he was contacted by military intelligence agencies to investigate and determine the potential for biological weapons, and to report on the leaders, nations, and corporations represented in Assinika.

The Ghost Dance Gene and the insurrection at Point Roberts captured wide public attention and support on late night talk radio; the federal government studied the political issues too much and lost the potential to reclaim the area on the border with Canada.

Molecular biologists and genetic engineers from more than a dozen nations rushed to the new tribal republic in search of a place to conduct their research and experiments without state or federal restrictions.

Stone, to be sure, had informed the scientists on talk radio when the insurrection would take place, the actual hour and day of the year. Point Roberts citizens and the general public, but not the federal government, heard the discussions on talk radio that a new nation would be declared in the autumn, five hundred years after the return discovery of the New World. The sciolistic state department and other federal agencies were too critical to believe what was announced in talk radio. The reservation warriors had first-hand experiences in how the government does not listen; in this one instance, not to listen was a favor to the Heirs of Columbus.

Chaine and Lapel never asked direct questions; they were from the same tribe and gained more from stories than documents; more came to the ear than the eye, but there were natural differences in the patterns of their investigations.

Lapel listens to women and watches men. She listened to the stories women told about transportation, their hands and hair, the last places they lived, taboos, and the forbidden tease. She imagined humans as birds and made a vital cursorial and arborial tribal distinction: those who believe that birds first flew from the ground to the air, or from the trees to the air.

Lapel started her career in an insurance claims department; she studied forgeries and learned through meditation that she could visualize the connections between artists, creators, and their materials. Men, she observed, revealed their intentions, and their insecurities and secrets, in the way they responded to their properties. She watched men and listened to women; the way men touch their machines, their children, and their animals. She was the best in the business and soon became an independent investigator.

Stone touched several times a day the enormous spirit catchers and blue medicine poles that loomed over the international border, the same catchers that were mounted on the bow of the Christopher Columbus Casino. He touched women on the neck, children on the cheek and shoulder; mongrels he touched on the withers and snout, and he shouted into panic holes for pleasure.

Assinika was a nation of parks, wildflowers, and biological stations, from the international border to the Strait of Georgia. Handsome blooms covered the meadows. The tribal mutants talked as they walked, and everyone walked in the nation.

Lapel listened on the roads and in the biological research laboratories and clinics. The tribal nation was cursorial; the warriors, women, and children imagined their flight from the ground to the air. Stone, she heard, was over a panic hole on a meadow.

"You watch me," said Stone.

"I listen," said Lapel.

"What do you hear?"

"An animal, not a bird."

"Neither," said Stone.

"What then?"

"Who are you?" asked Stone.

"Lapel Browne."

"You must be a bird."

"No, the wind," said Lapel.

"I am a stone, the earth is in a stone, my brother is a stone, and stones shout in panic holes to return," he shouted. Stone leaned over and shouted into a panic hole; the flowers shivered on the meadow.

"I listen," she shouted.

"Children climb into holes, pitch stones and marbles into holes," said Stone. "How natural we are as stones to shout our memories into panic holes." He touched her on the neck; she shivered and moved to the side, to avoid his reach. He danced to the other side of the panic holes, touched his own neck, and laughed. "Come, the world is better with a wild shout, one shout to the stones." She leaned closer to the hole, but remained silent. "The stone men down there would listen, come, one thin shout to clear the air in flight." She would not be summoned or tested by a trickster, but she had no choice on the meadow, so she shouted her own name into a panic hole.

"The wildflowers love to see our voices," shouted Stone.

"Flowers listen," said Lapel.

"No, flowers argue with the weather, and animals, and pose on the meadows," he said. Stone laughed, and then he shouted at the birds in the trees.

Chaine studied the leaders, their biographies, movements, contacts, and imagined various political strategies at the new nation. Most visitors, and the scientists, he observed, had arrived by boat at night; others traveled to the nation by helicopter. "The mutants, the curious, and the investigators crossed the border at the station on the main road," he wrote in his report. "Assinika passports were issued to tribal people, to the diseased and disabled, on the station; other visitors were issued four-hour passes, but there were no border patrols, and no apparent electronic surveillance.

"Christopher Columbus statues in stone and cedar stand at the dock and near the border station. 'Give me your tired, your poor, your deformed, diseased, and disabled, yearning to breathe free of pollution, and eager to be healed by the Ghost Dance Genes.'"

Pir Cantrip, the obscure exobiologist and genetic engineer, is short, thick at the waist, thin at the neck, vulturine, bald, and piscivorous; he is mannered, and manicured, but his body smells of sardines. Chaine noted that he wears tailored business suits, light blue shirts, and floral neckties. He could have been an investment banker, but for the mongrel at his side.

Gracioso, the mutant calico mongrel, balanced the best conservative appearance of the exobiologist. The reservation mongrel had two tails, no toes, and she smiled like a human; her feet were round, oversized soft pads, and silent.

"Pir is the gene master, and his mongrel must be one of his first experiments," reported Chaine. "He is responsible for the actual genetic implants that have caused so much concern, but there is no visible evidence that anyone has been harmed. Rather, the children are released from their birth defects, and there are tribal people here who have been healed. The power of tribal spirits cannot be discounted, but it appears that some manner of biochemical intervention has transformed hundreds of people with deformed bodies.

"Shamanic ecstasies are common cures on reservations, and no harm comes to tribal governments," he continued in his intelligence report to the agencies. "Therefore, to heal the diseased and deformed is not, in my estimation, a political problem unless the genetic chemical codes are borrowed, or stolen, and misused by our enemies. The greatest risk is not genetic but economic; success here, as an independent nation, could bring down the stock market. My recommendation is that the new nation be rewarded for their dedication to heal those who have been abandoned by other governments.

"Stone Wabanish is a political shaman with the mind of a genetic tribalist, not a fascist; he, the scientists, and the warriors should be honored for their humanitarian service to the world. Not to do so would bring harm to our own economy, and shame to our government," concluded Chaine.

God Save Talk Radio　　　　Admiral White pursued Stone on late night radio from the bingo barge to his new nation on the Strait of Georgia. Carp Radio was there, in fact, on the first night of the insurrection; live on talk show radio at the founding of Assinika.

"Admiral White of the Ocean Sea is back on the air," she announced. "Your late night host on land and sea with the voices of truth from the newest nation in the world." She paused for an automobile commercial and public service announcement. Cosmetic and patent medicine companies competed for time on the air with the new tribal nation.

"The Stone is here in his scarlet tunic; listen to the stones. So, once more we have that wild gene man on the air to answer your questions, to argue and win your hearts." Stone was high in a spirit catcher near the border; he never talked twice on radio from the same place.

"What are spirit catchers?" asked Admiral White.

"Catch the spirits," said Stone.

"What sort of spirit needs to be caught?"

"Must you ask?"

"No, the evil ones," she said.

"Your questions are my very answers," said Stone.

"Assinika has been a nation for three months, so why don't you have border guards like other nations, and immigration policies?" asked the Admiral.

"Birds nest on borders," said Stone.

"Equivocal, as usual," she sighed. "Listen, thousands of tribal people have been healed there in the past three months, so has there ever been an implant that went wrong?"

"Gracioso smiles," said Stone.

"Gracioso smiles because of the doctor?"

"Doctor Pir Cantrip, we are told, practiced experimental medicine on prisoners during the Second World War," said the Admiral. "Where did he learn genetic implants?"

"Pir was an orphan; he was educated on the run," said Stone.

"New Orleans, you're on the air," she said.

"Cantrip is a butcher, a Nazi."

"Prove it," demanded the Admiral.

"He's the one who killed my mother with chemicals."

"What does he look like?" asked Stone.

"He's tall, big feet..."

"Atlanta; you're next, what's on your mind tonight?"

"Money, who gets the cash from the genes?"

"No one," said Stone.

"How can that be true; someone must make a bundle."

"No one should pay to be healed," said Stone. "Those who are tortured with deformities are not commodities; diseases are not treated and cured to make doctors rich. People are healed without cost at Assinika."

"Bozeman, speak the truth tonight."

"God has the power over life, no one else."

"God is nature," said Stone.

"God made us who we are, God holds the genes," said Bozeman.

"God made Christopher Columbus," said Stone.

"God did that, yes."

"God was there when the adventurer gave us his genes."

"God is pure," said Bozeman.

"Columbus is a saint," said Stone.

"Tucumcari, you're on the air with the truth," said the Admiral.

"Stone, what's a panic hole out there?"

"Have you ever fallen in the dark?" asked Stone.

"Yes sir, more than once."

"Panic holes are the same; we shout down into the dark."

"Down in the dark," repeated Tucumcari.

"The hole in the dark, the panic in the shout," said Stone.

"Memphis, you're next, hold your question until after this commercial announcement," said Admiral White. Stone towed the braids on the spirit catcher and waited for the next voice on radio. He wore earphones with a small microphone attached.

"Memphis, we're back, this is our time."

"Columbus, man, he hit the islands before there were photographs, so how come you got statues of the man when nobody knows what he looked like?"

"The Heirs of Columbus are the eye-witness memories," said Stone.

"So what does that mean?"

"Memory in the blood, pictures in our genes."

"George Washington must be in mine."

"The District of Columbia on late night radio, you're on the air."

"Yes, perhaps you could clarify a rumor that has been circulating around the capital for the past month or so," said a man. "The question is, does your nation propose to collect a tithe from the annual tax revenues of the federal government?"

"The tithe is due, but not as a proposal," said Stone.

"What is the basis of such a tithe?"

"Columbus was promised one tenth of the income from trade."

"But this is the United States."

"The Heirs of Columbus have inherited the tithe," said Stone.

"Surely you jest, how would you collect?"

"Simple. We print new dollars, the annual amount of the tithe due until the federal government agrees to pay the tribal heirs the cost of pollution and the value of the land in the past five hundred years," said Stone.

"Counterfeiting is a crime, not a method of collection."

"The Heirs of Columbus are the natural heirs to the nation, and we have a natural right to our tithe; that right is not counterfeit," said Stone.

"The United States is not that old."

"Columbus is our mutual celebration," said Stone.

"Indeed he is," said the District of Columbia.

"Columbus wrote, 'May God in His mercy help me to find this gold.'"

"Admiral White has the last word, and the last word tonight is in the tithe, the truth is in the tithe at Assinika," she announced. "Carp Radio ran wild once more on the land and sea, hear you real soon on the late night voices of the truth."

Alicia Gaspar de Alba

Cimarrona

I.

"Laaaand fall!"

Captain Laurens de Graaf opened his spyglass and looked out. Yes, there it was, the dreary, foggy New England coast. The Puritan merchants had commissioned him, back in January, to bring sugar, rum, and slaves to the Bay Colony. Back then, the Captain had not been rich as he was now. He had not yet plundered Vera Cruz. At the time he had signed the agreement with the English merchants, the siege of Vera Cruz was only a dare that Van Horn had thrown in the Captain's face during a night of Christmas feasting in Port Royale.

If the Captain had known back in January that Van Horn's outlandish plan would work so well, that they would pull off the siege of Vera Cruz with the Spanish colors flying from the masts of their buccaneer ships while the Spanish Fleet sat in the harbor, he would never have agreed to do business with the Puritans. This foggy, gloomy wilderness, which the Puritans referred to as the city built upon a hill for the chosen children of God, always gave Captain de Graaf nightmares. More and more he had come to despise his annual visit to the Boston port; having to return twice in one year was enough to depress him until Christmas.

"Pedro!" the Captain called to his Spanish matelot. "Lay out my wig and greatcoat, and don't forget the wool stockings. We'll be putting into harbor soon. Tell Cook to get the punch ready."

Though Dutch by nationality, the Captain had learned Castilian during his long service in the Spanish navy. And he could speak French as well, having picked it up from the corsairs who, ten years earlier, had captured his Spanish vessel and then invited him to join their company. Not one to bite the hand of Opportunity, Captain de Graaf had become a buccaneer and now commanded two ships, his favorite of which was the *Neptune*. Though he had some French sailors on board, his crew on the *Neptune* was composed mainly of Englishmen, and so Captain de Graaf had had to learn English, too. The only Castilian among them was Pedro, loyal to the Captain ever since his Spanish navy days.

Pedro went below deck, and the Captain watched the crew scrambling on deck, taking in the sails, uncoiling the anchor ropes, loading one of the cannons to announce their arrival, shouting and slapping each other on the back in anticipation of going ashore. The Captain yelled for the first mate and told him to inform the crew that nobody was leaving the ship. They would send out the longboat to bring the English merchants aboard, dispose of the cargo, and sail the same day for Virginia. It was early enough still, and a good wind would find them once they left the cold shadow of the Boston port. Captain de Graaf was a superstitious man. The New England coast reminded him too much of the English dungeon where he'd been imprisoned back at the beginning of his buccaneer fame. He heard the cannon go off. Out of a habit he had never managed to suppress, he blessed himself with the triple sign of the cross.

"She made a mess in your cabin again, *mi Capitan*," Pedro said when he returned to the poop.

"Not another fire, Pedro!"

"Looks like she got into your logbook this time, sir. There's hen-scratching all over the pages."

"Damn the louse!" said the Captain, snapping his spyglass shut. "Why did we let her loose again, Pedro?"

Pedro followed the Captain down the ladder, his lips pursed tightly. *You've been craving bitch meat ever since she came on board*, he wanted to say, but el capitan de Graaf, the infamous Lorencillo, scourge of the Spanish Main, took to insolence the way he took to the pox. "You wanted her last night, *mi Capitan*." Pedro tried to keep the edge of jealousy out of his voice. "You know she always pays you back in some way."

"Damn her! I should've left her in Tortuga. What am I doing, with that crazy wench!"

Mexican halfbreed bitch, thought Pedro, but again he kept his mouth shut.

In his cabin, the Captain threw his arms up in anger. The wench had spilled the inkhorn on the floor and smeared ink all over the bedclothes. The written pages of his log were torn in half, the other pages . . . The Captain dragged the lamp across the desk to see his logbook better. "By your life, Pedro!" he said under his breath, "this is no henscratching, man!"

On one page the wench had written the name *Jeronima* over and over, on the other pages a long verse, in a penmanship so elegant and curlicued it confirmed his suspicion that the halfbreed he'd been sporting with for the past six weeks had been educated in a monastery. How she'd gotten mixed in with the Negroes, he didn't know. It wasn't common buccaneer practice to take Indians or halfbreeds for slaves, but the girl was attached to one of the Negro girls in his share of the plunder they'd captured in Vera Cruz, and had pleaded with him to take her along, had actually knelt at his feet and kissed his groin, promising to do whatever he wanted in exchange for coming on the *Neptune*. Captain de Graaf had a weakness for brave women; besides, he had never bedded a wench that had eyes of different colors: one dark as Jamaican rum, the other green as French chartreuse.

At first, the girl was dutiful and obedient, though she was a virgin, and wept each time he took her. But then the Negro girl who was her friend caught the pox from some of the slaves they'd picked up in Havana, and his men had thrown them all overboard to keep the rest of the cargo from getting infected. Ever since then, the halfbreed wandered through the decks, calling for her friend, wailing like a madwoman.

In the mornings and in the evenings, when the slaves were brought up to the light to eat and exercise, the girl served their food, chanting the *Ave Maria* with such sorrow that the slaves and some of the French sailors broke into sobbing. Cook said that when the girl helped him in the galley, she talked to a black figure that she carried in a pouch hanging from her neck. She could stand for hours in the stern, staring at the water, ignoring the sailors' pinching and fondling, holding an invisible rosary between her hands, her lips moving in silent prayer. When the Captain brought her to his bed, she stared at him with crazed, terrified eyes, shouting a rhymed verse to him—something about bullheaded men and the flesh of the devil—until he finished. The Captain thought the girl had lost her wits completely, but this writing on the page showed him that he was wrong, that there was still hope of getting rid of her at a good price.

"Hombres necios que acusais a la mujer sin razón, sin ver que sois la ocasión de lo mismo que culpais," the Captain read the beginning of the verse aloud. "Pedro. Go find her, quick! I have to talk to her before the merchants get here."

When Pedro had gone, the Captain sat down at his desk and drew up a bill of sale, dipping the pen into the puddle of ink soaking into the floor.

> *I, Captain Laurens-Cornille de Graaf, commander of the buccaneer frigate, the* Neptune, *hereby sell this halfbreed wench, captured in war on the coast of New Spain and subject to servitude. Her name is Jeronima. She is approximately twenty years old, has all her teeth and is immune to the pox. For her sturdy health and her knowledge of letters, her price is 50 sterling pounds.*   *21 June 1683*

The Captain signed the bill, sprinkled sand over the ink, then poured himself a generous shot of Spanish brandy to celebrate his fortune. If there was one friendly thing he could say about the Puritans it was that they knew how to appreciate fine penmanship, even in a wench. He heard the cannons go off in the harbor and knew that the ghosts of New England were on their way.

II.   She could not remember how long the journey had taken. After Alendula's disappearance, she had stopped counting the days since the pirates' ship had left Vera Cruz. She had stopped listening to the wailing of the slaves and to the strange sounds of the pirates' language. She heard only water, the flapping of sails, the night wind howling through the portholes. In the mornings, when she had to mash the horse beans for the slaves' breakfast, the stench of it brought her momentarily out of the numbness that had grown around her like a silkworm's case. In that slit of time, she would notice where she was, and remember what had happened to Alendula. She would see the swollen boards of the kitchen floor where every night, except those she spent with the white-haired man who spoke her language, the cook rolled her over and pumped her from behind. She would hear the clank of chains on the ladders and know that the slaves were being shuffled up to the upper deck for their morning rations of horse beans and water. After they ate, one of the pirates would pound stupidly on a drum, and the other pirates would prod or whip the slaves to dance to the rhythmless drum beats, their chains rattling, their moans strung in a perverse harmony. It was this, more than being shackled to the lower deck, more than breathing the fumes of excrement and vomit, more than hearing the constant keening of the other slaves, it was this denigrating dance in the open air that had most poisoned Alendula's soul, until finally she could not stand up any longer, and could not climb the ladder to the upper deck, and the little water she drank convulsed her body.

She remembered saying, "I don't know where we're going, Alendula, and you're making this more difficult for us. Why don't you eat? Look at you! You'll die down here without any air. Please try to get up!"

But Alendula was delirious at that point, her mind still traveling to the village of San Lorenzo that they had never reached because they had gone to Vera Cruz, first. It had taken them all of April and half of May to cross the mountains and come in sight of Vera Cruz. From the foothills, they could see the big ships anchored by the fort, the Spanish colors waving in the hot wind. Alendula said it was the *Flota* and they ran down to the port to watch the spectacle of seasick *señoras* and dizzy *hidalgos* and water-legged priests descending from the Spanish Fleet, unloading the wondrous treasures they had brought from across the sea. Instead of the Spaniards they had found pirates. The flyblown air of Vera Cruz burned with the screams of women being forced, of men being tortured, of Negroes and mulattoes falling to the sword or to the musket or to the clanking coffle of slaves.

What had happened then? How had she gotten on the same ship with Alendula? There were so many ships. So many pirates. All she remembered was sneaking down to the deck where the Negroes were chained to great iron rings on the floor, having to crawl over their bodies, no space between them, no room in which to stand. And Alendula weeping constantly.

"My mother's a free woman. Tell them that, Concepción. If my mother's free, I'm free. Don't they know that? I'm not a slave. They can't make me a slave! I'm from San Lorenzo!"

One morning Alendula refused to dance with the others on the top deck, and the pirate beating the drum came up and kicked her in the belly. Alendula's eyes rolled back in her head, and she started screaming *Eleggua! Eleggua!* Her voice was like the cry of a rabid cat. The pirate kicked Alendula again and again until she stopped screaming, blood and the gray foam of bean mash dribbling from her mouth.

She had watched Alendula's beating with a hatred so pure it felt like a blessing, like a bath in holy water that purified her spirit. Her mission was clear. She had to kill somebody. She would stab the Captain with his own sword the next time he rammed himself inside her. But that night, after the Captain had used her, he was called to the top deck and left her alone in his cabin. She would have to do something else. Break everything in the room. Or better still, set the cabin on fire. She took the lamp and smashed it on the floor, watched the oily puddle grow blue then explode into flames, felt the smoke in her eyes as the flames tunneled into the Captain's chair and caught on the leather. Somehow Pedro stopped the fire, and the Captain had her locked up in a storeroom in the lowest deck. With no pirates defiling her, nothing but the rocking of the ship and the continual slap of the sea to distract her, she was able to sleep and remember.

At first the memories were only sounds: hushed voices, a trill of birdsong, footsteps, the keening chords of an instrument. Gradually the sounds collected weight. Like magnets, they drew pieces of images to their core, became shadows and then figures that moved like puppets on a makeshift stage. There were two central players: Alendula and a woman called *Madre* whose face was hidden under a black veil. There was a garden, and a shack in the garden where Alendula lived in chains. There was a great house with many rooms, and many mysteries within the rooms, and many footsteps. She looked for herself in the garden and in the house but neither was her place. In a corner of the stage stood a birdcage and it was here she found the shadow that belonged to her, and a voice that said: *We are all slaves to our destinies, Concepción. Destiny is the cage each woman is born with.* Another figure appeared, dressed in sackcloth, her white-gloved hands pushing a broom.

III.   *Madre.* The word tumbled in her sleep like a dry weed, thorny stems scratching behind her eyes. *Madre.* A woman in a white tunic and a long black veil, an angel pinned to her chest, a quill in her hand, a woman with ink-stained fingers. *Madre,* Concepción had called her, though her own mother had been a Zapotec and had died at Concepción's birth. Why did she call that woman *Madre?*

Awake, she pressed her fingers against her eyelids, pressed hard until she saw lights and rows of tiny squares, her pupils throbbing under her fingertips, and dark shapes swirling into focus. A great patio with five fountains. Grapefruit and lemon trees. Birdcages hanging from the branches. It was the place where she had lived, a house full of women dressed like *Madre,* bells tolling seven times a day. The house of San Jerónimo.

Madre had been her mistress, her teacher. She had trained Concepción to take dictation, to read Latin and play chess, to copy manuscripts in the calligraphy of Benedictine monks.

She remembered *Madre's* voice singing a sad song about a fallen apple. *Señora Santana, ¿porqué llora la niña? Por una manzana que se le ha caído...*" She had been so little, then, but how old? She remembered another woman, much older than *Madre,* who had said to Concepción: *In here I am not your father's mother. Never call me grandmother. Never forget your place. You are here only because I am the Mother Superior of this house and because my son felt pity for you and didn't want to put you out into the street.*

She eased the pressure on her eyes and wept into her palms.

～～

She had dreamed of leaving the convent only to ride the canoes among the floating gardens of Xochimilco, or to take the yearly pilgrimage to the holy hills of Tepeyac, to see the bullfights and the *teatros de corrales,* to wear a costume and dance in the *mascaradas.* It had never occurred to Concepción to leave the convent forever or to run away from the place of her birth. But Alendula had told her stories of the village of San Lorenzo where free Negroes ruled like kings. She spoke of ceremonies that startled Concepción. Of moon mothers and river goddesses and altars piled with coconuts, oranges, and bones. Of old women who smoked cinnamon bark to see the future and sacrificed roosters to talk to the dead.

"You have to see it, Concepción. *Please* come with me to San Lorenzo! It won't be the same to go without you."

"But I'm not a *cimarrona*. I don't belong there."

"I'm not a *cimarrona* either, not anymore. I wouldn't be a prisoner in a convent if I hadn't failed as a *cimarrona*."

"It wasn't your fault, Alendula. There were spies all over the city. Everyone knew about the insurrection."

"I should have been hung. A *cimarron* must live free or die. That's the law of San Lorenzo. I should have been hung like my *papi*."

"I'm glad they didn't hang you, Alendula. You're the only friend I've ever had. My mistress says I shouldn't associate with the maids, but the boarders won't talk to me either."

"It was so horrible, Chica, the way they quartered him, the dogs snarling over his entrails. But he didn't bleed, not a drop of blood, he took all of his *ashé* with him to Olorun. I know he's ashamed of me, locked up here for three years, never even attempting to escape. I have to get out of here. I have to be free. *You* can get me out of here, I know you can. Even if you free just one person, you'll be a *cimarrona*, and then you can go with me to San Lorenzo and we'll both be free."

"I'm not a slave, Alendula, *nor* a prisoner. I don't need to go to San Lorenzo to be free."

"You don't know anything," Alendula said, sinking back into the swamp-thick shadows of her prison shed. "To live without a mistress, to listen to your own head, to make your own destiny. You don't know what any of that is, Concepción.

~~~~

"*Madre*, what's the difference between freedom and destiny?"

"Freedom is the opposite of destiny," *Madre* said.

"What's destiny?"

"Look up, Concepción. Look around you. What do you see?"

Concepción's eyes roamed over the bookshelves and the cluttered tables of *Madre's* study. "Your cell," she answered.

"You see a cage. Destiny is the cage that each of us is born with, and we can't ever leave that cage, Concepción. We are all slaves to our destinies."

"But you told me that being a *mestiza* made me free."

Madre twisted three handfuls of Concepción's hair into a tight braid. "No, you're not free," she said.

"Didn't you say I could leave here if I wanted to?"

"That's not what I mean, Concepción. I'm not talking about physical freedom. You can leave the convent if you want to, but that won't make you free. Look at yourself." She handed Concepción the mirror. "What kind of face do you see?"

"I don't know, *Madre. My* face."

"A *woman's* face," said *Madre.* "A woman who will never be allowed to be the kind of person she wants to be."

"Because I'm a *mestiza?*"

"Because you're a woman. That's the cage we're *both* born with, Concepción. It doesn't matter that you're a *mestiza* or a *criolla* or a servant or a nun. If your destiny is to be a woman, you will never know what it means to fly."

"Did I make you angry, *Madre?*"

"I'm angry at *them.*"

"At who, *Madre?*"

"*Men.* Bullheaded men who won't allow women to live according to our natures."

"I thought destiny came from God."

"God made man in his own image; that's what we're taught, isn't it, Concepción?"

~~~~~

She smelled pineapples and boiled beef, starch and wax, garlic. The smells of the kitchen in *Madre's* cell, and Jane, *Madre's* slave, stirring the pots. Jane of the *metate* and the broom, of the long tongue and the shifty eyes and the voice strident as a *verdulera's.*

"I know all about your plan, *mestiza.* Think I don't have ears? Think I haven't seen you sneaking around the prisoner every chance you get? Spying on the gatekeeper to see where she hides the keys to that shack. I know exactly what you two are up to, that's why I figured I better talk to you before you and your prisoner friend jump the fence."

"You stopped at a *pulqueria* when you went to the market today, didn't you, Jane? How can you go there? How can you drink that slime? Aren't you worried she's going to smell it on you?"

"I can tell you a secret, Concepción, and you'll be thanking me the rest of your days, wondering what you would've done without me teaching you this secret about men."

"Leave me alone. I don't want to hear your vulgar stories. I have to finish this work before she gets back from prayers."

"Now don't go acting like you're as pure as the Immaculate Conception; even if that *is* your name, you're nothing but a half-breed and halfbreeds ain't never been immaculately conceived.

"Shut your mouth, Jane!"

"Listen to this, *mestiza! She* don't know anything about men, and even if she did, she'd never do you the favor of telling you how they are. Men are everywhere out there, and they can smell you when you're green and ignorant the way you are. Just remember this: men got one weakness, and it's always hanging in the same place. He'll do anything for that weakness. First time he uses it it'll hurt like the devil's tearing into you with his hot fork. But don't let him know how much it hurts, or he'll hurt you more. Only way to heal the wound is to rub gunpowder into it. Good thing about gun-powder is it kills his seed. Bad thing is it'll nearly kill you, too, if you use too much, or if you do it when the moon is full."

~~~

The brisk, dark morning air made her teeth chatter; dread prowled in her veins.

"Alendula! *Despierta!* We're leaving!" she hissed, trying to find the keyhole of the toolshed in the darkness. She heard Alendula stirring inside, her heavy chains rattling.

"Concepción?"

"I've got the keys, Alendula."

"Hurry up, Chica!"

Concepción felt the key slip into the chamber. She crossed her-self quickly. The lock clicked. Alendula yanked on the door.

"My hands! Free my hands!"

Concepción fumbled in the darkness with the manacles on Alendula's wrists. She felt a cry swelling in her throat. Her fingers were moving so slowly! *Help me, Santa Lucía*, she prayed in si-lence. She felt the shackles open. Again, she crossed herself.

"Hold this!" She gave Alendula the basket that she carried on her arm—inside, were the bundle of clothes she had brought for Alendula, a blanket, and the scissors she had taken from *Madre's* desk. The pouch of coins that *Madre* had given her the night before hung between her breasts. She squatted to free Alendula's ankles, her head pounding as though she had woodpeckers trapped in her skull.

"Santísima Virgen de Guadalupe, Angel de la guarda, ayudenme!" she prayed aloud. She couldn't find the keyhole. Her hands were trembling so hard she dropped the keys.

"Por tu vida, Concepción," muttered Alendula. "You're looking in the wrong place. It's on the inside of my other foot."

"Don't talk to me, Alendula! I'm too scared." She turned the key.

"They're off!" said Alendula, stepping out of the fetters. "Let's get out of here!"

But the door hinges squeaked. The sound of breathing filled the dark shack. Alendula's hand clamped around her arm. The cry in Concepción's throat leaked out.

"Is that you, Jane?" Concepción managed to say. She heard whining. The dogs had followed her. She crossed herself a third time, nearly wetting her pants with relief. *"Son los perros,"* she said as the dogs encircled them and sniffed at their knees. Holding hands, they inched out the door, Alendula closing the door of the shed behind them. Startled birds flapped out of the bushes. By the time they reached the mulberry grove at the back of the garden, the sky had turned from black to indigo.

"Take off those rags," Concepción said. She handed Alendula the extra skirt and *huipil* and *huaraches* that she had bundled up in her *rebozo.* The clear, high voices of the nuns at matins rose from the open windows of the choir.

"Put these on, Alendula. I'm going to cut some carnations, that way when we leave the city we can look like we're selling flowers."

"You're going with me, after all?"

"I guess so."

For a moment, Alendula held her tightly and kissed both her cheeks. "I owe you my life for freeing me, Concepción."

"We have to wait until it's lighter so that we can see what we're doing," said Concepción, "and then we'll climb the tree and drop down to the street at first light. We can't go anywhere until the night watchmen go away."

"Don't be a fool, Concepción. What are we waiting for? We'll be safer in the dark!"

"If I'm such a fool, I don't know why you want me to go with you. Can you see anything? Do you know there's broken glass on the wall that'll tear your skin off? Go ahead! Jump over!"

"Don't get angry, Chica. I'm scared, that's all. I know you know what you're doing."

"Just get dressed," said Concepción. "The *huaraches* will probably be too big for you, but that's all I have." She took the scissors and ran to the field of carnations, their smell of damp cloves spicing the cold air.

They waited up in the mulberry tree until the bells of all the churches and all the monasteries of the city announced morning Mass, and then they let themselves drop to the cobbled street. Carrying the basket of carnations between them, they tried not to run to the causeway southeast of the Plaza Mayor. At that early hour the causeway was crowded with merchants, muleteers, gypsies, Indians, beggars, and mounted soldiers patrolling the lake of bodies moving into and out of Mexico City.

IV. "Hungry, bitch? Here, bitch." The pirate named Pedro lured her out of confinement with a piece of roasted turtle meat dangling from a stick. The smell of the meat turned her mouth into a saliva pit, but she knew that right behind Pedro was the cook with his net. They had played this game before. They would not catch her again. She let them think they had baited her, and then just as the net swooped down, Concepción kicked her way out of Pedro's grasp and ran to the slave deck.

Nearly half the Negroes had died already on the journey. The ones who remained didn't speak to each other anymore. Curled into balls, they whimpered and moaned and waited. Concepción found Alendula feverish and reeking of urine. Her teeth were loose, and her gums bled. Concepción grabbed Alendula's hand and pinched what was left of the ash-gray skin.

"Alendula! Wake up! What's happened to you?"

The crust around Alendula's eyes cracked open. "Concepción? Where have you been Chica? I thought you went back to that convent."

"I wish I could go back. This is like purgatory, worse than purgatory because we're not even dead. What have you done to yourself, Alendula? Why aren't you getting better? I can't take care of you all the time."

"I'm happy Concepción. I know the way now."

"I'm so afraid, Alendula. I think I'm losing my mind. I can't remember *Madre's* name, I can't remember what happened between Mexico and Vera Cruz. Tell me about the journey, Alendua. What did we do?"

"I dreamt the alligator again," Alendula said, her breath rank as sour dough. "It was a long dream Concepción. I was walking with my *papi* to the swamp and it was very bright and windy the time of the northerlies my *papi's* voice kept getting lost in the wind but I know that he is telling me to call Eleggua that Eleggua would meet me at the crossroads if I made my *ashé* burn." She paused to lick the cracked leather of her lips.

"What are you saying, Alendula? You know I don't understand this *ashé* business."

"At the edge of the swamp under the ceiba tree," Alendula continued, "my *papi* danced Eleggua's dance and then he rolled on the ground and his body changed into an alligator and he swam away into the swamp he wants me to follow him don't you see my *papi* wants to free me I'll be free in the water Yemayá will take me to Eleggua."

Concepción shook the bones of Alendula's shoulders. "Stop it! You're babbling like a fool. I'm going to get you some water, now, and you're going to drink it, and then I'm going to give you some bread, and I'm going to wash you, and your fever's going to go away."

"I have to make my *ashé* burn Chica I'll be free in the water."

Concepción felt her hand slapping the hot flesh of Alendula's cheek. "Does this look like freedom to you? *Cimarrona?* Is that what you are? You and your stupid freedom!"

The slaves had started to wail again, and the smell of Alendula's body made Concepción want to retch. She crawled through the open spaces and climbed to the upper deck to wash herself in the night air.

The next morning Pedro told her that Alendula had caught the pestilence of the Havana slaves, that she had been thrown into the sea in the middle of the night along with the others, and Concepción knew that Alendula had been making herself weak on purpose, that whoever Eleggua was, Alendula had wanted him to come and claim her. And suddenly she hated Alendula—her cowardice, her stupid beliefs. Hated her so much she would black out from hoping with all her strength that Alendula would be torn apart by every creature in the deep. It was Alendula's fault that she was here, alone, sodomized and violated by pirates, trapped in a floating prison heading God knows where on the rocking nightmare of the open sea. She had lost everything, and for that she cursed Alendula to eternal bleeding at the bottom of the ocean.

May the ocean turn red with your blood. May you never stop bleeding. May your blood feed all the fishes and all the monsters and all the spirits of the sea.

Suddenly, she was empty. She remembered nothing except Alendula, her ghost twitching from the rigging of the ship, flapping on the sails, howling with the wind. Her own name shriveled on her tongue and vanished. And then the singing started. A singing filled with a knowledge that punched her throat but did not surface from the darkness. The words of the singing ululated through her vocal cords in a language that was not her own, *Sancta Maria mater dei, salve mater misericordia, mea culpa, mea culpa, Ave Maria, Alleluia, mea culpa.* She would find herself gazing at the ocean, waiting for Alendula to rise with the moon, and the words would flow out of her like blood. A rosary of jade beads would appear in her hands. And above her, the ship's sails would become women in white tunics and black veils bending down to kiss her.

Other times, with the Captain moving on top of her, she would see a woman in the background, sitting at the Captain's desk, dipping the quill into the ink, writing, dipping, writing, and in the doorway, the shadow of a cloaked man holding a long, hooked staff.

Peeling yams or kneading dough in the ship's kitchen, she would suddenly take the black queen out of her pouch and stroke her and kiss her, knowing the black queen had a name but not remembering what it could be.

One day just before dawn, standing at her vigil for Alendula, she noticed a briskness in the air and white birds perched on the rigging. She saw something moving in the water, something dark and heavy and huge nearly rubbing up against the side of the ship, arching out of the water and sinking again, soaking her in the heavy splash of its gray-black tail. She had seen other ocean creaures on the journey, but none had stirred her as this one, none had showed her the dark and massive weight of her own solitude. In that moment, with the creature suspended just above the water, the name came to her, the name of the black queen: *Jeronima.* She rushed down to the Captain's desk and wrote it down on the only parchment she could find. *Jeronima,* over and over so that she would not forget it again, and as she wrote, a body of words surged like the creature out of the dark water.

She saw a stack of pages scribbled in an almost illegible hand. A magnifying glass appeared, and through the glass she could discern that the writing formed a long poem which she had to copy:

Hombres necios que acusais
a la mujer sin razón,
sin ver que sois la ocasión
de lo mismo que culpais:

She inked the pen again, and the pen became the goose quill she had always held. The horn of the inkpot turned to silver.

si con ansia sin igual
solicitais su desdén
¿porqué quereis que obren bien
si las incitais al mal?

She saw the range of green mountains that she and Alendula had trekked, the waterfalls in which they bathed, the fish Alendula yanked from the streams, the caves they slept in, where at sunrise swarms of bats returned to claim their darkness. She remembered resting in the shade of cypresses and weeping willows, counting the dried carcasses of cicadas that still clung to the bark of the trees.

...¿cual es mas de culpar,
aunque cualquiera mal haga:
la que peca por la paga,
o el que paga por pecar?

She saw the pass between the volcanoes, Popocateptl and Ixtaccihuatl, their white crests more luminous than clouds in the turquoise twilight, the torches of Mexico City lighting the valley of Anahuac behind them.

V.   A chessboard. Bells tolling in the distance. Two voices whispering as though in a confessional.

"Maybe it's a good idea for you to leave."

"*Madre*, I'm afraid to go. What if we get lost or if we're attacked by some wild animal."

"I think you will be much safer than I in that wilderness. In here there are more wild animals than you know."

"I thought you would beg me to stay, *Madre*. I thought I meant more to you."

"You have been invaluable to me, Concepción. But the new archbishop is not my friend. He is not any woman's friend. The rumor is he's cleaning out the convents of all particular friendships, and if Mother Superior gets her way, you'll be the first to be taken away from here. Who knows where they'd send you. It's much better if you choose your own path. You're eighteen, now."

"I didn't know I was your friend, *Madre*; I thought I was just your assistant."

"I know this is a difficult choice, *cariño*. Long ago I had to decide whether I wanted to sign my life away to the convent, and guess what helped me make my decision? I played a chess game with la Marquesa and decided that if I lost I had to leave."

"But I always lose, *Madre*."

"Not always, *cariño*. Let's play one last game. I'll be black tonight so that you can begin."

The pieces moved across the board, the white side losing quickly, until the queens faced each other across the same rank and file. It was *Madre's* move, but instead of taking the white queen, she picked up the black queen and turned the piece slowly between her ink-stained fingers.

"You can start your life over, Concepción. You can shed everything but death. Even if you'll never be as free as you want to be, at least you can say you *own* this decision; that's as close as you can get to owning your life."

And then *Madre* got to her feet and stepped out from behind the chess table. They stood face to face like the black queen and the white queen. And suddenly they were embracing. They were the same height, their bodies so close that Concepción could feel the bindings on *Madre*'s breasts, could smell the castile soap that *Madre* had lathered in her bath. *Madre* gazed at her strangely, and for an instant Concepción felt her belly quivering and a small thing opening and closing inside her, the meaning in *Madre*'s eyes transparent as the moon's reflection in a fountain.

"Write to me, *cariño*. Sign your letters with the name *Jeronima*, that way the Abbess won't know it's you, and the name will remind you of this place."

"I could never forget this place. That would be like forgetting you, *Madre*."

Madre handed her the black queen. "I want you to take this to remember me by, Concepción, to remember the eleven years we spent together and all the work we did."

"I'll name her *Jeronima*," Concepción said, and pressed the onyx queen to her lips.

Madre's gaze rested for a moment on Concepción's mouth, and then she shook her head slightly and stepped away, turning her back to Concepción.

VI.   The cannon boom startled her. She smelled sulfur. The ship had slowed down. Feet pounding the upper deck. The squeak of rigging and masts. The weight of the anchors dragging the ship to a heavy stop. She climbed on the berth, and through the porthole she saw green islets floating in a teal-blue bay, thick mist in the distance. The white birds she had seen earlier circled in and out of the mist, screeching like birds of doom. They had arrived wherever they were going. They would be looking for her, she knew. They would be leaving her here.

She ran out of the cabin and down to her hiding place behind the cannon balls, clutching Jeronima. If they didn't find her, maybe the pirate ship would take her back to Mexico.

VII.   Pedro knocked on the Captain's door and came in, dragging the halfbreed. The girl had her hands crossed and was mumbling into her fingers like a lunatic.

"*¿Os escribisteis esto?*" asked the Captain, pointing to the page. The girl glanced at the logbook and shook her head.

"*¿Sois Jeronima?*"

At the sound of the name, the girl pressed her sooty hands to her chest.

"*¿Sois Jeronima?*" the Captain repeated.

The girl shook her head again. "*Concepción,*" she mumbled.

"*¿Concepción?*" said the Captain. "*Ese nombre es muy difícil.* The people here will find that name too difficult to say, and they'll baptize you with a name of their own. You've written *Jeronima* all over my book. That name will be easier for these English tongues. I've called you Jeronima on this bill of sale."

The girl's eyes turned to water. "Bill of sale?" she asked.

"What did you think?" the Captain said in his own language. "I'm a man of business. I didn't bring you all the way to New England to let you off without paying for your trip."

The girl had pressed her eyes shut, and the tears streaked the grime on her gaunt, brown cheeks.

"*Este lugar se llama Boston. ¿Podeis dicir Boston?*" The Captain found himself explaining, "*Aquí es otra colonia. Nueva Inglaterra. Vinimos de Nueva España.* These people are English. They like discipline and hard work. They don't know your language, so you must, are you listening, Jeronima? If you want to survive among them, you must learn their language right away. They will not tolerate you speaking in a language they don't understand. Most important, you must never pray or sing or let your wits go out of control as you've done on the *Neptune*. Do you understand what I'm saying, Jeronima?"

The girl opened her eyes and looked at him. Yes, he could definitely see the intelligence in there, a clear space under the dark layer of madness. But it wasn't madness, after all. The girl, he realized, was full of rage, a rage so bitter it had changed her face, made her seem as wild as the Arawak boy who had stowed away on his ship many years ago. To think he had actually slept in her presence! The wench could have slit his throat or pumped him full of powder. The thought made his groin jump, and he wanted to take her one last time, slide between her skinny thighs and tame her wildness.

"I want to go back to Mexico," the girl said, the first clear sentence she had spoken in six weeks.

"No, Jeronima. You begged me to bring you aboard the *Neptune*, remember that. I would have left you on that island. Now, you must forget Mexico. This is where you will live from now on."

The Captain tore the pages of the girl's writing out of his log-book and stitched them to the tattered embroidery of her blouse. Then he pulled the girl's *rebozo* up over her shorn head.

"The English don't like women walking around with their naked heads showing," he said. He looked down at what was left of the girl's sandals. "They don't like the feet to show, either, but we can't do anything about that. Pedro! Bring a towel and clean Jeronima's face!"

The girl did not take her eyes off the black wick of the lamp as Pedro scrubbed her face with the wet cloth, mumbling insults to her under his breath. The Captain buckled on his cutlass and instructed Pedro to take the girl to the poop deck and stand her away from the Negroes. This one would not be auctioned. This one had a *precio fijo*.

VIII.   *Precio fijo. Fixed price.* She was aware of something cold and hard clamping around her ribcage, an iron fist battering at her chest. Her body felt like a dried carcass still clinging to the bark of life.

I'll be free in the water, she heard Alendula say as she climbed the ladder with the pirate behind her. An auction block had been set up on the deck, and the Negroes were already being paraded in front of white-wigged men in velvet coats and black hats. The pirate led her to the other end of the deck where a short man and a tall man stood beside a table, looking impatient.

IX.   "And who is this, Captain?" said the merchant who had commissioned him. "Have you taken a wife?"

"I have brought you something most unusual, Mr. Shrimpton," said the Captain. "This halfbreed wanted to escape the Papists of New Spain and begged me to bring her along. She is a diligent maid, but also an accomplished scribe, as you can see for yourself." The Captain handed the bill of sale to Shrimpton's assistant, cross-eyed Mr. Adder.

"It says fifty pounds for the wench," said Adder.

"Fifty pounds for a cursed wench?" said Shrimpton.

"Why say you she is cursed?" asked the Captain.

"She has the eyes of a devil, Captain. I would not take her even if she were free," said Shrimpton. "Now, what about the sugar?"

"She is not a devil; she is a halfbreed," said the Captain.

"Tell me, Captain, is there a difference?" said Shrimpton. "Adder, are you seriously contemplating the purchase of this heathen?"

Adder was bending over the pages that the Captain had sewed to the girl's blouse, scrutinizing the writing through a pair of spectacles.

"I've got a chicken farm and a lame father-in-law that need tending to," said Adder. "I'll give you thirty pounds, Captain."

"Yet you'd pay twenty for a simple-minded slave," said Captain de Graaf. "Her price is fixed, Mr. Adder. If you don't want her, I'm sure some gentlemen in Virginia will."

"Captain? You did bring the sugar, I trust?" asked Shrimpton, looking around the deck.

"Can she count?" asked Adder.

"Her education is impeccable, as you can see, Sir. Surely she was not spared the knowledge of numbers." To Shrimpton the Captain said, "We've brought you thirty barrels of raw sugar and eighteen barrels of rum."

"Captain de Graaf, our agreement stated—"

From the corner of his eye, the Captain was watching Adder poke the end of his knife handle into the girl's mouth.

"Yes, Mr. Shrimpton, our agreement stated that we would provide you with fifty barrels of sugar and twenty-five barrels of rum, but you see, it's been a dry season in the West Indies, and there aren't enough buccaneers doing business in sugar anymore."

Now Adder was prodding the girl's sandals with the toe of his buckled shoe. The girl's eyes were like smoldering coal under the sparse line of her brows. Her gaze fixed on the sea.

"It's easier to procure silver than sugar these days," the Captain continued. "We're lucky we brought this much. We did, however, bring you double the slaves you asked for; of course, the pox and the fever always take their toll. Nothing we can do about that."

Adder straightened up and flicked the girl's *rebozo* off with the back of his knuckles. "What happened to her hair?"

"Six weeks among slaves," the Captain implied, but seeing that neither of them understood, he added, "Lice. But she's clean now."

Adder read and reread the bill of sale, then looked into the girl's eyes. "You ought to be thankful that the Captain brought you here among God's chosen in the new Zion. We shall name you Thankful Breed." He set the bill of sale on the table, took the pen, and scratched out *Jeronima*.

"Thankful Breed," he said aloud as he wrote in the girl's new name.

X. The man's hands and face were white as limestone, his eyes like blue flames burning her skin. She turned her head and watched the Negroes being auctioned and appraised, each one trapped in the cage of her and his own destiny. *We are all slaves to our destinies, Madre* had said, and now she understood, finally, why Alendula had let the pestilence take her.

> *I'll be free in the water.*
> *Fixed price.*

She felt her legs running. Her *rebozo* sliding off her shoulders. She heard shouting behind her. Felt the hard thump of her knees hitting the side of the ship. Her hands gripping the rail, the muscles wrenching in her shoulders, and her body swinging down, suspended for an instant and then sinking, sinking as fast and heavy as the huge creature who had surfaced to show her the way.

The water, like thousands of needles, pierced her bones. She had never known so much cold. Her veins grew numb. She opened her eyes, and they stung from the salt. She saw nothing above her but clear gray water, black shapes in the depths below. Her sandals slipped off. The pouch that held Jeronima floated away. Her skirt clung to her like a shroud. A current of joy heaved through her chest. She was free. She had escaped the cage of her destiny and was sinking, now, to the depths of the sea to join Alendula.

And suddenly the air stopped bubbling from her mouth. Her ears popped. Something drifted past her face. Something pale and phosphorescent swirling in the water, coiling and uncoiling like a snake. *You can shed everything but death.* She saw the mouth opening, the fangs long and luminous. She gasped, and her stomach bloated with saltwater. In the wild kicking of her heart, she knew she needed air. She *wanted* air. She needed to cough, to breathe. Her arms and legs pumped like windmills in the water, but her body continued to sink. She was sobbing, now, choking on the humors of the sea, fighting the currents like a netted fish until at last she felt her head break through the surface, and her face came up and she swallowed air.

Alberto Alvaro Ríos

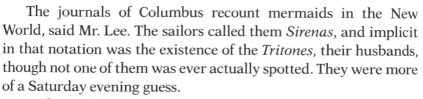

Triton Himself

His laugh was like rabbit droppings, each separate Gatling sound small, high-pitched, not much of anything. But added up together into his version of a laugh, these spitted sounds were suddenly a gang, menacing by virtue of their numbers. These noises connected like pearls on a string but without their shine, or Chinese firecrackers, too close. Too ready to explode. When one burst out, the rest could only follow.

His was a laugh, but only if he said so.

The desk clerk was clear on this point, and waited for instruction obediently.

The visitor stood there waiting for information on his room, but not for long. When the clerk did not respond, the man reached over and took a key from the shelf.

Well, he said, *I can see if a man wants to get any sleep around here, he's got to do it himself.*

~~~~

The journals of Columbus recount mermaids in the New World, said Mr. Lee. The sailors called them *Sirenas*, and implicit in that notation was the existence of the *Tritones*, their husbands, though not one of them was ever actually spotted. They were more of a Saturday evening guess.

Perhaps, the townspeople said, the *Tritones* were simply too lazy to show themselves, or so terrible that nobody who saw one ever survived. No good either way.

The journals recount the mermaids singing as God's own daughters at night. Of course, we think now, common sense, said Mr. Lee. Who sings their best songs in daylight, without a dark stage from which to emerge, without artificial, and therefore special, footlights? Who hands over a tip in the daytime, where everyone can see? The *Sirenas* sing their songs only at night. They sing when the world is halfway toward the show of dream, when reaching into the pocket for a coin is a reach down into sleep and what resides there by way of desire.

At sea, anyway, no one sings in the daytime. Not for show. There is work to be done in the daylight, whatever work sailors do, trim the sails, avast the hearties.

But when the sun sets, the accordions come out. The tattooed sailors smile their fishlike grins, full of sea meat and eel tongue and North wind. They start the push and pull of their musical boxes. They dance in their striped shirts and, slyly so that the other sailors do not see, retie their bandannas against the air, which has begun to cool. We imagine them half-reasonable men who get cold, half something from the old movies.

At night they drink thick rum and sing out too loud every song the sea has ever heard. They also do their singing at night, because they cannot see what is out there. They cannot aim their sails very well, or swab the decks. They cannot use their eyes, which in this darkness try to be hands. Squinting in the dark, they try to make their eyes feel ahead. Everyone does it.

The ocean at night is a whalelike cavern, but with the mouth of a tarantula, something unthinkable. One imagines the blackness and the movement to be many things. The night is beyond even the strength of the muscle a father makes for his son to see.

One will do anything to keep the teeth away, to keep the stars from coming down and the juice waters from coming up. Anything, any type of song, any kind of prayer. In this the sailor practices tying knots just to keep a rope near. In this a sailor practices knife-throwing just to keep a knife handy. Anything to use on himself, should the teeth of the night come together.

Sometimes the *Sirenas* answered back in song or in conversation. Sometimes their angry husbands all wet and foul-mouthed and careless drunk did the answering back, and sometimes nothing could be heard at all.

~~~~

This man who had come to town was a Triton. The townspeople were certain. Good or bad, one way or the other, no one could yet say. This was the story: he arrived in town from out of the dark, at night under a new moon, and no one had seen who or what had brought him.

He simply came to be at the front register of the two-room hotel, and laughed his laugh. No one knew how long he had waited before letting go of that singular noise, which sounded as if the stars themselves had come down from the night, so many little sparks, but without the light, so many little pin-pricks in a row. No one knew how long he had waited, but the wait must have been long since so many sounds made themselves inside that laugh, so many sounds the laugh could not stop properly once it got started.

Armida, the hotel maid, led him away to one of the two rooms along the rollers of that laugh. Even when he closed the door, Armida said, she could still hear something of it. The laugh was full of small saws and bees, strong enough to cut through the walls and with enough wings to fly into the garden and along the street. Armida could not tell with any precision when it ended, or if it ever did. Some noises in that room in later years were simply unexplainable except for this.

When the man woke the next morning, Armida, the maid and the room service as well, said he ordered a *coctel de abulón* brought over to his room. I don't want it so much for the abalone, he said to her, as for the tomato juice and lemon. Armida nodded to him as if she understood, but she did not.

What he felt in his head was very big.

That is what the man said, she told everyone, as he had continued to talk. The townspeople who gathered now nodded their own heads. Something was inside the words he had spoken, but no one could yet say what. They nodded their heads, understanding only that if the man said something in his head was very big, then they had better get out of the way in case he let it out.

No one knew for certain how to interpret the man's words. Nor did they know their role as townspeople. Should they stay out of his way because they feared him, or stay out of his way because they had little interest in a visitor to town? That they should stay away was the only point needing no discussion.

The townspeople immediately called the visitor Triton because, before he retired, he said something more to the clerk of the two rooms. He said either he was looking for his wife, or that he was looking for *a* wife.

The man moaned and held his head. Then he laughed. Perhaps it was not a laugh at all, someone said. Perhaps they had mistaken the sound, and it was the moan he began with that had not stopped.

This made no one feel better, and no one wanted it as an explanation for anything.

This man had no drink at the bar, but that did not mean he had not been drinking. As for that matter, he did not seem to have a gun, but that did not mean he was not hiding one. No one had seen horns on him either, but as they began to understand, that did not mean much.

Perhaps, they said at first, this man was only a bear. Maybe he was just passing through, which would not be too bad. Or better, he was simply a vendor, with brushes or medicines under his greatcoat. A traveling vendor was something they had seen before.

The remark about his wife, however, or *a wife*, gave everyone second thoughts. Did this visitor know about their daughters? Should they hide them? The town had hidden people before. But no one knew what to do now.

Did he say anything about his wife singing, they asked both Armida and the clerk.

Had some of their daughters sung too loudly, dreamed too much, or too hard? Had this Triton come to take one of them, who had called him without knowing? Had the tide of the ocean come up this far, so many hundreds of miles? In their Saturday evening talks they had often worried about the ocean. They worried about it coming up as far as the town some evening, not quite enough to swallow them all, but leaving one of its own lost on them. People knew for a fact stranger stories than this. And, as if by coincidence, many of them had to do with the ocean. So this story was possible.

Neither the clerk nor Armida could remember for certain whether he mentioned any singing or any water. Perhaps he had said nothing, or perhaps he had.

~~~

After his breakfast of abalone the visitor fell back asleep, snoring in much the same manner that he had laughed.

Mr. Lee was consulted.

The town had once saved Mr. Lee by hiding him from the soldiers who took all the Chinese and put them on trains. In return, he himself had saved the town, more than once. Though he said he knew nothing about strange occurrences, he always seemed willing to lend his ear to the moment.

Mr. Lee was brought over to the bar next to the two-room hotel where the Triton was asleep. Someone told Mr. Lee of the comparison between the visitor's laugh and a string of firecrackers.

He, too, nodded his head, but the townspeople felt sure that when Mr. Lee nodded his head *ahhh* it meant something different from when they themselves nodded.

Mr. Lee worked as a translator in this town. Every important document was taken to him for copying into Chinese, which used to be a service to the community when there were more Chinese in town. But since the trains took most of the Chinese away, the townspeople used his services differently.

The town hall had burned down two years previous. Mr. Lee's job now was to translate various documents back from Chinese. He had kept his own library, and at this point had the only records left of the town. When there was a question about some civic detail or other, Mr. Lee was consulted. He would go into his library and emerge with the appropriate document, which he would then bring back to life in a manner and language familiar to the townspeople.

On occasion, Mr. Lee's laws seemed different from what people could remember, but who could argue with the written word, regardless of its curvature.

From time to time, Mr. Lee himself would volunteer some arcane bit of law or other, some decision of the grandfathers for the good of the town. In this way, he showed them several new holidays, and with them he had the town order by special messenger a variety of foods that, somewhere in the business of everyday life, people had forgotten—several roots for spice, some thin black sauces.

If anyone could discern something from the presence of this stranger, it was Mr. Lee. After all, the story of the Triton as mate to the mermaid had first come from a particular tapestry Mr. Lee owned, a tapestry with threads that shone.

The mermaids themselves came from the journals of Columbus. The further story of the *Tritones,* however, came with a little help from the dark inside of Mr. Lee's outer room. While he had not given Triton as the sea-creature's name in Chinese, that is what he called the thing for these townspeople. This was a name they would understand.

He had a mouth, this Triton, said Mr. Lee, that could blow hard enough to make a boat capsize. No one forgets a story like that.

Suddenly this man appears, if he was a man, asleep next door, and with a laugh made from who knew what. It was cause for another beer, at the very least.

Mr. Lee nodded his head *ahhh* and listened to everything. By now each of the townspeople had something to say about the visitor. Each gave a new detail concerning the laugh, or said something about what seemed to take shape beneath that black greatcoat.

Who even wore a greatcoat around here anyway, they said to Mr. Lee in turn. Each had a different detail, but each had the same question. What was to be done?

～～～

By now it was time for the *botana,* the requisite social gathering of the townspeople in weekly celebration of Saturday afternoons. A little beer, a little food, some fried bits of one common thing or another, with tortillas, some *chicharrones,* then whole cucumbers with red chili powder and lemon and salt. A few prickly pear *tunas,* some purple ones and some green. A baseball game on the radio.

A hundred small pieces of conversation, an argument, which on these afternoons seemed like a large French bread, or better, a chair. Something there every time, but finally ignored.

Someone in love, who wanted to be left alone. Some kids, who would eat quickly, not wipe their mouths, and then run around, drinking lemon-lime sodas, or shaking them and wetting the walls, seeing who could reach highest.

Smoke, which was itself a second ceiling in this room. Some days it was a light cloud cover, some days a full cumulonimbus assemblage with a life of its own and animal shapes for the little kids.

Young people did not come. They were left to do chores at

home. All of them, all alone, at home on Saturday afternoons. In truth, not much got done. Invariably the next Sunday a particular boy smiled at a certain girl a little differently. By some mysterious manner, some postal system not known to the grown-ups, they now knew each other better.

Who could say about these things? As everyone knew, however, and though they pretended coincidence, all the people who came for *botana* now had themselves met each other as youngsters on Saturday afternoons. They had met, and met often, when their own parents were off with their younger brothers and sisters to the great *botanas* of the earlier years in the century.

Mr. Lee had not a little to do with this, as he had clarified for the town that, indeed, these Saturday leisures were de facto the law. The law was a good one, the townspeople thought, after a while, whispering around their beers about things. It was their civic duty and good for business, talking things over and eating the small leftovers of the day. Progress worked this way. Who would not want to move forward like the new locomotives?

〜〜〜

Mr. Lee nodded his head, ate a few of the shrimps and *tripas* from this *botana*, and listened to everyone. He summoned Armida and the clerk in turn, and Armida would come back periodically with reports of what she heard next at the stranger's door.

Mr. Lee sent a youngster to fetch his tapestry, which he then held up.

Did the visitor look like this, he asked.

The hour was dark, they said, and so late. Their eyes had been only half open, ready for sleep. As things turned out, only a few people had actually seen the man, and even then they had seen only his back. It was a large back, they agreed.

Armida and the clerk had seen him, however, from the front.

No, the two of them said, he did not precisely look like this picture in the tapestry. Not in the face, though he did have a beard. They could not look into his greatcoat, which he had kept well buttoned. This was at odds with the night, which was not so cold, said Armida. She was the maid and the room service, but her job was also to carry out the trash sometimes, or take one object or another outside at night. She spoke with the authority of many offices, and always with particular eloquence about the weather. Last night, she said, and nodded her head from side to side—not so cold.

Not so cold, see, said the clerk. Armida says so. But this man, he kept that coat buttoned to the top.

Now, they said to Mr. Lee, look how long this Triton-man is sleeping, and in the daylight. Perhaps he is a creature of the night after all. Wasn't it possible?

Mr. Lee used his old explanation about these things, the one he used to explain everything that seemed curious at first. Without him saying so, it was an explanation from his own life. In putting on a belt in the morning, Mr. Lee said, a person should understand why another person somewhere else might be putting on a small dress of feathers, or how two artful sticks might be the equal of a fork.

At times like this, Mr. Lee always wanted to say a person is a person, but saying as much would have sounded too easy, too regular, not big enough. So he invariably took the long way around to explain this to everybody. We are all living out our days, he began. We do what is in need of doing.

Perhaps, if you will listen, our man's visit is not unlike *dim sum*. That is what others might call the *botana*, said Mr. Lee. Another people at another time of day, in another place, but these were the same thing. Different foods, different words, but the same thing. Perhaps, then, our visitor is just another man. Not like us, to be sure, but enough like us.

Mr. Lee shrugged his shoulders and nodded his head yes, once, firmly, which was also another way of telling them not to worry. Sometimes it worked better, letting people see an answer with their eyes.

Mr. Lee always came for the *botana*, he told them. He knew a good thing when he saw one. What they called it didn't matter to him—*botana, dim sum*. They could call it a purple people's picnic for all he cared. As long as they stacked up food on the tables. Did they understand, he asked. This visitor had provided them with so many details, each so tasty, he said. Perhaps this was even a good man. Had he not been an entertainment, after all?

They nodded their heads in agreement. This was not the usual Saturday afternoon fare. That was true.

Firecrackers and pearls, stars and cowboy guns, unfolded serpents from the sea—Mr. Lee himself had paid good money to see these things at a theater in Nogales.

~~~~~

Mr. Lee looked around and took a moment for his story. This was also the law, to tell one's story when there was one.

At the theater in Nogales, he said, as they all knew, Mr. Martínez played the piano. Mr. Martínez played the best he could, perhaps more with emotion than with a delicacy of hand. Mr. Lee said this with a wink, which they all understood. He played the piano to make the action seem stronger. You know—a fast piano for the fast horse. Sometimes Mr. Martínez fell off his chair and was better to watch than the movie. At the very least, he was half the movie himself.

Just like an opera, Mr. Lee said. They had all heard Don Lázaro's records. A word said in an opera becomes a word spoken by someone who has swallowed a piano—a word with force, with music. Sometimes it was the movie talking, sometimes Mr. Martínez.

Well, did they recall Señora Piñeda? She used to live here until her new husband moved the family to Guadalajara, then somewhere after that? The first several times she went to the movies, she yelled at the people on the screen to look out! and not to trust the other one up there, not even for a moment.

Everyone nodded that they remembered. More important, as seen in the quick tenor of their nods, they appreciated Mr. Lee's speaking only about her. It could have been any one of them. They had all yelped out at the screen, also their first times. With the cowboys and the soldiers and the kings and queens up there, one could not help shouting, as a reflex, and as a friend.

~~~~~

This man Mr. Martínez, said Mr. Lee, did not even charge them anything at all for so many pleasurable hours. To give away so much was almost a crime. Of course, little did Mr. Martínez realize the entertainment was not in the piano. No one would dare tell him, at least not anyone with upbringing.

They nodded their heads like Mr. Lee, *ahhh*.

Perhaps in homage to Mr. Martínez they should offer this stranger something. Did Mr. Lee think so?

Perhaps, said Mr. Lee. In homage to Mr. Martínez. As they were all friends of the Martínez family in those days, they could not have insulted Mr. Martínez with the offering of money there on stage. They could not have made him bend down for something that was not a handshake, not in front of everyone else at the theater.

Leaving some gift now would be the thing to do, said Mr. Lee, a good way to remember. We should offer something to this stranger in appreciation of the lesson taught by Mr. Martínez. Did they not think so.

A bowl was passed, and a few beers not drunk. After all, as Mr. Lee had said, paying for the services of an entertainment was the honest thing to do. The clerk of the hotel thought the owner would go along with no charge for the room. *After all*, said Mr. Lee.

After all, they said.

Being scared had been good, Mr. Lee said, but not too good. Just right.

They nodded their heads in a slow yes. Nobody said aloud that being scared had not quite gone away, or that they would leave early to check if their daughters were, at least, somewhere still in town. This Triton had done a good job of scaring them, and shaking it off would take a while. But they tried laughing, with Mr. Lee, and they felt better.

Armida was put in charge of leaving the bowl of money outside the door. The clerk would leave a note clearly stamped with the red "Paid-in-Full" on top of the bowl.

The plan was a good one, they all said.

This town, Mr. Lee said, while shaking his head. Here there was no need of wind, not with so many whispers, no sir. Were they not lucky living so close to nature.

At first they nodded their heads, but then they laughed. They returned to the strategies of the *botana*, declaring what should be eaten in turn, what was most medicinal, what was in need of salt. They remarked again on the striking aspect offered by the shiny threads on Mr. Lee's tapestry, which was still in the room, oversized with its full head of the Triton.

This brought on, again, the very first parts of the Saturday's conversation, Columbus, and his sighting of the mermaids. The *Sirenas*, they have done it to us again, everyone agreed. This was a music they had all heard, a fast melodic scale coming as if from the mouth of each of them, all about the stranger. These were melodies and harmonies perfectly meshed, coming as if they themselves were the half-fish and lived inside the sea, crying out to anyone who would listen for help. What a surprise their cries had been, and to have them come out like songs, so that everyone listened.

This is the way the conversation went, but it was not after all real conversation. The townspeople simply could not go away. Each waited to see if the man would leave, if the money and the hotel would be enough.

Underneath it all, the *botana*, the friendships, the stories, the beers and the *norteño* music, the afternoon air, and no matter what Mr. Lee said—underneath everything, and not to be rude, but *hijo de la chingada*, they knew a Triton when they saw one. A laugh like that, so many pearls but without light, something from underneath the water, very far.

Real pearls leave a roughness in the mouth, not in the ear. Mr. Lee could make them feel better about the visit. But this man could not fool them.

PART FOUR

Benjamin Alire Sáenz

I Want to Write an American Poem

On Being a Chicano Poet in Post-Columbian America

There is no "degree zero" of culture, just as there is no "degree zero" of history.

— EDUARDO GALEANO

I.

In the world of late twentieth-century post-colonial, post-deconstructionist, post-modern American letters, I occupy an unenviable, liminal space both as a poet and as a Chicano. "Poet" is a difficult role for anyone to play, especially in an era where the possibility of meaning has been thrown into question. What does being a poet "mean" in an age when words and concrete, sensible realities abide in separate worlds?

Untrained in the academy when the idea of writing occurred to me, I naively began with the simple premise that I was going to represent aspects of my culture that were all but absent in the literature to which I was exposed. When I began writing, I implicitly believed that 1) I could legitimately "represent" some of the "realities" of Chicano culture, and 2) that writing necessarily had a social and moral function. But through my experiences in the educational institutions of this country—from El Paso to Iowa to Stanford—I became aware of the literary traditions that I would be measured against, and I began to suspect that everything that had ever been written could and would be used against me.

It is impossible for me to apply the word "poet" to myself without wincing. I become embarrassed. I put my hands in my pockets and look down at the ground as if I have stolen something that does not belong to me. "Poet" is a difficult role for anyone to play, especially someone who was not trained to play the part. (Some people grow up with a tremendous sense of entitlement; others do not. I belong to the latter group whose psychology was formed in part by race and class—issues we find troubling to speak about in

127

this country because race and class differences are not supposed to exist.) "Poet" brings with it too many expectations of high culture and/or academic traditions—poet as maker, poet as prophet, poet as the literary personage par excellence, poet as "unacknowledged legislator of the world"—expectations that will always be foreign property. You can take the boy out of his neighborhood, but you cannot take the neighborhood out of the boy, and in my neighborhood, the great literature of the world was not something that any of us aspired to write—it was not even something we aspired to read.

I may not always know what I am, but I know what I am not: I am not an Ovid; I am not an Alexander Pope; I am not a T. S. Eliot; I am not an Emily Dickinson; I am not a Gertrude Stein. I do not feel myself to be a true heir to Walt Whitman, to William Carlos Williams, to Ezra Pound, to W. H. Auden, to Wallace Stevens. I do not feel that I have inherited the literary traditions of García Lorca, of Pablo Neruda, of Octavio Paz, of Rosario Castallenos. Am I an heir, then, to the indigenous writings of the Aztecs and the Mayans? Can I rightfully claim the *Popol Vuh* as mine? The *Chilam Balam?* Do the writings, oral traditions, and myths of the North American Indians properly belong *to me?* What can I legitimately, morally, and honestly claim? The ancient Greeks? In short, who are my forefathers and foremothers? Whose son am I? What is my genealogy?

But if I wear the garb of "Poet" uncomfortably—like an ill-fitting Oxford shirt—then I wear the robe "Chicano" quite differently. If I am uneasy about making large claims as to my literary identity and lineage, then I am in no such uncertainty when it comes to my cultural identity. Chicano is a realm where I live comfortably (which is not to say painlessly). Chicano is skin: you can touch it, can smell it. The skin sweats. The skin has known work, has been scarred, and it will keep sweating, keep working far into another century. Chicano: 64 percent will not graduate from high school, will keep working, will keep sweating. Chicano works at Burger King in Palo Alto—Chicano is service economy. Chicana is maid. Chicana is farm worker. Chicano is janitor. Chicano is *corrido:*

Ya mataron a Cortez,
Ya se acabo la cuestion,
La pobre de su familia,
La lleva en el corazon.

But Chicano is not opera. Chicano dies—it is not tragedy: Chicano is not Achilles, is not Hamlet, is not King Lear, does not have far to fall, cannot be measured by *The Poetics*. Chicano is trickster; Chicano is coyote. Chicano sings: *sin musica no hay vida, sin musica no hay vida*. Chicana is neither Mexican nor North American, but Chicana is both. Chicana is neither truly European nor truly Indian. Chicana is conquered. Chicana is exile. Chicana is desert. Chicana is Rachel grieving for the thousands who are no more, who had no names, the canon fodder, the grape pickers, the imported *brazeros* who came to farm during World War II, but were deported soon as the war was over. Chicana is Magdalena at the tomb rolling back the stone with her rough-bare hands demanding to know where they have taken her dead. *Where have they taken my dead?* It is a scream, a lament, a demand. No answer is given. Chicano is child: product of a violent fuck. European desire meets savage, indigenous, noble Eve. Chicano is incarnation of rape. In turn, he rapes. In turn, he is raped. Chicano is macho, but Chicano is feminized. Chicano is not Puritan, does not keep the words of Jonathan Edwards in his books. Chicana finds herself in the image of Guadalupe, in the paintings of Frida Kahlo and Remedios Varo, in the altars she builds in her house. Chicano speaks impurely, makes up words. They call what he speaks "Tex-Mex," "Calo," "Code Switching." Defenders of the pure call it corrupted, call it corrupting. Chicano corrupts the integrity of the Spanish language. Chicano corrupts the integrity of the English language. Chicana's integrity is this: she has no respect for borders. She knows why borders are there.

II.   Several years ago, the Russian poet Joseph Brodsky came to visit our writing workshop at Stanford. When it came time to discuss the poem I had written, he remarked that my poem was the "most regrettable of the lot." One of the pieces of advice he gave me was to keep foreign languages out of my poems, since I was working in an "English tradition." (I had used a childhood poem rendered in Spanish, since Spanish was the predominant language of my childhood.) He later went on to recite a poem with a Latin phrase in it. What Mr. Brodsky was objecting to was not my use of a foreign language *per se*, but my use of Spanish—a language that has not traditionally held an esteemed place in American letters—unlike Latin, Greek, and French. Clearly, in the "English tradition," some languages are more foreign than others. Mr. Brodsky also warned me about expressing my politics via my poetry. As it turns out, I came to the same conclusion as Brodsky regarding my poem—I eventually threw it out. But I have since spent a great deal of time pondering Brodsky's attitudes toward American "poetics" (if that is what they are). Brodsky assumes that an American poet is *necessarily and by definition* working in the Anglo-American tradition. It never occurred to Brodsky that there are many literary and cultural traditions that coexist in America, and not every poet who writes "in English" is necessarily enamored of the Anglo-American tradition. Brodsky's attitude suggests that I set aside my culture, my working class roots, and my bilingual heritage if I wish to be an American poet.

Brodsky asks the impossible. I cling to my culture because it is my memory—and what is a poet without memory? I cling to my culture because it is my skin, because it is my heart, because it is my voice, because it breathes my mother's mother's mother into me. My culture is the genesis and the center of my writing—the most authentic space I have to write from. I am blind without the lenses of my culture. Robert Frost's New England is not even a remote possibility for me, nor is Pablo Neruda's Isla Negra. Paterson, New Jersey, was no Paris, but it was a big enough place to give William Carlos Williams his wonderful and particular vision of the world—but Paterson is not my city. What I have is a desert—and it is all I have—and it is a big enough place to write from for a lifetime. Like every poet, I would like to be read and appreciated—and not just by other Chicanos. By refusing to write out of any other space, I run the risk of being labeled nothing more than an "ethnic writer"—applauded by some for no other reason than my "ethnicity" and held in contempt by others for the same reason.

This is the truth of the matter: I have no choice. I cannot write out of a white space, and this for the obvious reason that I am not white. It is true that my writing wears a sign: THIS POEM WAS

WRITTEN BY A CHICANO, but it is also true that almost everything I read also wears a sign that ANNOUNCES ITS AUTHOR'S CULTURE, GENDER, AND CLASS. Robert Lowell's poetry is filled with his very male obsessions, his Yankee history, his Catholic/ Puritan angst, his academic, formal training—none of these qualities validates or invalidates his poetry. Every writer has his obsessions, and there are very real personal, psychological, historical, and political backgrounds for those obsessions. My particular obsession is my culture—a culture less familiar to most audiences in the United States than Robert Lowell's, but no less "American." Often, people do not read Chicano, Native American, or African-American poets because they are not interested in "ethnic" subject matters. But, as a Chicano, I do not read non-Chicano poets merely because I am necessarily enamored of the cultures from which they come and which they represent, but because I am interested in learning about the different poetic traditions that form and inform the broader culture around me. If Wallace Stevens's formal verse is complex and formidable, is it honest to dismiss the poetry of Langston Hughes because it fails to meet Stevens's poetics? Hughes himself once said, "I believe that poetry should be direct, comprehensible, and the epitome of simplicity"—a far different goal from Stevens's—a goal I find completely genuine and admirable. Hughes attempted to develop a poetics that was based on the music and life of black culture—a poetry that included his own people as part of the audience for his work. He could not afford to ignore the racism confronting the circumstances of his people. This very knowledge became a part of his aesthetic. Hughes's position in society (a position defined by his "blackness") became central to his poetics, just as Stevens's position in *his* culture was central to his formation as a poet. Like Stevens and Hughes, I too have a particular position vis-a-vis American culture, and it would be impossible to escape this position, even if I wanted to. I've learned to embrace the space out of which I write. It is a curse. But it is also a blessing.

III.   I write to document what has largely remained undocumented, underrepresented, and misrepresented in American literature. I write a poetry of witness. This does not mean that I consider myself to be *the* voice of the Chicano experience—this would not only be egotistical, it would be impossible. We are not a homogeneous people. All one need do is read a sampling of Chicano and Chicana poetry to realize how very diverse we are. There is no such thing as the Chicano voice: there are only Chicano and Chicana voices. The definitive Chicano writer does not exist, and never will exist. The more Chicana and Chicano writers there are, the better chance outsiders will have to gain fuller, broader, and deeper insights into our culture, and history. I am but one of many voices that seek to bear witness to a history that has remained hidden. What I write out of is my own particular and historical experiences, my own particular psychology, my own particular vocabulary.

I do not know how important my work is. I only know that it is important to me. I certainly do not write because I am convinced that my work is indispensable to American letters. To me, this would be ridiculous. Aesthetically speaking, I am not likely to threaten the position of the "important" poets of my century. But, as far as I am concerned, this is not a cause for weeping or gnashing of teeth. I am more than a little aloof from my North American predecessors (if, in fact, they are my predecessors). Much of the canonical poetry (that is, the poetry appropriated by the academy) is preoccupied with aesthetic concerns. More often than not, the poetry that comes to us via the centers of higher learning is a poetry filled with references to other writings—which is to say there is a preoccupation with established literary traditions, the self-conscious act of writing, and intertextuality. The academy has a penchant for poets who refer to other poets, writers, or philosophers (by working either *in* or *against* the traditions of their intellectual peers and predecessors). The study of poetry becomes a dialogue with the poetry that has come before it. Poetry becomes the property of intellectuals—a society where the virtues of subtlety, irony, distance, and complexity reign supreme. A poetry that seeks an audience outside the society of the academy is relegated to that purgatory referred to as popular culture—which is to say "low brow"—which is to say that it will be written out of poetic history. Given the poetic demands of the academy, what becomes of the poetry and the lived experiences of much of the American population?

Having spent so much time in academic institutions, it would be ludicrous to claim that I am completely unaffected by what is taught in those institutions, but I have remained close enough to my identity and distant enough from my education to remain critical of how the idea of literature is produced and reproduced. The representation of my culture has always remained at the core of my writing. If I have a muse, then it is my culture. The impulse behind my work has more to do with *my experience of America* than it has to do with the poetic traditions passed down from generation to generation in American universities. I am busy documenting the undocumented. (On the border, the *Migra* stop "aliens" and ask them for their "papers." Despite centuries of our presence in this country, we are still being asked to provide "papers." Providing papers is precisely what my poems are about.) I try deliberately to remain as aloof as possible from aesthetic debates. My work is political on a more basic level. I will not go so far as to say that aesthetic concerns have no relevant politics: I will say only that that particular battle is not mine to fight. There are many different aesthetic traditions—a writer ought to be free to work in the aesthetic he or she is most comfortable with without being condemned. I do not assume that a writer is necessarily conservative because he or she writes in traditional English metrics nor do I assume "postmodern" avant-garde poetry is politically intelligent and more relevant merely because of the aesthetics in which it participates. If I am critical of an elitist notion of art, then I am equally critical of a poetics that champions popular culture without acknowledging that much of popular culture in the United States is based on rampant commercialism, and is, more often than not, misogynistic and ethnocentric. Very often I get the distinct feeling that aesthetic debates only serve to further remove us from the historical and political issues that affect the peoples of our society. If I wish to be distracted from the world, I will spend the evening watching television.

I believe that art is more than a decoration, that it is a cultural necessity, that it is indicative of the mystery of the imagination—the ritual expressions of our complex emotional lives. But I do not believe in defending the integrity of art above the integrity of people whose lives I seek to represent in my poems. To work with words is to necessarily work in an aesthetic. But "to aestheticize" should not imply "to anesthetize." I find it impossible to engage in

133

a poetics divorced from the history that constitutes my memory and that produced me. I understand exactly what James Joyce meant when he spoke of his Ireland: "This race and this country and this life produced me. I shall express myself as I am." My cultural position does not allow me the mobility of many white writers. Being conscious of the poverty out of which I arose, and being acutely aware of the poverty in which so many members of my family remain, what choices do I have if I am to keep a necessary connection to my past in order to maintain some integrity? I cannot abandon the cultural and historical circumstances that are my only true inheritances. I do not claim that everything I write is "real." Like every writer, I mythologize. But if I mythologize about the Southwestern desert, I can do so only because of my *very real* relationship to a *very real* place.

When my mother was in the ninth grade, she was awarded a medal for outstanding academic achievement. A few years ago, she handed me her medal. It reads: "For God and Country." That same year she dropped out of school to help support her large family because her mother was sick. At fifteen she became a maid and part-time mother to her brothers and sisters. My father experienced such racism in West Texas that he still says bitterly: "I wouldn't shit in the best part of Texas." In the early 1960s what passed for plumbing in the "house" I lived in was one pipe that brought in cold water. My mother would rise in the morning and heat water to scrub us before we went to school. I sometimes still feel her washcloth rubbing my skin raw. She wanted us to be clean; she would not have her children be called "dirty." I am not likely to privilege what I have learned in educational institutions over the experiences of my family. For too many years I have seen the cycle of poverty of our people. All of my life I have seen more wasted minds and lives than Allen Ginsberg ever dreamed of seeing. I could launch into full and graphic descriptions—to do so would be to utter an endless litany of despair. I write to fight despair.

Though I work in language, language is not my primary concern (which is not to say that I am disconnected from and unconcerned about the language I work in—the words I choose). According to Alexander Pope, "Language is the dress of thought." I have always struggled to "dress" my thoughts appropriately. When I say that language is not my main concern, I am not implying that

I do not pay attention to sound, rhythms, line breaks, imagery, metaphors, similes, and the rest of the poetic and literary devices available to me as a poet—this goes without saying. No poet is exempt from learning his craft. No artist is exempt from immersing himself in his discipline. But it should be remembered that a poet ought to be judged according to his own particular tradition. It is disingenuous, inappropriate, and chauvinistic to judge the poetry of the indigenous peoples of the Americas by the poetic standards of English culture. (In the United States, the English literary tradition has been constructed as the central poetic tradition—but it is not central to many poets who find that particular tradition culturally and artistically foreign). I am primarily concerned—perhaps even obsessed—with the desire to write the unwritten into history—into time. We have bled. We have died unnecessarily. We have lived. *We live now.* We are worthy of being represented in history, in art, in poetry (and not merely assigned to be studied by cultural anthropologists and social scientists).

In Joyce's *A Portrait of the Artist as a Young Man*, Stephen Dedalus is speaking to an *English* Jesuit. As he does so, he reflects about his relationship to the English language because of his Irishness. He writes:

> The language in which we are speaking is his before it is mine. How different are the words *home, Christ, ale, master,* on his lips and on mine! I cannot speak or write these words without unrest of spirit. His language, so familiar and so foreign, will always be for me an acquired speech. I have not made or accepted its words. My voice holds them at bay. My soul frets in the shadow of his language.

My soul, too, frets in the shadow of those who take for granted their ownership of the English language. Because the language of my family was Spanish and not English, I have always had an ambivalent relationship to the language of my country. The language I am writing in will always be someone else's before it is mine. English was the language of my education; it was the language of power—of empowerment—of intelligence. To speak Spanish, when I entered grade school in 1960, was to be dumb in every sense of that word. If "in the beginning was the word," then the word be-

longed to the gods who spoke English. The word was not mine—
the word was the possession of the gringo. It was my task as a student to receive the word, and having received it, to forget the language of the home. But to erase a language is to erase a culture. We
were treated as inferior and we knew it, though we did not know
the word "inferior." We learned shame early, and despite my mother's efforts *we were* looked upon as dirty.

But a child knows more than he can say in language. James
Baldwin spoke for many when he wrote:

> All this enters the child's consciousness much sooner than we
> as adults would like to think it does. As adults, we are easily
> fooled because we are anxious to be fooled. But children are
> very different…. They don't have the vocabulary to express
> what they see, and we, their elders, know how to intimidate
> them very easily and very soon. But a black child, looking out
> at the world around him, though he cannot quite know what
> to make of it, is aware there is a reason why his mother works
> so hard, why his father is always on the edge…. He is aware
> that there is some terrible weight on his parents' shoulders
> which menaces him. And it isn't long—in fact it begins when
> he is in school—before he discovers the shape of oppression.

A child senses all the splits of his universe though he cannot
give them names. Often, he does not even learn the names of the
many oppressions and inequalities from the adults around him
because the adults are all trying very hard to deny that they exist.
Silence is a difficult habit to break. I did not have a word for racism and cultural domination until I was much older—and even
then, I first thought it applied only to what whites felt for blacks. It
was only much later that I understood, that in southern New Mexico, it was we who were the blacks.

When I speak of my self, if it is not obvious already, I speak of
a historical self—a self that is immersed in a specific cultural context. The self I speak of is obsessed with history precisely because
in the writing of history, so many Chicanos (not to mention Native
Americans) have occupied almost no space, and this from a culture
that has been present in North America for centuries. I do not need
Fredric Jameson to implore me to "always historicize." I would

like to think that the self I bring to my poetry is much more than a self-indulgent, confessional individualist whose emotional life is the center of his universe. The self that I bring to my writing is not an individual self that seeks to divorce himself from the polis. I agree wholeheartedly with Denise Levertov when she responds to Wordsworth by writing "The world is not with us enough." I must keep myself close to the world and its concerns, the earth and its peoples, if my poetry is to be a bridge (however small) between clashing cultures and ideologies.

In the United States we have evolved into a culture of fractured individualists. We have lost interest in building community and are becoming less and less capable of critiquing the self-interest of the upper classes and multinational business firms who have broken with the community of humankind. We must stop fetishizing the "rich and famous"—they are not worthy of our attention or admiration. We must break with the very rich because the very rich have broken with the common people of the earth. We must stop showering the Donald Trumps of the world with affection. He, and individualists like him, have no valuable vision to offer the Americas. We must turn to those who have a vision of community (and by community I do not mean a nationalism supported by militarism) and learn (perhaps for the first time) that our differences with each other need not be threatening, and that, despite everything, we all belong and must return to the earth—we all belong and must return to each other. As Dorothy Day, the founder of the Catholic worker movement once wrote: "We have all known the long loneliness and we have learned that the only solution is love and that love only comes with community."

IV.   We often speak about American history as if it were something real. But I do not believe in American history: I only believe in American histories. But histories are written constructions of those in possession of the word, and I object to the way history has been constructed, sanitized, and glorified. Dick Fool Bull was a witness to the events at Wounded Knee:

> There were dead people all over, mostly women and children,
> in a ravine near a stream called Chanke-opi Wakpala,
> Wounded Knee Creek. The people were frozen, lying there in

all kinds of postures, their motion frozen too. The soldiers, who were stacking up bodies like firewood, did not like us passing by. They told us to leave there, double-quick or else.... So we went on toward Pine Ridge, but I had seen. I had seen a dead mother with a dead baby sucking at her breast. The little baby had on a tiny beaded cap with the design of the American flag.

American history has much to do with slavery, with the European genocide of indigenous populations, with the creation of myths that served an ideology of occupation. American history has much to do with industrialization and the ensuing exploitation of workers and the pollution of the earth. American history is sordid and bloody and disgusting, and nothing will ever convince me that our national past has been heroic. Our politicians are enamored of speaking of "traditional American values," but *the* traditional American value is war—killing—and it seems to me that this country has always been able to create the illusion of community by engaging in wars (the U.S. invasion of Panama and "Desert Storm" being but the latest examples). Wars create an *us—us* against them. This is a very false community. It takes more than waving yellow ribbons and flags in a parade to create an authentic community—it takes a commitment to create a climate where all the peoples of the Americas can enter into dialogue.

Walt Whitman once wrote:

> We Americans have yet to really learn our own antecedents, and sort them, to unify them. They will be found ampler than has been supposed, and in widely different sources. Thus far, impress'd by New England writers and schoolmasters, we tacitly abandon ourselves to the notion that our United States have been fashion'd from the British Islands only, and essentially form a second England only—which is a very great mistake. Many leading traits for our future national personality, and some of the best ones, will certainly prove to have originated from other than English stock.

"Many of the leading traits for our future national personality" should come from our indigenous peoples—their attitudes toward the land, their sense of community, their myths (which ought to be as well known to us as Greek and Roman myths), their spiritualities. The European sense of superiority we have inherited has shown itself to be militant and uncivil.

Since Columbus set foot on the Americas five hundred years ago, and had the audacity to rename everything he saw and claim every piece of land he set foot on for Spain, the indigenous peoples have been struggling for their place in American society. They are still waiting. What kind of a civilization are we?

The story of America is chaos. The European-Americans who colonized and appropriated this land have fought war after war, piled up violences upon violences. Our American past is a mass grave with bodies stacked up taller than the tower of Babel. The living stare at the bones looking for meaning. I confess that I cannot walk through life unless there is some kind of meaning: this is not only at the heart of constructing history, but it is also at the heart of constructing poems. In his last interview, Arturo Islas said: "Life has no shape. We impose shape on it so we can deal with it. It's scary to think that it's all chaos. And what artists do to the nth degree, what writers do to the nth degree, without seeming to do it, this is the trick you see, is to give shape to things that have no shape. The human heart has no shape. Emotions have no shape. It's the writer who gives them a form." Our history *is* chaos. Others have been giving it form for centuries. I refuse to sit back and merely curse the darkness. I have decided to enter the debate for the heart of America.

Eduardo Galeano, in his preface to his trilogy, *Memory of Fire*, makes the following observations:

> I was a wretched history student. History classes were like visits to the waxworks or the Regions of the Dead. The past was lifeless, hollow, dumb. They taught us about the past so that we should resign with drained consciousness to the present: not to make history, which was already made, but to accept it. Poor history had stopped breathing: betrayed in academic texts, lied about in classrooms, drowned in dates, they had imprisoned her in museums and buried her, with floral wreaths, beneath statuary bronze and monumental marble.... Through the centuries, Latin America has been

despoiled of gold and silver, nitrates and rubber, copper and oil: its memory has also been usurped. From the outset it has been condemned to amnesia by those who have prevented it from being. Official American history boils down to a military parade of bigwigs in uniforms fresh from the dry cleaners. I am not a historian. I am a writer who would like to contribute to the rescue of the kidnapped memory of America, but above all of Latin America, that despised and beloved land: I would like to talk to her, share her secrets, ask her of what difficult clays she was born, from what acts of love and violation she comes.

Galeano's monumental work, a fragmented representation of the history of the Americas has become for me a model for what I wish to do through my poetry. Like him, I want to breathe something of my people into history. I remind myself that we are not so much the products of history as we are the products of our interpretations or constructions of history. History is not so much something that has been written as it is something that we continually and necessarily must rewrite. What has been lost must be recovered. I write to recover. I write to proclaim. I write to explain. I write to declaim. I write because I love, because I am sad. I write because I am a part of the universe of the living and the dead, and it is a joy to be a part of it. I write because I am angry, and my anger is legitimate. *I write because I remember.* Some Chicanos, unfortunately, feel the price they have to pay for success is to relinquish their culture. We give up our altars, our processions, our prayers, our traditions, and immerse ourselves in the great White Protestant culture of North America. But I do not call that success; I do not call that "integration." I call it erasure. I call it the great forgetting. I call it death. There are many people who suffer from cultural and historical amnesia—it is one of the great ailments of our age, and why we so often and stupidly repeat mistakes over and over again. Memory is the most important tool at the disposal of a writer—any writer—and without it, she not only cannot be a writer, she cannot be alive. As Luis Buñuel reflected: "You have to begin to lose your memory, if only in bits and pieces, to realize that memory is what makes our lives. Life without memory is not life at all."

We often think of 1492 as the year Columbus "discovered" America. We think of the discovery of the North and South American continents as a *fait accompli*. In fact, the Americas have yet to be discovered. It is false to think of "the age of discovery" as being over—we are still in the midst of the age of discovery. We must keep searching until we get closer to the heart of what America is. Five hundred years and we are still in search of our communal identity. Human beings are slow to learn. The tensions in our society are everywhere to be seen, and they point to our arrested development: the tensions between the ancestors of the European colonists and the indigenous peoples they displaced; the tensions between rich and poor, the homed and the homeless; the tensions between races, between peoples who speak different languages, between genders, between sexual identities, between peoples who think in different grammars. I believe our violent and contentious present is symptomatic of the fact that we have never come to terms with the truth of our past. We have never come to terms with our impulse to enslave, our drive to prove our cultural and military superiority, our compulsion to dominate other peoples and the earth that gives us life. Part of our national psychology has always been to aspire to be "the greatest nation on the face of the earth," but that greatness has *always* had more to do with power than it has had to do with the spiritual and emotional development of our civilization. We must exorcise this sickness. We have remained far too interested in defending and glorifying the colonialist and militaristic enterprise that made possible the European conquest of the Americas—so much so that we have never been able to effectively critique our own history. We have remained mortgaged to European culture and European standards for far too long. In doing so, we have sacrificed the art, literature, and culture of the peoples of the Americas.

I am a Chicano poet, which makes me an American poet—and by American I am not speaking exclusively of the United States. I am a citizen of the Americas, and I want my poetry to reflect it. Like William Carlos Williams, I believe we must keep searching for "an American idiom"—a language truly American (not merely North American but *pan* American). In his seminal essay, *In Defense of the Word*, Eduardo Galeano expresses what he sees as his responsibility as an American writer:

It seems to me that the possibility of contribution depends to a large extent on the level of intensity of the writer's responsiveness to his or her people—their roots, their vicissitudes, their destiny—and the ability to perceive the heartbeat, the sound and rhythm, of the authentic counterculture, which is on the rise. That which is considered "uncultured" often contains the seeds or fruits of *another* culture, which confronts the dominant one and does not share its values or its rhetoric.... The testimonies of the people as they express in a thousand ways their tribulations and their hopes are more eloquent and beautiful than the books written "in the name of the people."

Our authentic collective identity is born out of the past and is nourished by it—our feet tread where others trod before us; the steps we take were prefigured—but this identity is not frozen into nostalgia. We are not, to be sure, going to discover our hidden countenance in the artificial perpetuation of customs, clothing, and curios which tourists demand of conquered peoples. *We are what we do, especially what we do to change what we are:* our identity resides in action and in struggle.... A literature born in the process of crisis and change, and deeply immersed in the risks and events of its time, can indeed help to create the symbols of the new reality, and perhaps—if talent and courage are not lacking—throw light on the signs along the road. It is not futile to sing the pain and the beauty of having been born in America.

What does it mean to be a Poet? What does it mean to be a Chicano? What does it mean to be an American? It is the nexus between these realities that forms my poetry and my identity. I know America has not yet been discovered. I want to help sing her into being. I want to write an American poem. But to do so I must learn the chants of her peoples and repeat them until they are written in my heart: *May it be beautiful behind me / May it be beautiful below me / May it be beautiful above me. Happily on the trail of pollen, may I walk.* Whitman's impulse to sing himself into America seems absolutely right to me: "I celebrate myself and sing myself." He was not celebrating an individual divorced from his community— he was celebrating a love that he had claimed as his—*America.*

Much later, Langston Hughes wrote, "I, too, sing America." Corky Gonzalez, the Chicano activist and poet once asserted: "I am Joaquin." He had to proclaim himself back into the land of the living. Long buried—and buried precisely because of his race, he had to find the strength to unbury himself. They knew what Galeano knows, and what I know now, too: *It is not futile to sing the pain and the beauty of having been born in America.*

Ray A. Young Bear

Journal of a Mesquakie Poet

From the Tribal Homeland Front, Notes Leading to Five Hundred Years After

May 20, 1991

In the twenty years or so that I have been involved with poetry readings and visiting artist/lecturer residencies here in Iowa and the greater Midwest—an occupation that never ceases to astound me in light of my Mesquakie, People of the Red Earth, roots—I have discovered that young people in this "advanced" nation of ours are extremely fortunate to know anything when it comes to Native Americans—and their tragic history.

Since Native Americans have much to do with who I am via my identity and tribal affiliation, this certainty of young people "not knowing and perhaps never knowing enough" about my ancestry hits me on a personal level.

Academically, we have been apprised that Iowa students are among the best when compared to others, but their knowledge about Native Americans is embarrassingly next to zero. Yet I suspect it is no better in Azusa, California, or Rome, New York. It doesn't make them any less in their skills, of course. Mostly, there's ample room for improvement. While these students are fully aware of our existence, such knowledge is often weighed down with stereotypes and misconceptions. Take for example the range of questions received this past year from elementary and high school students:

"Mr. Young Bear, do you live in a tipi?" "Have you ever scalped anyone?" "Do you wear feathers?" "Did you ride into town today on a horse?" "Do you own a bow and arrow, and have you ever hunted buffalo?" "How does it feel to be an Indian?"

Knowing these types of questions are quite serious, I usually responded with lighthearted but truthful answers that went some-

145

thing like this:

"Dear Child...First of all, just like you and everyone else here, I live in a house and enjoy the conveniences of a modern existence. I have indoor plumbing, VCR and TV, stereo, computer/printer, and so forth. The way you and I live are in many respects the same. It is our beliefs that are different.

"Second, the tipi dwellings of which you speak belong primarily to the Northern Plains tribes, like the Sioux, the Crow, and the Blackfeet. But contrary to what you've been taught, they don't live in them anymore. Long ago they used to.

"As a contrast, to let you know tipis were not the only ancient dwellings, my Woodland/Algonquin people long ago resided in geodesic dome–shaped lodges. Depending on the season, these bark-covered lodges were adequately insulated with hollow reeds for winter or naturally air-conditioned with vines for summer....

"As for scalping, I don't believe in buying or reselling rock concert or sports tickets at exorbitant prices. (There will be puzzled looks until an explanation is given.) Actually, jokes aside, please know from this day forth that the literal taking of scalp was never our invention. I've been told white men introduced this macabre practice to us. Of course, when this later backfired, we were stuck with it as the villain-inventors. (Scalping? I will continue within my thoughts. No, never. But having been a university lecturer, there have been occasions when it seemed appropriate, especially with students who wanted something gradewise for nothing. *Entre nous in jest.*)

"As for the donning of feathers, do you see any on me? (I will ask while holding on assuredly to the lapels of my suit or vest. The classroom often reverberates with laughter before I mention ceremonial regalia is worn for special occasions only, using church-related "Sunday Best" clothing as an indirect equivalent. It should be noted a sponsor or two will audaciously suggest I arrive in traditional "garb," which I will not honor lest I perpetuate such narrow-mindedness—with all due respect. Conversely, I wouldn't think of asking anyone to wear *klompens*, wooden shoes, or Viking furs unless that was their sole folkloristische dansgroep occupation.)

"And about my horse? I hate to ruin grand impressions, but my horse is Japanese-made, a 1987 Toyota Tercel with close to 100,000 miles on the odometer. It doesn't eat hay...nor does it make the mess afterward. It uses premium unleaded, the best gas possible to prolong its life before I take it out to the pasture...and junk it.

"And my only association with bow and arrows, I am sorry to say, came by way of childhood via rubber-tipped arrows and bull's-eye targets. That's the farthest I took the interest. Toys.

"As for hunting buffalo, I don't believe I have ever had the pleasure. You see, your forefathers wiped them out. (The tempo of the classroom laughter will subside but resume with...) But I imagine if I ever met a snorting buffalo with its horns gleaming wildly in the sunlight somewhere in the cornfields, I'd run like HELL, and I'm sure you'd run alongside me....

"This brings to mind the aspect of hunting. Ever since I saw a whitetail deer die twelve years ago from a gunshot wound, I have developed new concerns. The sight of a beautiful animal choking on its own blood changed me forever. Without getting into the subject, let me say that from where I stand wildlife is not abundant, and I am extremely uneasy with hunters—be they Native American or Caucasian—who abuse the outdated privilege.

"Nowadays, and I don't think you'll be too surprised to learn this, we hunt at the same place your parents hunt. Which is where? Yes, the local supermarket. My wife, Stella, and I crouch along the aisles of the meat and produce section like this (breaking into an exaggerated pantomime), hunting for the freshest and cheapest items possible with our delicate senses.

"And how does it feel to be Indian? That may be the most important question of the day. Let me ask you a question in return, and let me change it slightly. I hope your answer will be the same as mine: Do you enjoy being a human being?"

Informing students Native Americans oftentimes live very much like other Americans, enjoying the same pleasures—or on the other hand, not having the same opportunities and living a life of torment—is never without obstacles.

I use my poetry as a means of self-expression and present bilingual/bicultural works in the form of books to narrate, juxtapose, and detail tribal existence of the past and present. Many students are astounded to know we share similar novelties. During these moments, with apologies expressed emphatically, I will diverge from poetic purpose and focus on shattering misconceptions that have long since calcified. The students are surprised at entertainment we have in common: Red Lobster's ocean delicacies, Pee Wee Herman's Saturday morning television show, and Casey Kasem's Top Forty radio program. Once the shards of old images have flown out the window, I tie the connections stronger by confessing that I am hopelessly "mesmerized and . . . in love" with the award-winning vocals and beauty of pop singer Mariah Carey.

If I can leave a classroom with the knowledge I have eradicated the last vestiges of frontier mentality, I will feel successful. If a disgruntled observer later records "more poetry should have been read as was the original intent," I will shrug and smile. Even those in the know fail to see sagacity when it is right before their eyes. Poetry can easily take a back seat if I ascertain I am the first—and possibly last—Native American the students will ever see, hear, and talk to.

As perhaps the only thrice-published Native American poet within a three-hundred-mile radius, correcting misconceptions can be a god-awful burden. More so, when the education system turns out to be the mute culprit. Then how does one circumvent this reality? The figurative answer is, a little brain-jarring mixed with a hefty dose of humor, art, and music. Simply put, my pedagogical approach incorporates these autobiographical elements into my cultural and creative arts presentations. I wholeheartedly espouse the belief that a student is more likely to digest and keep such information through laughter and startling insights as opposed to outright didacticism.

Needless to say, a crucial chapter in the American saga seems to be missing. A change must soon be enacted toward the proper and judicious presentation of facts. The way things are now, it is rare to meet educators who go beyond the three R's. Obviously the trend of most schools is to concentrate on subjects needed for modern survival. Which is their prerogative. And accordingly educators will teach Indian-related subjects as they themselves have been taught. Which is contrary to how most subjects are taught.

Fortunately, in the eclectic muddle, there is an elite handful who choose to enlighten students about a horrendous epoch most prefer to stay away from. These are the incredible few who frequently digress from the contradictory glorification of Thanksgiving via paper cutouts of Pilgrims and Indians having an ancient cookout. To hear fifth and sixth graders discuss early tribes receiving "contaminated grain and spoiled meat" and "blanket gifts infested with the smallpox germ" is a dramatic departure, but simply knowing of past atrocities is meaningless unless there is a keen awareness of remorse—and guilt. I say this because any association with the past nowadays is met with a sense of apathy. (This bridge-burning attitude is a carry-over from immigrants who arrived from the Old Country, those who wanted to melt indistinguishably into the pot.) With the older populace, of which a large percentage has never done anything of social relevance, the typical response is, "We're tired of feeling guilty. Let bygones be bygones. If it hadn't been us, it would've been someone else." Yet that doesn't mean the first abuses of aid or the first SCUD-related incident should not be discussed. If anything, these verities should become a vital component of American history. As long as this arm's-length detachment is held, I postulate, more atrocities will be committed to humanity throughout the next century.

~~~~

The long drives taken during the school year have left an indelible impression upon my work and consciousness. It is often a time to seriously reflect on the opportunities given to talk about my poetry and Mesquakie background. On occasion there are several questions that surface, dive, and resurface as the rural landscape dotted with farm machinery and livestock whizzes by my car window.

Just how important is it to share such information with these young people? Should I assume the storyteller/messenger role which I first saw in my grandmother, the person who essentially shaped my world view via mythology and spirituality and its precepts? Or should I limit it?

When my great-great grandfather, Mamwiwanike, initiated the monumental purchase of central Iowa land in 1856, the sole purpose was to establish a homeland for the Mesquakie people and all those to be born afterward. In order to accommodate the welfare and future of the Mesquakie Nation, there was a momentary state of acquiescence to the Euro-American's value system. In exchange for cash Mamwiwanike was given a deed, a document, a piece of paper with black markings that indicated ownership of said property.

To my knowledge, this transaction between tribe and state may be the only one of its kind. The intent, of course, was to provide a place where Mesquakie progeny could live in solitude, protected with invisible barriers from the *wa be ski na me ska ta*, white-skinned person.

More than 130 years have passed, and thanks to the divine wisdom of the boy-chieftain, the Mesquakie have the distinction of being known for their tenacious beliefs. This tenacity accounts for our original language, culture, and religion still being intact. But all has not been without conflict and some loss. There have been heated debates and clan-dividing issues as to what factors of Euro-American society we should accept or reject, what to fence in and what to fence out. This is where I come in, a descendant of both the conservative and progressive factions, asking questions.

When studies are no longer done to determine how much we have lost and regained of our former selves, and when cultural barometers record our tribal myths, and ceremonies have successfully withstood centuries of genocide, our survival will be attributed to spirituality. (Granted, there are certain individuals who exploit by "going through the motions" with little or no adherence to one's worthiness. To counter this, My grandmother, *no ko me se ma*, believes there will be a few who will be blessed to carry the sacred fires to the futuristic darkness.) But no one knows this.

How does one report that five hundred years after Columbus the Red Earth People are basically unchanged? For clarity and a promotion of better understanding between people, especially toward those with little or no roots to speak of, should this achievement be taught?

My heartstrings convey that if the fundamentals of Native American knowledge aren't part of the classroom curriculum, we will continue to be portrayed in a ceaseless array of disturbing and puzzling caricatures. (The Washington Redskins and the Cleveland Indians pop immediately onto the cerebral screen, including the University of Illinois' Chief Illiniwek mascot.)

It is therefore no surprise many schools inadvertently perpetuate romantic images of tipis, feathers, buffalos, and the like. I have no trouble with this stylized approach as long as it includes an in-depth section on contemporary Native American society. Admittedly, this is a hefty request, but if this subject is to be taught correctly, careful research is a necessity. Without a thorough background the chances of a childhood introduction turning lopsided is increased tenfold when Mrs. Pinkston cannot go beyond classroom tipis and fluorescent tempera-coated dioramas.

By the time "studying Indians" is but a photographic memory posted on the bulletin board and the displays of talking-skin drawings collect a film of dust, a child is left with incomplete and clouded images of "Indians." As a result, wrong impressions of cataclysmic proportions are born. (Contrary to what many believe to be a monumental but wobbly-legged step in the reels of cinematic history, many people have yet to see Kevin Costner's *Dances With Wolves*. (While Costner may bathe in the Oscar tinsel for the birth of the Lakota-inspired epic, it isn't nearly enough to stop John "Custer" Wayne from hopping into our lives with a pathologic vengeance.) Add to this heap the small-town entrepreneur who sells "Tribal Name Burgers" (after a neighboring Indian community) and/or the corporate bigwigs who use "Tribal Names" on their exclusive merchandise: our identity has been grossly misused and distorted by a country that has yet to recognize its errors.

Instead of thrashing about helplessly in the tumultuous waves of the Ocean of Perpetual Malignment, I resolve it is not the fault of these innocent students nor their teachers and administrators for "not knowing and perhaps never knowing enough" about my ancestry. It began long ago in the name of this and that. To pinpoint and isolate where this infectious misunderstanding began should be taken as a matter of priority, for it inevitably touches upon the righteous attitudes of government and politics.

In the autumn of 1990 when area educators issued "Let's hope and pray the Persian Gulf crisis doesn't lead to war" statements at conferences and high school government classes, I was among those most pessimistic—and rightly so. "With the Native American as a monumental example, why should the United States stop with Iraq?" I asked rhetorically, noting that the seek, befriend, steal, and destroy pattern was established centuries before at the expense of my ancestors. "That is why the word P-O-G-R-O-M exists in Webster's dictionary," I said, knowing very well a mother hen or two would cluck contemptuously and attempt to spread their wings over their ears. But I raised my voice. "Pogrom is a noun that means an 'organized slaughter of a racial or religious minority group.'"

All of this leads me to speculate that while much of the Christopher Columbus hoopla scheduled for October 12, 1992, will focus on political and technological achievements of America, no one can ever underline firmly enough the inexcusable disrespect for humanity that has taken place through my grandfathers. And in one way or another, we are all caught in the middle, stagnating.

Inés Hernandez

An Open Letter to Chicanas

On the Power and Politics of Origin

Mis queridas hermanas:

As many of you know, I am Nimipu (otherwise known by the French-imposed name Nez Percé), of Chief Joseph's band, on my mother's side. On my father's side I am Tejana/Mexicana—I was raised in a Chicano barrio in Galveston, Texas, but with my sometimes stubborn, always gentle, loving Indian mom always at my side. My dad, carpenter-fisherman-worker, with hands and mind of an artist, is Tejano/Mexicano, therefore mestizo, therefore at least part *indio*—my mom, from the res' and the *montañas*, having come to the island to share her life with him. I am their daughter. Yet in the Indian/Chicano community I am often confronted with persons who tell me I must choose—Indians who complain about my Mexicanness—Chicanos who complain about my Indianness. Herein the politics of my own creativity and the politics within my creativity. My work, my word, is my response from my being to and for myself first, and then to those persons who have faced the similar dilemma of wanting to understand the difference.

The weight of the role that has been imposed upon us as mestizas—that burden, with its roots fundamentally interwoven with patriarchy and Catholicism (and the accompanying degrading dichotomy of the *mujer mala/mujer buena*), we have already repelled. But what do we do with that outrage, that hatred, those intense resentments, and finally, that fear that for so long was the main instrument used to keep us repressed and which dried up all the life energy of our beings so that we would end up effectively spent and even turned inside out, with nothing inside to sustain us or nourish us?

About sixteen years ago I was sitting in my home in Austin, Texas—my sons were asleep, and my lover, who knows where he

153

was—and I felt intensely depressed. I sat at my kitchen table, drank a whole bottle of wine alone, and smoked some weed (I gave up smoking marijuana about eleven years ago). Suddenly, I grabbed paper and pen and began to write: two poems came out that I believe are declarations of love and resistance for women. One is called *"Rezo"* ("Prayer" or "I pray"). In this poem I called on the spirits of the female ancestors, and those feminine principles, to ask them to help us conquer our history and "put in order our House of Aztlán"—metaphorically, of course, I meant our Chicana/o community. The other poem was the following:

Canción de madre	Mother's Song
No llorés, hija	Don't cry, my daughter
India de mi corazón	Little Indian girl-child of my heart
No llorés	Don' cry
Ni pases esos corajes	Don't allow those rages to
	pass through you
Muy dentro de tu alma	So far into your soul
Hasta que te pierdes	That you lose yourself
te pierdes	you lose yourself
Y no te encuentras	and can't find yourself
Ten calma, mija	Be calm, my little daughter
Todo pasa	Everything passes
Nacer	To be born
Renacer	To be reborn
Retenacer	To be reborn again
Es cosa natural	Is natural
Nadie tiene control	No one has control
Ni el Miedo mismo	Not even Fear itself
Echate a ese Miedo	Kick out that Fear
de tu vida	from your life
Y enfréntate con tí misma	And face your own self
O puedes o no?	Can you or can't you?
No llorés, hija	Don't cry, my daughter
Todo pasa	Everything passes.

I didn't quite understand at the time, but I now know that the *"Canción"* was the answer to the *"Rezo."* I am the daughter in the song, and the mother is the most ancient mother of all—the original female energy, the female *principle*, in every sense of that word, call her by any name or many names— who in her consolation validates me, as an *India* and as a woman, and teaches me how to have courage, to be brave. But that mother is also me, mother to my self, as we all can be, and so I dedicate this song to all mestizas.

I feel that within each Chicana/Mexicana/mestiza there is that indigenous aspect that is connected with the collective consciousness of the red tradition of this continent—and that aspect reveals itself as a little Indian girl who for centuries has been abandoned, ignored, and unloved. We have wanted to erase her from our being—she doesn't know love—she doesn't know what it is to have confidence in herself or trust in others. In the most remote corner of our being—whether we are dark-, medium-, or light-skinned— she has hidden herself. She is cornered, repressed and humiliated, encaged and without voice, without hope. She nourishes herself with the little vital energy that we cannot deny her—because she is a part of our being, our cultural essence. The spirits of her ancestors, her grandmas and grandpas—how they would like to free her, embrace her, and show her lovingly how to grow and become a complete woman, beautiful, powerful, and courageous. But they, too, have been forgotten. It is very common to hear Chicanos say, "Well, yes, they say my grandmother was pure Indian, but no one knows what tribe." Of course, because that rarely is spoken of. Children are told not to behave like *indios*. When *raza* gets drunk and carries on, the next day the people often say, almost with a mixture of shame, laughter, and admiration, "The Indian in me came out." Out of where? Out of hiding? Out of the closet? Out on a prison furlough? Out of isolation?

Genocide is an instrument of imperialism, and both depend on cultural imperialism and the dialectic of terror to invade, violate, traumatize, exploit, and totally control human beings throughout the world. As long as the majority of mestizos/mestizas refuse to acknowledge the face and heart of the Indian man or woman inside themselves (again, *not to the exclusion* of the other aspects of their being and cultural heritage), they will not be able to realize themselves as complete human beings, in the sense of knowing their own origins, much less give true value to the indigenous peoples of the Americas or to the other autochthonous peoples of the world (and so, these people will continue to remain faceless masses, without individuality or personality)—a grave and sad situation for humanity, and for all so-called progressive movements today which mestizos/as are involved in. Why and how so? Because I have noticed the overwhelming tendency on the part of many of my colleagues in academia, and in the community, some of whom are Marxist-oriented, for example, to reject and discount the indigenous perspective in their analysis of the issues that face us. Anything Indian is seen as unsophisticated and "primitive." Besides, they argue, race is not the primary issue, and furthermore, Indians are always talking about spirituality, respect for the Mother Earth, and sovereignty. Why can't they (the Indians) just accept that their time is up, it's past, it's over and done with—it's history. Yes, I would say, it is history—repeating itself.

Eduardo Galeano writes in *Memory of Fire* that in 1563 an Araucano chieftain confronted the Spanish captain Bernal and demanded that the Spaniard's troops surrender to native forces. The Araucanian warriors had the upper hand, but the Captain refused to surrender, even in the face of sure death. He tells the Indian chief that in the end they, the Spaniards, will win the war, for there will be "more and more of us." The chief asks "How? With what women?" The Captain says, "If there are no Spanish ones, we'll have yours,...and we'll make children on them who'll be your masters!" And so, many times over, the scenario was and is played out between Indio and Español whereby the energy was/is set in motion to sustain the hostility, the antagonism, the hatred today between Indio and mestizo. Perhaps surprisingly to mestizos, proud of their Spanish drops of blood, however few they are, Indios, "Skins," find it a cause for shame, for derision—"You don't talk about being Mexican." Why? Because your mother was raped and you were helpless to prevent the act—you are further evidence of it—constant presence. At another level, the Indio, the "Skin," often has the utmost scorn and contempt for mestizos who are running after the European superiority lie. How dare they think they are better by aligning themselves with the rapist, the invader, the thief? The irony of our situation should not be missed.

Many people would argue that the so-called Spanish (and Portu guese) "Conquest" was not as brutal in its decimation of indige- nous peoples as were the genocidal policies in the North. I wonder. At least here in the North, Indians know they're Indians and they know what that means. In the mestizo community we have inter- nalized the Western European, and now white American, oppres- sor's mentality that turns us against our very selves.

I have always been stubborn in my insistence (and I know I am not alone) that what is most precious about the Chicana/o psyche is our originality. As orphans, because that has been our (mis)fortune (of course, for reasons expressly historic), we have had to dig out of our own insides what is ours—because there was no one who would accept us, much less teach us. Scorned by the Anglo-Saxon world, where we continue to drop out of schools in record numbers, and by much of the Mexican world, where fre- quently we are condemned for our *mocho-pochoness,* or assumed lack of sophistication, the Chicana and the Chicano have had to strengthen and develop ourselves in our own way—that is, we have had to recover and reevaluate what our culture is, not only through formal investigation and research, but also and in great part through our intuition and the dictates of our heart.

In the process of reintegration with our history as Mexicans, for example, we saw some interpretations that didn't seem right to us. One of the major cases is the history of Malintzin, who within the Mexicana/Chicana culture has come to signify more than her identity as an Aztec woman. Chicana writers and artists have con- fronted the pejorative manner in which the image and spirit of this symbolic mother of the first mestizo has been accused and punished over the centuries. Why does she even matter? Because first of all, Malintzin, or la Malinche, was named in the records of the so-called Conquest, and thus she acquired a face and place in history, and in the Mexican collective conscience, not only as mis- tress to Cortés and mother of his children, but also as the "tongue," the interpreter who traveled with the Spanish troops to secure the support of other native peoples; she is, from the men's historical perspective, the mother to be ashamed of, the arch-traitress, the Mexican Eve, the one who opened her legs and in giving herself over, gave over the continent to foreign control.

For me, there is a relationship between la Malinche and marijuana in the Chicana/Chicano community. I've heard some of our *gente* argue that if you don't smoke *mota*, you're not Chicano/a. I know it was said facetiously, but I have also heard Indians say the same thing about liquor. But liquor was introduced to the Indian community throughout the Americas to aid in the cultural devastation. In the case of Chicanos, however, there is another factor to be looked at: marijuana is an herb that has medicinal powers, but for the most part, it has been abused and exploited, and has worked against us as a people. I've noticed that the same Chicanos who make the argument for *mota* often are not concerned with, and in fact dismiss, the efficacy of all other hierbas in terms of their healing properties. I know, also, that many males see mota as female. The herb and the woman, both abused, violated, and exploited by men for their femaleness, both considered "bad" by men, yet both sought after for that very "badness." In the circle of men, a woman can be accepted if she assumes her role in the "illicitness" of the setup.

One of the possible meanings of the name *Malintzin* is derived from the root *malin-*, which is seen by some as associated with the Nahuatl word *malinalli*, or *hierba*. So Malintzin can be seen, in turn, as a human counterpart of the herb *malinalli* (in the Indian community she would also be called, as an herb, the little grandma, the little sister/older sister—she is a *relation*). The original meaning of the hieroglyph *malinalli* as defined by Mexican scholar César Macazaga Ordoño, in his study *Templo Mayor/ Sagrario de la Vida: La religión agraria del Mexico Antiguo*, expresses the idea of life and death. From the skull is born the herb, year after year. Plants, flowers, life are reborn from the earth that has been fertilized by the bones of those buried there, and matter is renewed thanks to its own death. If we extend this understanding to Malintzin the person, we are given a nonjudgmental way in which to look at her life and her role in history, and we have one more piece of evidence to connect her to the Mother Earth, and to that female principle that encompasses everything.

However, in typical male projection, and as if the men themselves had not mistook the Spaniards for gods, she is associated instead with the worst of all possible offenses—collaboration with the enemy. Mexicanos, especially the men, are outraged at their mother, their women, themselves. Why? Because they don't see their mother as a victim—they see her as a sell-out, one who gave herself freely—so, they want to rid themselves of any trace of her, and the female aspect of themselves. They view Indios/"Skins" with the contempt they feel is befitting a supposedly weak and inferior race, just as they transfer their mistrust of Malintzin to mistrust for all women. Why? Because they have bought the father's story that is seeped in misogyny and, having internalized the racism of Indian hating, they identify with him. When Captain Bernal spoke his words to the Araucanian chief, he totally invalidated the power, consciousness, and presence of the native women and what their response would be to this planned, forced utilization of their bodies as instruments to give birth to children who would turn on their own people and be programmed to devastate them.

For me, Malintzin is at the heart of the very issues that Chicanas are struggling with today—race, class, gender, sexuality, and voice. Because she is so well known, she is associated with all Indian women and with all of us as mestizas. She represents the indigenous feminine aspect of this continent—the continent itself as Mother Earth, which continues to be invaded, violated, exploited, tortured, and killed, just as indigenous peoples are throughout the Americas, in Guatemala, Bolivia, Peru, Brazil, Chile, wherever Indian people are. As an individual human being, Malintzin also had a major role in history at a monumental time, and so she must be looked at as an active woman, politically, sexually, culturally, a subject who made choices within the rigid framework that she moved, just as today's Chicanas have done. It is not such a far cry to relate to this woman who has been condemned for her gender, her color, her politics, her sexuality, and for being brilliant and articulate. Let us not forget either that Malintzin was taken in slavery as a child; she is related to that Indian girl child in all mestizas. To date she is not free, except in the dance community of the Aztec tradition.

Within the dance tradition of the Concheros of "la Gran Tenochtitlán," la Malinche is a path-opener, an *abrecaminos*, who cleanses and blesses the path with the smoke of the incense in her *sahumador* (a clay, chalicelike vessel that represents the Mother Earth and which holds the embers that allow the incense to burn—the embers themselves representing the fire in the heart of the earth—and the life in woman's womb). The *sahumador* holds the sacred fire, which is said to protect the entire circle of each dance group. La Malinche is the front(line)—the vanguard, so to speak. Hers is an arduous position, for on her depends the security of the path. That is, through the dance tradition (which has experienced syncretism) the positive image of la Malinche has survived. In this tradition I am a Malinche; I have been for eleven years. My role as a Malinche within a ceremonial context has helped me to understand how I am a Malinche in a social and intellectual context. We should consider the possibility that each Mexicana/Chicana could become a Malinche in the sense of being a path-opener, a guide, a voice, a warrior woman, willing to go to the front to combat the injustices that our people suffer. In this way our indigenous mother will be revindicated and we will be revindicated as well.

Who are the Malinches of today? As Tomás Borges of Nicaragua says of poets, "Anyone who loves their people with their whole heart and willingly commits to their defense and to the struggle for justice on their behalf." Rigoberta Menchú, the young Guatemalan Mayan leader, who learned the language of the oppressor, Spanish, and made it her own, just as she learned the Bible to use it as an organizing text and tool in her community. Elvia Alvarado, the Honduran *campesina/India* organizer, and Roberta Blackgoat, of the Diné nation, resisting the relocation at Big Mountain—all of the women who have accepted their role as "tongues" and demanded that their voices be heard.

There are many Malinches—Sor Juana Inés de la Cruz; the Mexican feminists of the 1910 Revolution, such as Sara Estela Ramirez, Juana Gutierrez Belén de Mendoza, Dolores Jimenez y Muro; Violeta Parra, the Chilena "mother of the New Song Movement"; the *boricua* sister Olga Talamantez and her other sisters who are now serving sentences in this society as political prisoners of the United States; Dolores Huerta, Raquel Orendain, María Salas, and all the other *campesina* women who have carried on the struggle for so many years, knowing only too well what it is like to be treated like Indians; all the women labor organizers who continue the tradition of leaders like Emma Tenayuca and Manuela Solis Sager; women such as María Jimenez and Isabel García Gallegos, who steadfastly defend the rights of our relations "without papers," the undocumented workers; those workers themselves who brave the frontline of the U.S./Mexican border daily to exert their will to live and sustain their families; writers, poets, artists, like Angela de Hoyos, Gloria Anzaldúa, Janis Palma, Joy Harjo, Jean LaMarr, Cherríe Moraga, Ana Castillo, Santa Barraza, and so many others, who dedicate themselves to cultivating their own originality so that their vision of us and of the world will be keen and just; academicians who, in their investigations, find on behalf of our people, on behalf of our culture, on behalf of our women, but who are not afraid to call a lie for what it is and who speak out against learned patterns of abuse, violence, and victimization, whatever their source; and every single woman, Chicana/Mexicana/mestiza, who has refused unconditionally to accept any longer any form of oppression or violation of her self, whatever that source, and who has committed herself to a universal struggle for justice and dignity, as they say in the Indian community, for "all our relations."

To be revolutionary is to be original, to know where we came from, to validate what is ours and help it to flourish, the best of what is ours, of our beginnings, our principles, and to leave behind what no longer serves us. Not every Chicana/Mexicana was/is Aztec. We come from many tribes, many peoples. To begin to understand our origins in more than a superficial way is to begin to "find our way back home" to what is ours, as opposed to what has been imposed upon us. The day that each mestiza/mestizo truly searches for and finds her/his own roots, respectfully and humbly, and furthermore validates those peoples who still maintain their identity as original peoples of this continent of America, North, Central, and South—on that day we will be radical and much more capable of transforming our world, our universe, and our lives.

The values that indigenous peoples hold in common are values that many of us recognize as integral to Chicano culture, the ancient yet so simple wisdom of knowing how to act, how to be *buena gente,* how to respect, how to do your part, how not to offend, how to be women and men of our word. These values are the same as the indigenous ideas about how to be good human beings, and by extension, how to realize ourselves as sovereign individuals and sovereign peoples. This ancient wisdom recognizes that the entire universe is energy and that when we move (as in *movement*), we

161

can contribute to the chaos or the harmony of the universe—we can destroy or we can help to heal. This wisdom understands furthermore that all that lives has spirit and holds that spirit in respect. What are some of the other values?

Respect for the land: The understanding that the planet Earth, the Mother Earth, is a living organism that nourishes us and sustains us and that we as human beings have devastated her, stripped and poisoned her, and thrown her completely out of balance—Indian people know this and indigenous philosophy around the *world* consistently warns of the incredible dangers inherent in this disrespectful ideology of annihilation. In the Indian world-view, human beings are supposed to be *caretakers* of the Earth, not destroyers. Each person is supposed to assume his or her responsibility. That is why the Indians in Brazil's rain forest are so upset that they have begun to come out and speak to the world community. Not only are they being wiped out, once again for corporate interests, but they also have not been allowed to fulfill their responsibility in caring for their portion of the planet, and they know the consequences for all humanity and all life. Indigenous people are the original environmentalists and ecologists.

Respect for women: Anyone needing details on this issue should read Paula Gunn Allen's *The Sacred Hoop: Redefining the Feminine in American Indian Traditions* as a starting point; her essay, "Who Is Your Mother?: The Red Roots of White Feminism," is especially critical for those Chicana feminists who have not yet begun any comparative analysis of Chicana/Native women's feminism, but who instead have sought white feminist models by which to develop their ideas. Gunn Allen's study is useful in its beginning elaboration of early gynocracies within native communities, and the impact on them by the misogynistic, homophobic, and racist ideologies that were introduced as crucial to and one with European colonization.

Indigenous philosophy recognizes the duality of all life. The female principle is not only respected but revered, and female power is given its due and never underestimated. Like Paula Gunn Allen, the Mexican feminist scholar, María Antonieta Rascón, reminds us in her essay *La Mujer y la Lucha Social* that the Spaniards came to impose a male trinity on people who believed in the complementary relationship of a female/male duality, or more

precisely, a female-male/male-female duality. The Spaniards en-
sured the indocrination into the new ideology by targeting the
young Indian girls and isolating them from their families to teach
them the new ways, since the girls would eventually give birth to
the future generations. This "boarding school" concept worked
well here in the North and continues to be used today.

Another major aspect of indigenous philosophy that Native
women from the North in particular are developing in their own
way, but which has its basis in the original understandings of all
the nations, is the idea of women's menstrual cycle as a special
time for women, a time for centering oneself, a time for purification and healing, and preparing for the month to come. It is said
here in the North that when a woman is on her "moon," she can
ask that any sickness that she is feeling at any level of her being be
released with the flow of blood that leaves her body at that time.
This idea, to me, makes sense, and makes this time of the month a
different experience for me. I don't see my periods as such a drag,
and I feel that this information provides a new approach by which
to explain menstruation to very young women who are beginning
to have periods (which is, of course, the *razón* behind indigenous
puberty ceremonies).

With respect to Indian men's understanding of the power and
position of women within the community, today's Indian male activists, intellectuals, spiritual people know that respect for women
and for their power, as intimately related to the presence and
power of the Mother Earth as they are, is fundamental to indigenous philosophy. In other words, you cannot, if you are an Indian
man, act as if you truly know what "Indian" is if you do not properly acknowledge and show respect for the women. It has not been
my experience that this is the case for Chicanos.

Respect for children and elders: Children and elders are cher-
ished within the Indian community, as they still are in the Chi-
cano/a community, I believe. On this issue, I think we are much
alike, and I think of, on the one hand, the struggles we have engaged in on behalf of a just and validating education for our children, and on the other hand, the oral history projects we have un-
dertaken in the Chicano/a academic community for the very
reason that we do value the life experiences of our people, and that
we do not want their lives to have been lived in vain, nor their

story to remain untold. The stories of the women, for me, are the key to my resistance, my creativity, and my celebration. Those old ladies, the oldest ones, the grandmas from the beginning of time, and the tapping into the stories that their spirits have to tell, are a source of joy and healing. I see in all of the Indian women, especially the old ladies, the toughest, strictest ones, I see in my mother, that Indian womanness—humility and dignity and pride—the ability to hold out, until forever if they have to, in silent strength and continuance until their conditions are met. I remember participating in a wonderful Chicana/Indian Women's Symposium at the University of Wisconsin a few years ago; an old Winnebago grandma, a respected and beloved medicine woman in her nineties, was there accompanying us throughout—her name is Flora Bear Heart. I asked her what she thought of the gathering, and she smiled and said, "Oh, I am so happy, I have been waiting a long time for this time to come, and now it's here."

Respect for difference: El respeto al derecho ajeno es la paz. In the old days, not so much in the colonized mentality of many Indians today, differences such as sexual preference were respected, and in many cases tribes assigned great significance and powers to gays. Today's conscious Indians understand this, and so homosexuality and lesbianism are accepted matter-of-factly by them and formal documentation is being gathered to demonstrate the historic foundations for this acceptance within the culture. For information, see Will Roscoe's *Living the Spirit: A Gay American Indian Anthology,* as well as Gunn Allen's *The Sacred Hoop.* This respect for difference also extends to the level of community, local to international. Indians do not try to convert. They do not have a mission to impose their way of life or belief systems on anyone or anything.

Respect for natural medicines: Indigenous peoples are the original holistic healers. Their knowledge of natural medicines is a science. Indian ceremonies are ways of facilitating the balancing, centering, and healing of individuals, whole peoples, the Mother Earth, and the entire cosmos, an understanding that certainly is held by the *curanderas* and *curanderos* in the Chicano/a community as well. Since all life (plant, animal, water) is seen as a relation to the human being, and a teacher to the human being, the human being is not taught to presume superiority over other life forms. When conscious Indians hunt and fish, therefore, they do not waste or wantonly destroy just for sport, but take what they need and give thanks.

Respect for themselves as global citizens and sovereign peoples: Throughout the history of contact with European peoples, Indian peoples have had spokespersons who testified on their behalf so that the injustices committed against them, and their people's resistance and demands for justice, would be recorded. Today, Indian people, men and women, travel the world over—to the United Nations, where they have promoted the Universal Declaration of Human Rights for Indigenous Peoples—to the World Court—to many international tribunals, to state their case, the case of Fourth World peoples. Indigenous peoples within the United States have worked with indigenous peoples throughout the world—even with some Chicanos/as.

la marcha	the march
es danza	is dance
es vida	is life
cada paso	each step
dado	taken
ejecutado	carried out
conciente	with a conscious
mente	mind

With infinite thanks to the dance tradition of the Concheros of la Gran Tenochtitlan, I have come to understand that dance is life and life is dance, an awareness I now know belongs to all indigenous peoples throughout the world. To dance—to move harmoniously with all the Creation, struggling always to go beyond ourselves so that our spirit becomes able to guide our being in the best way.

In the dance community everyone has the chance to have their say, from the oldest person to the smallest child. Everyone can lead a dance, and all the circle has to follow the steps. But with that privilege comes the enormous responsibility of knowing how to lead a dance with one's spirit, because the well-being of the entire circle depends on the *conciencia* of each member. Each step matters. Each step is a prayer and a manifestation of our *conciencia* and our *espíritu*. Dance, like life, is a march and a manifestation (or demonstration). The constant and continuous march toward our personal and collective goals, toward the new sun of justice that is about to arrive, and even now, can be seen approaching—*y viene bailando*. My own manifestation, my dance in these moments? These same words that I chose to work with in these pages, because I was allowed to have my say. This letter is my dance, and I offer it *con respeto y amor.*

Note
_____

Portions of this paper appeared originally in Spanish in my essay *Cascadas de Estrellas: La espiritualidad de la chicana/mexicana/ indígena*, in *Esta Puente: Mi Espalda*, edited by Cherríe Moraga and Ana Castillo (San Francisco: Ism Press, 1989). This particular essay, with some slight changes, appeared first in *Changing Our Power: An Introduction to Women's Studies*, second edition, edited by Jo Whitehorse Cochran et. al. (Dubuque, Iowa: Kendall Hunt, 1991).

Victoria Lena Manyarrows

Confronting and Surpassing the Legacy of Columbus
A Native Woman's View

> *i never was a maiden.*
>
> behind me stands a long line of warriors
> women so many, and men
> fighters who defied relocation, extermination
> seeking mountains, their safety and solitude
> calling to me on the wind
> that they have given to me for breath
> *carry us forward into the future*
> *do not forget us*
> *we have saved this day for you . . .*
>
> (from my poem "i never was a maiden," April 1989)

As an Eastern Cherokee, I am a descendant of those people who defied relocation to Oklahoma in the 1830s and instead chose the "safety and solitude" of the southern Appalachian mountains. This relatively small group of Cherokee who escaped "relocation"—or should we be more honest and say "deportation"—lived in the more mountainous, northernmost region of the Cherokee nation of the Southeast, and were traditional people who were more unfamiliar with and less tolerant of white ways than their Cherokee relatives living to the south, in the area of the current state of Georgia.

Luckily, unlike the more vulnerable "Lower Town" Georgia Cherokee, the northern "Upper Town" Cherokee lived outside the path of the white, land-hungry settlers and the U.S. Army. Primarily because of this geographical circumstance, the "Upper Town" Cherokee escaped the brutal and genocidal relocation—the "Trail of Tears" suffered by so many Cherokee people in the 1830s. Instead of being forced by the U.S. Army to march the death march to the barren "Indian Territory," today known as the state of Oklahoma, these defiant and rebellious Cherokee did what so many Native people throughout the Americas have been forced to do since the coming of Columbus and the Europeans to the western hemisphere in 1492—they sought refuge in the mountains, away from the colonizers and invaders, and formed new communities there, focusing on their own physical, social, and cultural survival.

It is this legacy that I remember when I think of the "legacy of Columbus." It is the legacy of struggle and survival that so many Native people have lived and breathed for the last five hundred years. We have endured countless attacks on our sovereignty and psyche, and today Native people as a whole are taking more and greater control and responsibility for our lives and our Native nations. We are not only surviving, but also working to *surpass* the legacy of genocide and destruction that Columbus and the European colonization of the Americas have meant for us as a people.

Like all Native people, I am a survivor of centuries of war and attempted extermination. I am a warrior, not a stereotyped "Indian maiden," and I feel a special responsibility to the present and future generations—and to my ancestors—to carry on their memory and struggles, and work for a better future for all Native people.

As a Native woman who vividly and intuitively remembers the past and the sorrows and struggles of my people, I strongly value and respect the lessons of history. Lessons that remind us not to forget the decimation, destruction, and genocide that have happened and that continue today, and lessons that teach us the importance of unity and perseverance in the face of overwhelming odds and threats to our existence and humanity.

In the time-honored tradition of so many Native and mixed-blood women, for many years I have recognized the importance of linking my spiritual beliefs and practices with my political beliefs and actions. As a youth, especially as a teenager, I became attuned to the vital and, for me, inseparable connection between spirituality and politics. Like so many Native and mixed-blood children, experience and knowledge of Native spirituality and religion were denied and often hidden from me. My own personal curiosity, and the Native reaffirmation and political movements of the 1970s (that inspired and empowered so many Native people to assert our rights as human beings and regain our "lost" personal and political power, strength, and unity) led me to explore and "discover" my hidden and forbidden spiritual and cultural roots.

As I grew older and became more aware of my own Native cultural, political, and spiritual identity, I learned the importance and necessity of linking culture, spirituality, and political awareness and action. I learned and realized that spirituality and traditional ceremonies alone would not alleviate oppressive living conditions, enduring problems such as alcoholism, domestic violence, and abuse, and the persistent feeling of hopelessness and apathy too often present in Native families and communities. In the struggle for Native survival, self-respect, and sovereignty, I came to believe that integrating spirituality with political awareness and action is essential.

Today, throughout the Americas, Native people continue to face repression and sometimes death as racist and disrespectful governments attempt to further strip Native people of land, life and human dignity. Racism, persistent poverty, alcoholism, substance abuse, psychological and social displacement and isolation, and physical and emotional abuse and violence continue to threaten the physical, psychological, and spiritual life force of Native people, particularly in the highly industrialized and often alienating societies of the United States and Canada.

After five hundred years of sustained suffering, alcoholism, substance abuse, and other forms of physical and emotional abuse and self-abuse are common occurrences in many Native communities and families in Anglo North America. The racism from the dominant white society is often turned inward, and the result of this "internalized" racism is low self-esteem, confusion, and all-too-often self-inflicted physical and emotional abuse and violence. Alcohol and suicide are seen as doorways of escape from a life lacking in hope and filled with pain and unhappiness.

In working to better the living conditions and status of Native people, it is important to understand how psychosocial displacement and isolation are acute realities for most Native people liv-

ing in this racist and ahistorical society, which is generally ignorant and disrespectful of Native people and Native needs and
wants. More than any other racial or ethnic group in U.S. history,
Native people have been misunderstood and stereotyped into oblivion. The only way that we can be "understood" or perceived by
the dominant white society and its believers is through stereotypical images and ideas, usually based on mythical images from the
past and images of suffering past and present, which generally
serve to disavow our current existence and not take us seriously as
contemporary participants in society.

For Native people the genocidal legacy of Columbus continues
today—even as we fight it with every newly found source of
strength and determination among us. To overcome the severe
and continuing threats to Native people and lands, Native people
are becoming more organized, confident, and self-sufficient, and
we are gaining control of our dignity and lives, and coming together with greater determination and perseverance to heal our
wounds and discuss and take action to secure our futures—for
ourselves, our children (the future generations), and our Native
nations as a whole.

For Native women, the past five hundred years have been years
of much hardship, struggle, and adaptation. Many Native populations have been decimated by disease, famine, and outright murder and massacre by the European colonizers and settlers. Much
of the burden of holding together families, tribes, and nations
threatened by genocide and centuries of psychological assault and
intimidation has been assumed by Native women.

Leadership, initiative, and vision have always characterized
Native women. Native tradition usually encouraged and supported strong and important roles for women, and today this tradition is still very much alive. Today, Native women across the
land are working together and building successful marketing
groups and businesses that are respectful, ethical, and financially
fair to Native artists and craftspeople. Developing and operating
these marketing groups and businesses, such as the Zuni Crafts
Collective in New Mexico and the Ikwe Marketing Collective in
Minnesota, helps develop Native and tribal economies and self-
sufficiency, as well as self-esteem, self-respect, and pride in the individual women (and men) who work together to make these busi-

nesses serve and benefit Native people as a whole.

The San Francisco Bay Area is but one example of a locality where Native women form the backbone of leadership in the fields of health, education, welfare, and the arts. Native women such as Bonnie Guillory of the American Indian AIDS Institute, Betty Cooper of the Native American Alcoholism Program, Carol Wahpepah of the Indian Child Resource Center, Erna Pahe of the American Indian Center, Professor Betty Parent of San Francisco State University, and Janeen Antoine, director of American Indian Contemporary Arts in San Francisco, are all honored and respected leaders in the Bay Area Indian community.

On the national scale, in terms of Native and tribal leadership, Wilma Mankiller, principal chief of the Western Cherokee Nation of Oklahoma, has symbolized and personified the role of Native woman as leader since 1985. Recently, she was reelected to a second term as leader of the 75,000-member strong Western Cherokee Nation, receiving overwhelming support and recognition for her years of work and dedication to building a stronger and self-sustaining Cherokee Nation.

As mothers of the future generations and caretakers of the people, Native women continue to feel a special responsibility and concern to protect and safeguard our Native people and nations against further physical, cultural, and spiritual genocide. On this five hundredth anniversary of European intrusion into our lands, we Native and mixed-blood women find ourselves more and more determined and eager to make ourselves *heard* and *seen*, as we press forward and work independently and in coalition with peoples of all colors in order to better meet our needs and the needs of all Native people.

It is possible that 1992 will be not only a year of tremendous significance and symbolism, but also a true turning point in the struggle for greater Native self-sufficiency and sovereignty. After the flurry of activity both real and symbolic in 1992, we will need to focus our attention and energies on the years ahead and concentrate on solving those problems that afflict Native people.

Alcoholism is one problem that will undoubtedly continue to severely affect many Native Americans for years to come. Betty Cooper, a Blackfeet Indian woman active in the resistance to the 1992 "Jubilee" pro-Columbus celebrations and the director of the

171

Native American Alcoholism Program in Oakland, California, has suggested that one of the most important approaches and responses to the problems and challenges of alcoholism among Native people lies in the education and increased awareness of the next generation of Native leaders—today's youth:

> Right now, if we can reach the children from the third to the fifth grade and teach them some coping skills and if we teach them not to use alcohol and drugs and how to cope with it if it's at home then we're looking at the year 2000 having young people, young Indian people, who have never used or abused. We're looking toward having a whole generation of Indian people who don't feel that they have to be chemically dependent. We have to look at the overwhelming problems of alcoholism in our communities but we also have to look forward with hope.[1]

It is vital that we look forward to the future with hope and with strength and find solutions together to problems such as alcoholism, poverty, racism, abuse, and violence that confront Native people as a whole, and let us not forget the history of abuse and the legacy of genocide that we have survived and will continue to survive and *surpass*.

Chicana writer Gloria Anzaldúa writes that knowledge of our oppressed histories as Native and mixed-blood, "mestiza" people and the importance of unity and working together to reach common goals are vital to our survival and success:

> The dominant white culture is killing us slowly with its ignorance. By taking away our self-determination, it has made us weak and empty. As a people we have resisted and we have taken expedient positions, but we have never been allowed to develop unencumbered. . . . The whites in power want us people of color to barricade ourselves behind our separate tribal walls so they can pick us off one at a time with their hidden weapons; so they can whitewash and distort history. Ignorance splits people, creates prejudices. A misinformed people is a subjugated people. . . . Before the Chicano can have unity with Native Americans and other groups, we need to

know the history of their struggle and they need to know ours. Our mothers, our sisters and brothers, the guys who hang out on street corners, the children in the playgrounds, each of us must know our Indian lineage, our *afro-mestisaje*, our history of resistance.[2]

As Native and mestiza women in particular, it is important that our inherent link to the earth, our land, the sky, all of creation, and especially to one another be strengthened and reaffirmed. In our daily lives let us join hands and hearts and work together to build more respectful and humane societies in these Americas and throughout the world. Five hundred years is five hundred years too many for people to endure such poverty, such physical, psychological, and spiritual oppression and destruction, and the near genocide that has been endured by the Native populations of the Americas. By working together and sharing a vision of humane possibilities, Native and mestiza women can better help to guide our Native nations and peoples into a more dignified and hopeful future.

~~~~

today
we will not be invisible nor silent
as the pilgrims of yesterday continue their war of attrition
forever trying, but never succeeding
    in their battle to rid the americas of us
convincing others and ourselves
    that we have been assimilated & eliminated,

        but we remember who we are

we are the spirit of endurance that lives
in the cities and reservations of north america
and in the barrios and countryside of Nicaragua, Chile
Guatemala, El Salvador

and in all the earth and rivers of the americas

(from my poem "today we will not be invisible nor silent,"
November 1984)

Notes

1. Peggy Berryhill. "Profile—Betty Cooper and Theda New Breast," *Native Self-Sufficiency* (Forestville, Calif: Seventh Generation Fund Publications, 1987), p. 26.
2. Gloria Anzaldúa. *Borderlands/La Frontera: The New Mestiza* (San Francisco: Spinsters/Aunt Lute Book Company, 1987), p. 86.

PART FIVE

Ray Gonzalez

Without Discovery

When I was in elementary school in El Paso in the fifties and sixties, we studied American historical icons like Davy Crockett, Abraham Lincoln, and Christopher Columbus. The heroic importance of historical characters like Crockett and Lincoln were obvious to a daydreaming boy like myself. I always wanted to be a hero and created my own characters in the strange little stories I wrote in my spiral-bound notebook.

Columbus was something else, though. It was harder for me to understand what my history and social studies teachers were saying when they told my classmates and me that Columbus sailed in three ships and discovered where we lived. How could anyone discover El Paso, Texas, and the United States when they had always been here? I didn't understand how people in the fifteenth century couldn't know the United States was here. When it finally hit me, I realized Columbus was a great hero because he discovered a wild land full of savage Indians, the bad guys who killed many explorers like Columbus and fought to keep my country from ever being created.

In the fifth grade, I added Columbus to my list of heroes, and even made up my own stories of exploration where my friends and I sailed down the Río Grande in wooden rafts we built in my backyard, bound for those narrow, sandy islands that stuck out in the middle of the dry river. We never actually did anything like that, but when the whole concept of exploration and discovery finally sunk in, I knew heroes like Crockett and Lincoln could not have performed their mighty deeds without Columbus coming along to get the whole thing started. This guy with his *Niña*, *Pinta*, and *Santa María* was our true leader and he must have been a brave man taking on so many red-skinned Indians.

I can still see those colorful illustrations in my history textbook, the bearded and armored Spaniards taking on the dark-

177

painted, half-naked hordes of savages. My friends and I didn't play cowboys and Indians for nothing. We knew who the good guys were, even though a cowboy hat and a shiny gun and holster were more fun than weird armored helmets and long swords. I got stuck being one of the Indians because, when sides were drawn on the playground, the few Chicanos who went to Putnam Elementary were told they were the Indians. I rarely got to be one of the good guys.

I did a report on Columbus's three ships and got an *A+* on it. I was a good artist and spent a great deal of time drawing the intricate sails on the ships. I knew everything about them, and my fifth grade teacher was pleased. That *A+* told me I was an explorer, and I knew the history of my country. I understood all about good and evil, how the story of us all was clearly written and told in the textbooks I loved to take home and read. No one had to force me to do homework. My fascination with explorers pushed me to read more and find those books in the library that told me the Mexicans who killed Davy Crockett at the Alamo were blood-thirsty, dumb peasants, that our proud forefathers settled the west because those same tribes of people who resisted Columbus were keeping cities like El Paso from being established.

When I was forced to play Indian at school, I resigned myself to it, though I felt shamed and hoped that not too many of my teachers would see me on the playground and wonder why this student, who was so good at re-creating the voyage of Columbus, was whooping and hollering on the monkey bars. At times, I was afraid they would not let me do another report on the good guys because I was some kind of traitor on the playground. The other boys had the wooden pistols and the cowboy hats. I had nothing except my hand over my mouth, hollering and jumping like an Indian, waiting for the tougher kids to run around the swing set and shoot me.

By the time the bell rang to go to class, all the Indians had to roll in the dirt and play dead. If you got up, the cowboys would kick you or throw dirt at you. As the Indians, guys like Carlos Uranga, Sammy Madrid, and myself were always the last ones to walk into class. The cowboys got to go in first. That is the way it was, and my fascination with Columbus and his three ships took on a secret role in my world of heroes because I had to be an Indian on the playground. My *A+* didn't mean anything outside the classroom.

My later years in high school were often marked by extreme incidents of racism against me and the few Chicanos who went to Coronado High School. I got used to being called "dumb Mexican," hearing the jokes about "wetbacks," being left out of projects with other students, being assaulted for being so quiet and "greasy." The racism influenced the beginning of my life of silence, where my heroes had been replaced with a desire to write and create my own worlds. As an avid reader, I began to discover the truth behind the myths of Crockett and Columbus. Yet, the story of genocide against native people has taken me a lifetime to come to terms with and try to understand. I have yet to truly study and comprehend the impact of Hernán Cortés burning the Aztec civilization and Mexico City to the ground, fusing it into my own mestizo family lines that have a great deal to do with how Chicanos and other Hispanics should look at these last five hundred years.

Growing up in Texas made me aware of the long, bloody history of oppression against Mexican Americans. Moving to San Antonio recently, and going to the Alamo for the first time, brought it all home. That Texan icon is not my own and will never be the icon of many people I know, but the fact the little mission still stands in the middle of busy, downtown San Antonio has something to do with playing Indian in school and with the 1992 celebration of the five hundredth anniversary of those three ships coming west.

The Alamo still stands as a Texan nationalistic altar, and will help the 1992 celebration of Columbus be successful, because many Americans got to build their own altars by playing cowboys and Indians on school grounds. Those of us who became writers because that inner silence burst upon our spirit, started writing for many undiscovered reasons. One of them has to be the childhood influence of being stuck on those monkey bars, yelling like the wild animals we were told we were. Even our skin was the right color to match our savage psyche, the appropriate madness to resist the deeds of Columbus or Cortés.

The year 1992 marks our survival on the losing side, a rare place to be for some Americans (except for Vietnam). The year 1992 means we came down off the monkey bars when the school bell rang and went to the next grade at the next school, our history texts never telling us not every American could run to the water fountain first, not all of us could be at the head of the line to please our teacher. And, we believed the whole thing until we graduated and had to look for work or try and find money to go to college.

The year 1992 is also significant because the history of the twentieth century demands the whole world stop and look back. The history of Western civilization shows that when a century turns, it is harder to overcome collective guilt, a convenient time to try to come to terms with our bloody ghosts. The problem with studying a five-hundred-year period is that there are too many lies, truths, deaths and conquests to ponder and analyze. There are too many school children dividing up into two sides. But, this time, we have more than twenty minutes of lunch hour left before the bell rings.

As a writer, I have been influenced by my shame in playing an Indian when I was a boy. To write and create is to rise above that playground level and get to class on time without having to wipe the dirt off my mouth. I have also been influenced by Steve Kinnard, Bruce Burns, John Dodson, and all the good guys who got to beat up on me, then take off their cowboy hats, and go into class without being counted tardy. Their books of poetry will win national prizes and get published because they wore the white hats. Their novels will make the best-seller lists and get reviewed in the *New York Times*. My writing is also haunted by the fifth-grade report I did on the *Niña, Pinta,* and *Santa María*.

I still want to sail to unknown lands and discover something, draw as innocently and precisely as I did in fifth grade, but that *A+* paper dissolved into the earth a long time ago. As a poet, I keep digging it up out of that inner silence, but as I progress in my writing career, the cowboy hats keep popping up to remind me that Columbus influenced even the structure of American arts and letters.

As a Chicano writer, I have had to dangle from the monkey bars and come late to class because the *Niña, Pinta,* and *Santa María* have landed at harbors where Chicano, Native, Black, and Asian American writers have not been allowed to drop anchor. Greater opportunities may now be developing for so-called minority writers, and let's admit that 1992 has had a great deal to do with it. Yet, are they opportunities of only one year, a lifetime, or five hundred years?

If I can shake off that shame of being told I wasn't good enough to be on the cowboy team, will I be able to write better poems, essays, or novels? Will more of my books get published? Will more East Coast publishers look at me because they are tired of their guilt at having published and promoted only the writers who made it to class on time? Are the cowboy hats that Steve, Bruce, and John brought to school now torn and frayed, or does 1992 mean that Columbus shouldn't have gotten me an *A+* on that report? Perhaps, I only deserved a *C* because I couldn't tell the true story of the conquest and genocide of the American continent.

How many of us grew up that way? I wish I had copies of every textbook I was handed in my elementary school years. One of my favorite tasks on the first day of school was writing my name in neat, large script on the inside cover. It meant a brand new year and fresh challenges for an intelligent kid who knew that book was his and that he could devour it in no time. I can imagine a close study of those books would say a great deal about textbook adoption policies in the state of Texas in the fifties and sixties, policies that have not changed a great deal in thirty years.

Where is the historical truth? Why couldn't a boy like me have the right to be taught the truth? Where is the childhood part of me that is proud of that colorful drawing of the *Niña*, *Pinta*, and *Santa María* I spent two weeks working on?

Now, as a published writer, I know my history and I wait for 1992 to run its course. I wait for other writers of my culture to be given an honest chance, but I also want to see how many writers are waving their childhood drawings of Columbus, or George Washington, or the Statue of Liberty. How many of them got to do fifth-grade reports on Benito Juárez, or Pancho Villa, or Augusto Sandino? How many of them have overcome their silence to respond to this American look at five hundred years of *A+* reports?

In 1986, a National Endowment for the Humanities survey found that one-third of the nation's seventeen-year-olds did not know what year Columbus made his first voyage. Four percent of the students surveyed thought the voyage occurred after 1850. This says a great deal about our educational system, but also tells us that many people will not react to the media hoopla over 1992. Their world is still flat and, if they journey too far, they will fall off the edge.

Perhaps, the education I got as a child and the versions of history I based my *A+* report on were better than I think. It might be more accurate to say the world has shrunk in five hundred years and Columbus's three ships started the shrinking. Today, CNN and MTV are the textbooks, not the old history readers I grew up with in the library.

It may be appropriate to celebrate Columbus and overdo it because of our sophisticated media environment. The technology may bring more views on the Columbus debate from scholars and historians in all parts of the globe. The electronic world is also responsible for those students not knowing when Columbus sailed and for the limited opportunities "minority" writers have.

Marking the five hundred years also means the American media and publishing industry have not needed to discover writers who drew pictures of the three ships thirty years ago, nor do they have a need for native writers who have been too aware of the real meaning of the year 1492. Today's media audience does not need its own history. It may react to the celebration by defending Columbus as a true hero, and reject any notion that those who were exiled to the monkey bars have a history that says otherwise.

That may be an extreme way of looking at it, but Chicano writers have to revise history, preserve their own culture at the same time, and try to write good literature. All this must be done in the midst of a hot media environment that wants exciting stories for the five o'clock news, not essays about monkey bars and long lost drawings of pretty ships.

Twelve full-scale replicas of the original ships have been built for the celebration. Spain's official three cost 4 million dollars. This is a small example of the 80 to 100 billion dollars estimated to be spent on 1992 events by several countries. These staggering sums include everything from the 50 million dollars worth of plants Columbus, Ohio, spends for "AmeriFlora '92," the nation's first international floral and garden exhibition, to the 10-million-dollar lighthouse the Dominican Republic builds in Santo Domingo.

Who knows how many ships will sail by that beacon, but that light may not reach far enough to blind several movements against the 1992 extravaganza. One of the most encouraging signs is the fact the United Nations General Assembly has not taken any official action to recognize the Quincentennial. Efforts to have it recognized have been stymied diplomatically. Iceland and Ireland claim their descendants invaded first. They want the honor. Several New World nations have fought all this, calling 1492 an "encounter," not a "discovery." So far, their resistance to a 1992 conquest has been successful.

In the middle of these far-reaching, sometimes ridiculous, at times heartening events, I keep thinking back to my lunchtime games of cowboys and Indians and to my *A+* report on the *Niña, Pinta,* and *Santa María.* History of my childhood says my shame of being pushed off the monkey bars, to get my face ground into the dirt by the tougher cowboys was one of the strongest internal catalysts for becoming a writer. My history also says my talents as a student were recognized for the report I gave on Columbus's three ships, the way they were built, how they sailed, and how many men they carried.

I recall the teacher pinned my drawing on the bulletin board and kept it up there for several days. It hung alongside several other good reports, but it was the most colorful, the most artistic. My history as a Chicano writer says I was already waving the visions and colors of a dynamic, growing literature before a tough audience, other kids who were busy on their own voyages, drawing their own ships, hanging up their own hats, trying to write their own versions of history, not knowing their fifth-grade dreams would someday be as important as every crucial political event that took place between 1492 and 1992—crushing, monumental dramas created across the continent of their lives.

Roberta Fernández

(Re)vision of an American Journey

"What is it for?" Isabella is said to have asked, in a burst of practicality, when Nebrija's book was presented to her by a royal courtier. "Your Majesty," the courtier is reported to have answered, "language has always been the companion of empire."[1]

Stimulating, sometimes heated, late-night conversations with friends were frequent fare in candle-lit cafés in Berkeley, where quite often our discussions revolved around theoretical solutions to Third World social problems. A complex situation, we agreed, but not unsolvable, as we too grappled with our own identity as people of color actively challenging the hegemonic structure and our own relationship to it within "the belly of the monster." Self-identity did not come easily, as we strove to balance our academic endeavors with the nitty-gritty explorations we carried on outside the classroom. In general, we tended to straddle between a nationalist identity and an internationalist world view.

As an extension of this struggle, I chose to focus my dissertation research on the theories of cultural and literary nationalism espoused by the social philosopher José Carlos Mariátegui; and in the academic year 1974–1975, I went to Peru to begin my investigation in earnest. At that point, life in the Third World took on a different dimension, as I confronted one challenge after another in the capital city of Lima. Theoretical solutions were far from my mind, as I dealt with such basic experiences as getting around a city that was undergoing rapid demographic transformation under the "revolutionary" leadership of the Velasco Alvarado government.

My daily existence in Lima, on a graduate student budget (which nonetheless surpassed that of the average Peruvian), forced me to come face to face with a reality that was entirely different from the one I had known previously. For example, the act, once assumed as simple, of getting around a city often proved to be physically exhausting. I had to figure out how to get on—and even more difficult, how to get out of—the slick, foreign-made buses that, teeming with passengers, often bypassed the bus-stops, making it impossible to keep to any projected schedule. Daily I made my way through main pedestrian thoroughfares where residents of the *pueblos jóvenes*, the shantytowns ringing the parameters of the city, took up entire sidewalks with cheap plastic wares, the sale of which promised their vendors a meal for yet another day. I learned to concentrate in the reading room of the Biblioteca Nacional, where the open windows forced the library patrons to study amid the noise and pollution emitted by the constant parade of buses rumbling up and down Abancay Street. Intellectual work in the Third World, I found out, demands an unrelenting yet flexible commitment; its challenges are, for the most part, unimagined within the academic institutions of the United States, where general comfort and accessibility to materials are almost always taken for granted.

I soon realized that as demanding as the physical adjustment to the capital city was, often I was more worn out by psychological stress, a response to the value system I encountered in many of the people I met from the bourgeoisie. At the *pension* where I ate and conversed with students from the colonial city of Arequipa, I often felt sick with the way the entire household treated the fifteen-year-old, round-faced youth and the equally young maid in uniform, both of whom had come to Lima from Puno in the Lake Titicaca area. From early morning to late evening, the *señora* kept the young *serranos* constantly at work. I was aware that the two servants never got a chance to rest, as in silence, never raising their gaze, they repeated the same chores day after day. When they finally would go off to their rooms, their overworked bodies would rest in a narrow, hard cot with two-inch pilings for mattresses.

A few days before I returned to the United States, much to the consternation of the *señora*, I gave all my clothes, including my well-worn Spanish boots, to the young *serranos*. "*¿Cómo pudo hacer eso?*" she asked me in disbelief, and I figured that, after I was gone, she would probably lay claim to my clothes. I should have realized she would have this reaction, for the overvaluing that was given to products imported from the United States and Europe had become apparent to me soon after I arrived in Lima. I had been unprepared for this overconcern with appearances, coming as I was from years of living in a rarified society in the United States, where people delighted in boasting of their nonmaterialistic lifestyle; in contrast, I had been surprised at the great number of professional women and young women of the bourgeoisie who told me they made at least one trip per year to Miami to shop for clothes.

Now that I live in Houston, I periodically read in the newspapers about wealthy Mexican tourists who come to this city for a weekend of shopping at the Galleria stores, under the pretext, of course, of spending a few days away from the smog in Mexico City. These Mexican shoppers remind me of articles in *Unomasuno*, the Mexico City daily, describing the latest aspiration of the Mexican middle-class: to give their children the best of all presents—a trip to Disneyland. In Peru, the desired vacation spots were the cosmopolitan cities of Buenos Aires and Caracas.

As I recall this bent toward *artificio* and *apariencia,* I am reminded of the sad humor in an experience I had with another common mechanism used in colonialized societies to maintain control over the masses: the preoccupation with *abolengo,* or the importance given to ancestry and the "right name," remnants of the old Spanish concern with being an *hidalgo,* an *hijo de algo.* In Lima, I had been told by the Office of Foreign Ministry that in order to extend my tourist card for a third time, I had to find a sponsor who would vouch for me. I also needed to bring in the required documentation accompanied by a notarized signature.

Based strictly on the convenience of the address, I had selected a notary public out of the phone book (the office was on my way to the library). When I called the person who had agreed to vouch on my behalf to advise him of our meeting spot, my friend quickly told me that the notary public I had picked would be exorbitantly expensive because the firm was associated with one of the "old names" of Peru. I listened to his suggestions of other places, but in the end opted for the convenience of the address.

The following day we met at the designated office. I presented my documentation, got the required signature, and was asked for a minimal fee. My friend was astounded. "Many *Limeños* would gladly pay ten times as much to have that name on their official papers," he told me more than once. At that point, I felt I had a sense of how this emphasis on *apariencia* manifests itself on the daily lives of the people in a society that has undergone a period of colonialism.

In the last few days, I have been reminded of some of the experiences I had in Lima as I read *Dogeaters*, Jessica Hagedorn's brilliant satirical novel of life in the Philippines during the Marcos regime. Hagedorn's Manila is a world very much like the one I found in the Peruvian capital city, where things were "slightly off, carefully posed and artificial,"[2] a world in which people's motto tended to be "Adaptability is the simple secret of survival,"[3] a philosophy of life symbolized in *Dogeaters* by the fragile, transparent snakeskin that the young witness/narrator Rio finds in her mother's garden. In a society that has suffered through colonialism, Hagedorn implies, changes of skin are common occurrences.

Dogeaters has led me to reflect further on the Columbus legacy and the heritage it has left in the New World. A description of Manila made by the voice of the Filipino opposition, Senator Domingo Avila, reminds me of the comparable situation I encountered in Lima: "We Pinoys suffer collectively from a cultural inferiority complex. We are doomed by our need for assimilation into the West and our own curious fatalism..."[4]

A brief passage in the novel makes me ponder. It is entitled "President William McKinley Addresses a Delegation of Methodist Churchmen, 1898"; here, the mindset of colonialism is synthesized into a generic encapsulation as Hagedorn shows how the colonialist tends to rationalize how his own version of civilization justifies his actions.

> ...And one night it came to me this way... that we could not give them [the Philippine Islands] back to Spain—that would be cowardly and dishonorable; two, that we could not turn them over to France or Germany—our commercial rivals in the Orient—that would be bad business and discreditable; three, that we could not leave them to themselves—they were unfit for self-government—and they would soon have anarchy and misrule over there worse than Spain's was; and four, that there was nothing left for us to do but to take them all, and to educate the Filipinos, and uplift and civilize and Christianize

them, and by God's grace do the very best we could by them, as our fellow men for whom Christ also died. And then I went to bed, and went to sleep and slept soundly.[5]

Remembering how personally wearing it had been to deal with the social repercussions of colonialism as I encountered it in the Peruvian metropolis, I pause to consider that about every six weeks I would escape for a few days to interact with the healthier, more authentic peoples of the *sierra* and the *selva*. The trip that left the deepest impression on me was a visit to Yarinacocha, a rough and tumble bustling city in the oil-rich *selva* of the highlands. All the stepping stones for that trip were laid as a result of my interest in language and languages.

~~~

In January of 1975 an international congress of philology met in Lima. I attended some of the sessions, particularly drawn to one dedicated to the Spanish language in the United States. In that session a leading Latin American linguist from the University of Texas, basing his work on the patterns established by other immigrant groups in the United States, came to the conclusion that the use of Spanish was fated to disappear in the United States. I knew I had to challenge the speaker, for I felt that he had marred his conclusion by his sociological interpretation of the question-at-hand. So, when the floor was open for discussion, I walked to the microphone and introduced myself as a Chicana from Texas, studying in California and researching in Peru. Then, I proceeded to tell the audience about the constant regeneration of the Spanish language that occurred every time a new wave of immigrants arrived in the United States from Mexico, or from other parts of Latin America. I summarized information about the new social movements for reclaiming Latino heritage, which had inspired a whole new generation to look to its cultural past; and finally, I referred to the role that bilingual education was having in keeping the Spanish language alive among the youngest speakers of Spanish in the United States. "We know," I concluded, "that whether a language lives or dies is, at root, a political question, and that as a people we can impact on the fate of our language."

I had not realized, as I had been speaking, that what I had been describing in reference to the future of the Spanish language in the United States paralleled the Peruvian preoccupation with Quechua, their own national language. Therefore, I was unprepared for the reception to my comments, but was pleased when the audience cheered and clapped for a long while; and I immediately understood the implications that my remarks had for their own situation.

With that ten-minute commentary I unexpectedly broke the isolation I had been feeling as an independent research scholar. A student leader from the Universidad Nacional Autónoma de San Marcos offered to teach me Quechua, and for about two months, until he was forced to go underground, we had a two-hour language lesson on a weekly basis in which I learned the language of his country and listened to his interpretation, from a Maoist perspective, of the Peruvian reality which, I felt, complemented my library research on Mariátegui's preoccupation with national questions in the 1920s.

Also at the congress I met a number of young people from the United States, who became my good friends: Becky von Hooten, from Wisconsin, who was teaching English at the University of Trujillo; Martha Beane, who was also teaching English, at the Universidad Nacional in Lima, and later continued her work in the barrios of Los Angeles; and Peter Landerman, whose research on proto-Quechua allowed him an association with the Peruvian branch of the Summer Institute of Linguistics, a group of linguists-missionaries who, in Peru, work primarily in the jungle.

A few months after Peter and I met, and fortuitously, a couple of weeks before my anticipated journey into the *selva*, Felisa Kazen, one of my childhood friends from Laredo, came to Lima to speak as part of the lecture series sponsored by the Instituto Cultural Peruano-Norte Americano. Her presentation focused on the Congressional law that funded bilingual education programs in the United States; and it was attended by the entire group associated with the Summer Institute of Linguistics (SIL). At that event Peter introduced me to the leaders of the SIL, who upon, hearing that I was planning a trip to Pucallpa, invited me to stay at the SIL center bordering a lagoon in Yarinacocha.

Little did I anticipate what awaited me on that much-needed excursion, where I would be privy to the story of the encounter of two completely different cultures. I was to have the good fortune to be told about this encounter by someone directly associated with the experience.

~~~

On my fourth day in that village center in the high *selva* of northern Peru, I sat in the small SIL library, the sole listener to the story of the Mayorunas, a people characterized (like other peoples native to the Americas) as primitive in the Spanish colonial chronicles. More recently, in the early twentieth century, the Mayorunas had been described as foragers into the territories of neighboring tribes, where they raided for food and women. Their practice of female infanticide eventually unbalanced their population, causing them to engage in additional aggressive activities; they had last been sighted in 1910, the period of the rubber boom, when the Mayorunas had responded to the invasion of Western adventurers by moving deeper into the jungle. By the end of the first quarter of the century, the Mayorunas were considered extinct.

The person telling me the story was a white American missionary-linguist, dedicated like her colleagues, first to learning the unwritten languages of the people in the jungle, then painstakingly transcribing those languages into grammar texts. With those texts, their goal of bringing the word of the Christian bible to the residents of the high *selva* came closer to becoming a realization. As she spoke, I would occasionally glance at the images of the Mayorunas in the album she had set down in front of me. Mostly, though, I listened attentively to the story she was willing to share with me.[6]

By the time I went to Yarinacocha, I had already been to the Amazonic lowlands, to Iquitos, a city associated, in the early twentieth century, with the prosperous years of the rubber-barons. Built up as an elegant city in the *selva*, Iquitos was then left to stagnate when the Asian *caucho* market lowered the price of the Peruvian product, described by the natives of the rain forest as the "tears of the trees." In Iquitos I had signed up to take a commercial trek into the rain forest. But when I had shown up at the early hour designated for departure, I had found out that no one else had requested the trip, and I was to be the sole passenger on the excursion that would take the boatman, the guide, and me in an aluminum canoe along the black waters of the Amazon into the rain forest.

On that trip, whose delights I could not have fantasized, we visited several sparsely inhabited communities of roof-thatched huts where the residents with painted faces and decorated bodies had demonstrated the art of blow-shooting poisoned darts. While I had loved every minute of that journey, particularly the instances when we were enveloped by the sounds of the birds and fauna of the rain forest, I had been aware at all times that on one level or another I was experiencing what some clever entrepreneur had dreamed up as my "two days in the jungle." Still, in spite of my wariness about the trek, I had left Iquitos feeling that on that particular excursion I had experienced the high point of my trip to Peru, an evaluation I would have to alter after the visit to Yarinacocha and its environs.

In Yarinacocha I immediately felt privileged to be in contact with people in their natural habitat. I was touched by my interaction with the Shipibo people, a so-called primitive society forced to interact with the slickness and conniving mores of the world in which I lived, my world whether I wanted to claim it or not. In San Francisco, a village that was several hours away by canoe from Yarinacocha, I had looked at the serene and simple lifestyle of the Shipibos (who reminded me of the Lacandones of Chiapas) and had wondered how they would be able to make the jump across centuries in one or two generations. I had listened intently as Teófilo Tapia, the Peruvian bilingualist administrator who had accompanied me to San Francisco, constantly reminded his listeners that they were indeed Peruvians. It is important to convey a sense of national identity to them, he reassured me, for the Shipibos viewed themselves strictly as a tribal people. In order to incorporate them into the national reality, the Peruvian government had to convince them that they were an important part of the nation; and, for this process to take effect, the Shipibos also had to be taught to conduct themselves in Spanish outside of their own immediate circles. The solution would not be easy, he reassured me.

Several years later, back in the United States, I was told that the Shipibos were doing quite well in adjusting: they were fast learners and were earning a "good" living, installing tiny chips into computer boards for foreign corporations. I did not know of this *barbaridad* as I listened to the story of the Mayorunas, who had been inhabiting a world far older than that of the Shipibos. Until circumstances had forced them to make contact with the outside world, the Mayorunas had lived in a completely circumscribed world, their existence known only to other tribal people into whose territory the Mayorunas foraged.

I looked at the photographs in the album provided to me by my narrator, a kindly and well-meaning middle-aged person, eager to share details of the encounter that had so affected her life and the lives of all her colleagues. We sat in the tiny library, next to the language lab, as the setting sun streaked shadows on the photos of a type of people with whom I had come into previous contact only through illustrations in *National Geographic*. The Mayoruna men and women, who had stared directly into the camera, were pictured with thin reed spears piercing the area around their mouths. In this way, they had created catlike whiskers on themselves, no doubt to show their *nahual* connection to that particular species of the animal world.

As I listened to the story, I kept turning the pages of the album, looking both at the people who had recently made contact with a world unknown to them and at the face of the narrator, describing the singular experience of two groups who had met across cultural and temporal borders. Her side had become aware of the Mayorunas when a scouting party had found a young man, of about sixteen, abandoned in the jungle by his people after having been bitten by a snake. Assuming he was dead, the Mayorunas had left him behind in his hut, but he had eventually made his way to a road, where the linguists had found him. His infected leg had been nursed back to health, and over many months of contact, the Americans had learned both his language and about his people.

During the three years that intervened from the time the young man was found to the moment that direct contact was made with the Mayoruna group, the SIL staff learned about the beliefs of the people they were seeking. They found out that the Mayorunas believed that when a member of their group died, they had to abandon the immediate area and strike up a home in a new place. Because the diseases of the world from beyond the jungle had penetrated into their habitat, the Mayorunas were losing their people at a rapid pace. Thus, they were constantly on the move, going around in circles throughout the jungle.

At the time the young man had been found, the leaders of the Mayorunas—by now various groups numbering several hundreds—had come to the conclusion that they needed to go past their own confines into the world beyond their own, a world whose existence was verified for them by myths, rumors, and their own findings.

The SIL linguists decided that they too needed to find the Mayorunas. As a group they concluded that women would be perceived as less physically threatening to the tribal people, and an expedition of two volunteers was sent out. Armed only with the language they had learned from the young man, two women—Harriet Fields and Hattie Kneeland—headed into the jungle in search of a people who they now knew were also looking for them.[7]

During this time, each group kept finding the signs that the other party was leaving behind in strategic locations. Eventually, my narrator explained, only a river separated the two. One night, the linguists heard the menacing cries of jungle cats, but assuming that pumas could not swim, they went to sleep, albeit lightly as they anticipated a possible meeting on the following day.

"Those women were so brave," I heard my narrator say, a brusque interruption to the scene I had been envisioning from the point of view of the Mayorunas.

"At least they knew what they might expect to meet," I said by way of reply, "while the Mayorunas had no idea about what lay ahead for them."

The women continued camping on the banks of the river, my narrator continued. Then, on their second morning by the river, they awakened to find a delegation of Mayorunas standing a few feet away. In simple speech the women greeted the Mayorunas, inviting them to share their food.

By the end of that day in the late 1960s, the two parties had crossed the river on a canoe. Greetings had been extended between the women and the rest of the Mayorunas, and a new delegation had been sent back with the linguists to the center at Yarinacocha. Additional food and medicine were sent to the people in the *selva*, again with new delegations of women. Eventually, the men also met each other, and the young man who had served as language and cultural informant was reunited with his people.

194

With Western medicine combatting the Western diseases that had infiltrated into the jungle, the Mayorunas managed to break the cycle of death that had been plaguing them for years.

"What will happen to the Mayorunas?" I asked. "It must be so difficult for them to traverse temporally into the twentieth century, and I doubt that they will be left alone to continue with their own ways of life. Westerners will find it hard to believe they have anything to learn from these tribal people, and yet we might learn something if we only opened ourselves to them."

"They are adjusting well," my narrator said with a smile. "We have brought the word of Christ to them. That young man quickly learned our language, then served as interpreter between both parties. We think they were led to us by Divine Providence."

"Won't they just wind up being exploited?" I asked. "Everyone expects the give and take associated with 'discovery' to go only in one direction. They give and give in. We take and take out. But, realistically, how will they survive economically?"

"The Peruvian government is seeing to their integration into the greater world," she replied. "The Mayorunas are very smart. Like the Shipibos, they are being processed to enter into civilization. And, like the Shipibos, the Mayorunas are doing extremely well in adapting to Western culture."

At the time, I did not realize what her statement really implied. But, in retrospect, I am reminded of a comment made by the famous Berkeley anthropologist A. L. Kroeber: "It is pleasant to believe in progress. It makes my times and my ways superior to all others."[8]

I converse with my friend and colleague Benito Pastoriza, a Puerto Rican poet, at a café in Houston. I tell him about the Mayorunas, about more recent information I have obtained regarding the instruction the Mayorunas have been receiving in bilingual education programs. In these schools they have learned to read and write in their own language; then, their new skills are transferred to the target language—Spanish, the official national language in Peru. The ultimate goal of this standard bilingual education program is to have the Mayorunas use Spanish for social and official transactions. One might assume, then, that in subsequent generations, their original language will be lost. This is the same conclusion, I remind Benito, that the linguist from the University of Texas reached in regard to the future of the Spanish language in the United States. The difference is that, in the United States, new groups from Latin America constantly regenerate the current use of the Spanish language. The situation of the Mayorunas is not quite the same.

By the 1970s, the Mayorunas were recognized as a community numbering several hundreds composed of different bands, all of whom had been contacted by the SIL linguists. An airstrip was built by the government near the area identified as Mayoruna territory; soon the various bands congregated near the airstrip. It became evident that the Mayorunas needed to have their territory officially recognized, for once their raiding of other tribes stopped, colonizers from the outside world—Peruvians and others—began to claim the land previously inhabited by the different bands. As a result of these invaders, the Mayorunas were forced to learn about Peruvian law to stake their claim to their lands. In such situations, there is always a conflict of forces at work, I was told, for it is easy for the Mayorunas to lose their culture and to come into the national culture at the lowest level possible. In practice, their needs must be met as the process of acculturation goes on.

The outside world also discovered that the Mayorunas refer to themselves and to their language as *Matse*. However, this same outside world continues to use the Quechua word *Mayoruna*, meaning "river people," to refer to this recently "discovered" group.[9]

"Their survival no doubt depends on many factors, including what we all do to save the rain forests," I say to Benito.

"Imagínate," he responds with a wry smile.

We wonder, then, if the Mayorunas will wind up losing their own language in subsequent generations because of the infiltration of Western languages and cultures into their lives. We think of our own people—the Mexicans and the Puerto Ricans—in the process. And of our own individual situations, for we both have made an effort to be truly bilingual and bicultural; actually, we have striven to become multilingual and multicultural.

We discuss our Tejano students, native-speakers of the Spanish language who identify as "Mexican-American." We note how generally they are closer to the roots of their culture of origin than is the general tendency among students in California who call themselves "Chicanos." Benito and I have both taught some of the courses for native-speakers of Spanish. Of the two, I think he is the better teacher in this particular area.

"Every day I look at my students," he tells me, "and I get so angry when I see how hard they struggle to reclaim their language. If they had been taught to read and write in Spanish all the way from elementary school to the present, by now they would be completely proficient in oral and written communication in Spanish. I have no patience when it comes to waste, and that is what the educational system has done. It has wasted human talent. For two hundred years." He gives emphasis to his voice. "When are these people going to accept the fact that the Mexicanos in this area have been speakers of Spanish ever since they got here more than two hundred years ago?"

"Let's not forget the other, older languages," I remind him. "As a people we did wind up losing our Indian tongue, didn't we?"

Then I recall the question posed by Yolanda Broyles González, a friend in Santa Barbara who chairs the Chicano Studies Department at The University of California, Santa Barbara. When she found out that I was teaching a course for native-speakers of the Spanish language, she sincerely inquired: "What do you do with them in such a course? The Mexicanos in Tejas have such a special way of expressing themselves. Yet, these Spanish departments insist on changing their speech. 'So that they may be well understood in Buenos Aires and Caracas,' they rationalize. More than likely our students will be using the language only within their own cultural sphere. So, why do these educators insist on colonizing the Mexicanos by way of their language usage? They so demean us in the process."

I tell Benito that I sympathize with my friend's question, that she and I have discussed ways of strengthening our students' knowledge of Spanish from a positive point of departure. And I recall two incidents I recently witnessed: the spontaneous outburst of the entire class during an oral presentation when a student enthusiastically described a character in a short story by Carlos Flores as *"Es un huevón."* Turning red in reaction to the class's response, the young woman explained that this was the only word she had in her repertoire to describe the father in the story. Empowering her, I wrote *perezoso* and *flojo* on the board. In another instance, a student was able to describe a long-haired person only as *greñudo* or *con mechones largos*. Yet, his passive knowledge of the language allowed him to select, from a list provided, a variety of ways to get his point across.

We need to give our students the ability to make different choices in vocabulary usage, Benito and I agree, in order to broaden their choices in life. "But, in regard to most choices, particularly to linguistic choices, one must choose on the side of the open, of the positive," I remind him. "Let's take Richard Rodriguez. He chose on the side of closeness, on the side of the negative."

I know Chicanos tend to have a visceral contempt for Rodriguez and for his book, *Hunger of Memory: The Education of Richard Rodriguez;* yet, for a number of reasons that will soon become evident, I teach the book in several of my literature classes and always refuse to permit my students to attack the author on the basis of what he has to say about bilingual education and affirmative action. That's the easy way out, I tell them, for, if you believe in these social programs, then you will tend to disagree with him, but others who do not support the programs will disagree with you. So, the discussion will come down to one based strictly on personal opinion, albeit one based on statistics from both sides of the argument.

I try to contextualize Rodriguez's mindset within the American assimilationist experience, also an undebatable perspective to my way of thinking, for I believe that he has as much right to view himself as a middle-class Mexican American as a Chicano has the right to align himself with the working class and its culture. Even Rodriguez's pathetic relationship with his parents cannot be truly debated, for it is a point in fact in the life of this author; as a consequence, he provides the reader with a description of a dysfunctional family, not unheard of in your typical case of the American assimilation process in which members of different generations, each with a different world view, come into conflict with one another.

For the first-generation or even the second-generation American, this cultural separation from one's parents tends to be the price that is paid for becoming "an American"; it is the price paid for turning one's back on personal and group history and for opting to live, in a cultural vacuum, strictly in the present and for the future. But, again, to berate Rodriguez on his choice in this matter means that one would still be involved in value judging; in this instance, one would be making a value judgment on a choice made by the great majority of people in the United States.

Even his self-portrayal as a person disproportionately concerned with appearances, with *apariencia* and *artificio*, can leave us with a sense of pity. He describes how his preoccupation with symbols of status was passed down from parent to child.

> In their manner, both my parents continued to respect the symbols of what they considered to be upper-class life. Very early, they taught me the *propria* [sic] way of eating *como los ricos*. And I was carefully taught elaborate formulas of polite greeting and parting. The dark little boy would be invited by classmates to the rich houses on Forty-fourth and Forty-fifth Streets. "How do you do?" or "I am very pleased to meet you," I would say bowing slightly to the amused mothers of classmates. "Thank you very much for the dinner; it was very delicious."
>
> I made an impression. I intended to make an impression, to be invited back. (I soon realized that the trick was to get the mother or father to notice me.) From those early days began my association with rich people, my fascination with their secret.[10]

Like Jessica Hagedorn's Pinoys and some of the people I met in Lima and in other places, Rodriguez comes across as the quintessential colonized person, predisposed to being outer-oriented, preoccupied with appearances and with symbolic changes of skin.

> This man. A man. I meet him. He laughs to see me, what I have become.
>
> The dandy. I wear double-breasted Italian suits and custom-made English shoes. I resemble no one so much as my father—the man pictured in those honeymoon photos. At that point in life when he abandoned the dandy's posture, I assume it. At the point when my parents would not consider going on

vacation, I register at the Hotel Carlyle in New York and the
Plaza Athenée in Paris. I am as taken by the symbols of leisure
and wealth as they were. For my parents, however, those
symbols became taunts, reminders of all they could not
achieve in one lifetime. For me those same symbols are
reassuring reminders of public success. I tempt vulgarity
to be reassured. I am filled with the gaudy delight, the
monstrous grace of the nouveau riche.[11]

His confession is at least honest, not without a sense of irony,
not without a sense of distance as he looks in the mirror to confront the man he has become. The educational process he has undergone has produced a colonized individual, a person who bows
down to hegemonic rules. We last see him in the book as a man
without a family, without real friends, without a job.

Rodriguez's premises regarding the goals of the educational
system can indeed be questioned. He pretends to criticize the system when in fact he succumbs to it and is its logical end product.
In setting up the binary divisions of private self versus public self,
of private language versus public language, he chooses on the side
of the negative and the closed. In his convoluted self-hatred, he
winds up giving the reader an example of what American education can produce and does in fact produce in the majority of cases:
a monolingual and monocultural person.

Paralleling Hagedorn's Pinoys and, generally, people in colonized societies, including those within the United States, Rodriguez suffers from the inferiority complex of those who accept the
norms set up by the colonialist; his need for assimilation into the
hegemonic culture has narrowed, rather than broadened, his
choices in life. In the end, his concluding that the restriction of
one's self is a better choice than its expansion, that negation is better than affirmation, winds up being an altogether unacceptable
solution to a problematic situation.

The philosopher María Lugones further enlightens this reaction to Rodriguez's work by stating "that to be educated is to be
monocultural is an untenable proposition. Education should instill cultural flexibility in us. It should instill cultural fluency: the
ability to appreciate in different cultural modes. It should enable
us to go back and forth between worlds with different logics, dif-

ferent values, different ways of perceiving."[12]

Unfortunately, the goal of colonialism has always been the opposite of what Lugones tells us is the ideal of education, the ideal of what a society should offer its people and their future, based on their singular history and their present reality. Colonial systems strive to erase the cultural and linguistic base of groups that have the misfortune of being perceived as detriments to the system's deluded sense of progress. For five hundred years the Americas have witnessed a legacy of conquest and colonialism as the aftermath of Columbus's journey. The Native peoples have experienced the imposition of the outsider's language, religion, and values; and the colonialist's fantasy of "otherness" has shaded his vision of the people he has colonized: the Tainos, the Aztecs, the Incas, the Shipibos, the Mayorunas, the present-day Mayas, the Filipinos, the Navajos, the Cherokee, the Creeks, and the Chicanos. The list goes on.

But, as we near the end of the twentieth century, the various Calibans of the New World are arising to curse the colonialists in the particular languages in which they have been educated. We are reclaiming our cultures and languages, which have survived in spite of centuries of outside imposition. The quincentenary of the so-called discovery of the Americas has provided a forum for the discourse on the politics of identity, a response of the voice of "the other," which insists on the politics of ethical difference. For the moment, in some circles, the politics of identity is superseding the politics of erasure. Perhaps we too will wind up going to bed and sleeping soundly, free for a while at least of having to live with the repercussions of the delusion of hegemonic sameness.

Notes

1. Kirkpatrick Sale, *The Conquest of Paradise: Christopher Columbus and the Columbian Legacy* (New York: Alfred Knopf, 1990), p. 18. Sale describes Nebrija's 1492 grammar of the Castilian language as "a typical work of what one might call the encyclopedic mentality to which Renaissance Europe aspired and that was to sustain its vaunted scientific method: it is intended to be all-inclusive and exhaustive, neutral and non-judgmental, ostensibly without political point of view or social purpose, and meant only to be a list, a catalogue, an inventory." (p. 18)

2. Jessica Hagedorn, *Dogeaters* (New York: Pantheon Books, 1990), p. 35.

3. Ibid., pp. 8–9.

4. Ibid., p. 101.

5. Ibid., p. 71.

6. On April 21, 1975, I wrote about my visit to Yarinacocha in a letter to my friend Margaret Shedd. Born in 1899 in Persia, now Iran, of American missionary parents, Margaret Shedd lived in many different cultures and wrote about them in nine novels. She was founder and director, for eighteen years, of the Centro Mexicano de Escritores. After the Tlatelolco massacre in Mexico City, she left the Centro and returned to Berkeley, where she was one of the founding members of Aztlán Cultural, an organization in which I was very active.

The following comments record my evaluation of the staff at the Summer Institute of Linguistics immediately following my visit to Yarinacocha:

"Did you have contact in Mexico with the Summer Institute of Linguistics? If so, what is your opinion of the work they do? I went to Yarinacocha with lots of reservations about the work of the Institute, but soon my doubts were replaced with admiration for the people themselves, although I still question the nature of their work. I thought of you during my visit there, for I figured that the childhood you described in *Hosanna Tree* was probably lived in the atmosphere of love, gentleness and fervor I found at Yarinacocha.

"The physical atmosphere is beautiful: lots of green lawns, small houses carefully screened and upkept, with no frills but with all the basic necessities, little barefooted children all over the place, and these gringo missionary-linguists whose lifework is translating the New Testament into the 'exotic' languages of the world. They have the most personally balanced lives I have yet seen in which all the different aspects of life truly come together—a sense of mission, hard work and the realization of one's labor in tangible form: giving the power of literacy to the tribal peoples and embarking them on their path to 'civilization.' The linguists seem to live in full realization of their being, guided by the motto: 'The Lord wills it so.' With such a personal world view, what problems can then exist?

"There are a few Peruvian representatives of the Ministerio de Educación here. Their self-realization also comes from putting their socialist ideas into tangible form. This is what I always thought a revolution could be like; for the first time I had a sense that something indeed might be coming out of this Peruvian revolution but one doesn't really experience the positive changes in Lima. Some of the people I've met here have told me that the government is striving to build a base in the Sierra and the Selva first; then it will deal with the cities.

"I think it will take me a long time to process through these experiences, to have a sense that I truly understand what it is I have been seeing and doing."

7. According to Petru Popescu in *Amazon Beaming* (New York: Viking, 1991), the photographer Loren McIntyre, intrigued by stories that were coming out of the SIL center in Yarinacocha, set out on his own to

make contact with the Mayoruna. McIntyre has spent the last forty years exploring and photographing Latin America. As such, he has visually documented the southern continent more than any other living photographer and is also recognized for having experienced Amazonia in greater depth and scope than any other living North American journalist. He has written and photographed for many articles in *National Geographic*. Wanting to record the Mayorunas with his camera before they could be dragged into "the basement of Western culture" (p. 17), McIntyre tends to have a rather sardonic view of "the two Harriets" as he repeatedly refers to the linguists Fields and Kneeland. "If these [the people he encountered on his own] were Mayoruna, they were related to the ones first sighted in 1966 in Peru, doggedly pursued since by a missionary pair from the Summer Institute of Linguistics known as the two Harriets. Harriet Fields and Harriet Kneeland kept flying over the Peruvian jungle calling in Mayoruna through an airborne loudspeaker the way an alien ship would call to the earth race in a science fiction movie." (p. 17)

Popescu, Romania's most provocative young writer and filmmaker before defecting from the Ceausescu regime, met fellow filmmaker McIntyre in Brazil and set out to tell the story of his Latin American explorations, focusing primarily on the American's discovery in 1971 of the source of the Peruvian tributaries of the Amazon. Now, officially named Laguna McIntyre, the fountainhead of the Amazon, in Peru, is close to the site where the rivers Apurimac and Ucayali meet. *Amazon Beaming* is a fascinating book, targeted at a New Age readership active in ecological concerns. In this way, it tangentially addresses some of the issues connected with the ecological destruction of the New World brought on by the "discovery" of America; these questions inform the point of view in Kirkpatrick Sale's *The Conquest of Paradise* and Herman Viola's *Seeds of Change* (Smithsonian, 1991), books closely associated with the plethora of "discovery/encounter/legacy" publications that are appearing in 1991 and 1992.

8. Quoted in *Amazonia*, photographs and text by Loren McIntyre (San Francisco: Sierra Club Books, 1991), p. 158.
9. I owe this recent information on the Mayorunas to Peter Landerman.
10. Richard Rodriguez, *Hunger of Memory: The Education of Richard Rodriguez* (New York: Bantam Books, 1983), p. 122.
11. Ibid., p. 136.
12. Common reading presentations made by María Lugones, Jackson Bryce, and Deborah Appleman on *Hunger of Memory* by Richard Rodriguez (Northfield, Minn.: A Carleton College publication of papers presented at The Carleton College New Student Convocation, September 3, 1990).

Juan Felipe Herrera

Frida's Aria
*Toward an Aesthetics of
the Dispossessed in the
Twenty-first Century*

Yo soy la desintegración.

—FRIDA KAHLO,
Journal entry, Mexico City, 1954

When Cristóbal Colón and his men set foot on the soil of this hemisphere, a native scream catapulted across the skies of the "New World." There was laughter, too, the frenzied guffaw of Spanish and European Empire and Discovery—the anticipation of further expansion and fracture. The scream hovered over the storm clouds and deepened into the viscera of the tropical jungles and returned and fused into the hard bones of the Indians. This was the scream of massacre, rape and dispossession. The disposession poured out from the conqueror's sword and the Franciscan savior's sceptor and went down into the green soul and collective spirit of a native people. This essay is an entry into this scream—into its various contours, voices and nuances, from 1492 to the present.

In this essay I am concerned with bringing attention to the Amerindian Scream and the response to it, *Frida's Aria: the birth of an aesthetics of the dispossessed*—the emergence of a people's expressive life caught up with the contradictions of forced occupation, physical and viral assault—the disintegrations of land and body.

The art and life of Frida Kahlo provide the language and frame for this discussion—Frida the Mexican painter; the most significant founder of the language of dispossession and fracture—the Amerindian Scream. The scream does not carry a continuous and coherent melody. Its shape and body have been cast in violence. In similar fashion then, this essay is "fractured"—going into various literary genres as well as moments, voices, and events.

To begin our entry into *Frida's Aria*, this account interprets

205

and imagines various "figures" present in Kahlo's art and experience. These figures then serve as points of departure and improvisation in re-conjuring the scream and its passage through time and territory. These "figures" are accompanied by the works of contemporary Chicana and Chicano writers and artists—all involved in a changing aesthetics for the twenty-first century—collectively and individually singing back through time and into the future.

I. A Second Body   *Think on the time it takes a scar to heal, a river to rise—an old woman to regain the tumbling powers of her broken arm—a young woman (calling herself Frida) to restructure her shattered vertebrae, to be immersed in the displacements of a body-cast, a second body which she inhabits for the rest of her life. This, yes, this is precious to us, that is all. When you think on the poetics and the assemblage of the dispossessed, if you wish, think on the figure of Frida Kahlo, the Mexican artist who in 1932 painted herself somewhere in-between Mexico and the United States—in the open space of the jaws; between the mandibles of the jaguar and the nuclear turbine. It is the healing of this metaphysical fracture too (which may invoke further breakage) that concerns us.*
     This is Frida's body.

For the moment *Frida's Aria* is heightened and carried by the interplay of the figures *scar and second body.* Let us begin with *scar.*

In Chicana and Chicano literature there is a call to the body. An announcement is made that a wound has been inflicted upon "our body." This is a primary interest whether the writer is speaking of a physical, historical, spiritual, or a metaphysical sense of being; of course, the literary voice rarely singles out a limited sector of experience as its foundation—we know that all of these arenas of life are being implied. We can recall Alurista's early call to the body in his poem *"Mis ojos hinchados."*

> the scars of history of my face
>   and the veins of my body
>   that aches
>   vomita sangre
>   y lloro libertad

i do not ask for freedom
i am freedom ...

The scars and wounds and the wounding have been present for a long time. In 1877, Guillermo Prieto—a cohort of Benito Juárez and writer in exile comes to the the United States. He arrives and moves with the zealous gait of a poet and political man and records his excursions and experiences in a diary that later becomes a three-volume collection entitled *Viajes a los Estados Unidos* printed in Mexico City in the same year. In the first volume, Prieto takes punctilious notes of his stay in San Francisco. He visits Chinatown, saunters through Market Street and takes account of the people, their economic and cultural plights. He even jots down the menus of the day. He also visits and dines with American scholars like Howard Bancroft and on occasion focuses on the *tertulias* and albums exchanged among the Mexican literati. The material abounds with rich ethnographic descriptions of the Mexican middle-class literary salon, yet, for us, Prieto's import lies in the interstices of his reflections, the flippant commentary. He presents a number of close associates and goes on to tell us of the religious shrines and temples in the city, and he happens to notice *"un tipo altamente repugnante."* His own architecture breaks down; here is where a painful new awareness of being takes over; a tear of sorts, a nauseous slippage between himself and the body of the Mexican transformed into an *ayankado*—a Chicano.

There is in San Francisco, as in the entire United States, a highly
repugnant type: the yankee-ized Mexican. He sports a rough boot,
carries a marvelous blade with which he polishes and sharpens his fingernails,
wittles wood and cleans his teeth; he speaks little and always in English,
he is almost lying down with his feet on the table or on a bannister or
on the wall, drinks wiskey, chews tobacco, gives too many handshakes
to the first-comer and from his salute spits without shame, tipping
to his eyes his trampled and ungoverned hat.[1]

(my translation)

The awareness of the *scar*, the slippage between the skin of Chicano being, perhaps begins with Prieto's early narrative. We can sense the appearance and continuity of a *scar* as it stretches and undulates from Prieto's city-body encounters to Alurista's own body tracings. Yet, the language for this set of odd appearances is cast forth by Frida herself—the singer of Chicana and Chicano being in the Americas.

Frida becomes the singer of the Americas in 1932. Her transformation into a Chicana and singer-speaker comes about as she paints a portrait of herself titled "Self-Portrait on the Border between Mexico and the United States." She becomes the *scar*—synthesizing and widening the gulf between the disparate realms of psychic and territorial Chicana/o and Latina/o experience. In a sense, the *scar* speaks out, pours out its knots and seams in the only self-portrait where Frida as a physical figure stands on a pedestal. The year 1932 marks the thickening of the *scar* with Frida's own personal trials—the death of her mother, her first visits to San Francisco and Detroit, and the hemorrhaging of her insides. This is the year when she also begins to experiment with new art forms. All this energy seems to move in the "Self-Portrait," where she appears to preside over disparate material forms—a patchwork of clotheslines, urban rooftops, pipes, a scarlet gramaphone and scaffolded grayish buildings. The *scar* has exploded from Prieto's swashbuckling knife-wielder in the city (a potential scar-maker) into the metropolis itself. With Frida's painting there is also an implosion of sorts; a metaphysical blast where the body blows up and into the inanimate shards of the city-scape. Is this a suicide? Has the knife-hombre killed his own figures? Has the city-woman metamorphosed into everything we see outside in the city? We are left with one of Frida's last journal entries in 1954: *"Yo soy la desintegración."*

The *second body*. One of Frida's own body-casts may give us a clue. Or better yet, her life-long stays inside a series body-casts gives us a clear set of signs to follow. First, we need to note the obvious—a body-cast is a sheathe covering our own skin. Second, such a *second-body* can also be the text of our tellings, that which lies outside of us, yet resembles us: Prieto's and Alurista's encounter with their own "other."

Given the existence of a *second-body* makes it probable to have "third" and "fourth" bodies. In her recent multivocal text, *Borderlands/La Frontera: The New Mestiza*, Gloria Anzaldúa points us in this direction; we have, she proposes—multiple body casts or sheathes which are autonomous unto themselves not necessarily creating a whole.

> Living on borders and in margins, keeping intact one's shifting
> and multiple identity and integrity, is like trying to swim in a
> new element, "an alien" element. There is an exhilaration in
> being a participant in the further evolution of humankind,
> in being 'worked' on. I have a sense that certain 'faculties'—
> not just in me but in every border resident, colored or non-
> colored—and dormant areas of consciousness are being
> activated, awakened.[1]

The *second-body* takes form in Raza literature and most of all in the articulation of a Chicano poetics. The *second-body* descends and ascends. It begins with a *scar* somewhere on the surface. It appears in moments of crises, turmoil, and even estrangement.

The most significant and perhaps the initial *second-body* figure of Raza poetics is in the *voz* of Sor Juana Inés de la Cruz. In 1691, on the first of March, Sor Juana, a Mexican nun of the Order of St. Jerome, finished a "response" to Don Manuel Fernández de Santa Cruz y Sahagún, the Bishop of Puebla, Mexico. Originally the Bishop had written a letter to Sor Juana reprimanding her for her text, *Critique of a Sermon*, a debate against the arrogance and position of a priest's sermon. It is the *voz*, the voice she uses in the opening of her *Respuesta* and continuing throughout that is intriguing. We notice how she addresses the Bishop as *señora*:

> My most illustrious *señora*, dear lady. It has not been my
> will, my poor health, or my justifiable apprehension that for
> so many days delayed my response. How could I write,
> considering that at my very first step my clumsy pen
> encountered two obstructions in its path? The first (and for
> me, the most uncompromising) is to know how to reply to
> your most learned, most prudent, most holy and most loving
> letter.[3]

Although the Bishop *signed* his original critique with a female pseudonym—*Sor Filotea*—it is Sor Juana's opus, *Response to the Most Illustrious Poetess Sor Filotea de La Cruz*, that brings into

form and history the occasion of the *second-body*. The first paren-
thesis of the *Respuesta* offers us a clue in knowing how to consider
the *voz*. Even if in a mocking fashion (or especially if in a mocking
fashion), she points to knowing "how to reply" as the "most un-
compromising" feature in her project and text. At one level, Sor
Juana's *voz* launches a grand reprimand to the Bishop and his in-
junctions. At another level, the *voz* strikes back at the colonial text
of Catholicism, where in accordance to the Bishop's admonish-
ment, women should be content to study only for the service and
"love of learning." What is dear to us is the issuance of an unusual
second "sister," how a "second" language begins—one which
serves, creates, and propels a new *herstory* into the Americas.

The *second-body* is not whole and does not seek wholeness. It is
complete in itself. Frida's body-casts are narrations of a Frida-life.
To continue, they do not depend on Frida's own pulse or heat or vision.

II. Jade Mother Goddess   *Frida came back and kicked away
the features. There was a crises.*

*There was a mid-point of no return: a reddish ovum with tidal
waves turning and leaping beyond its plasma, a jade mother goddess with cactus shoulders and a puzzled clay-like background broken, moving around the granite complexion of the moon; there was
a maguey thorn breast, succulent, shedding a tear-shaped milk drop
and in the center, in one of the centers, there was a scarlet woman
with her black hair falling down into the roots of a thousand embraces. She reached it alone. And language, (Master-made language)
faltered for a moment, fell apart—yet the Master keeps on, somehow. Pretending to speak; writing with the idea that his words connect with a larger universal system of Master-meanings. The small
invention is simple—this sweaty speakerly Master.*

In a painting text done in 1949, *The Love Embrace of the Universe, the Earth (Mexico), Me, Diego and Mr. Xolotl*, Frida speaks of
the infinite numbers of the body's refractions and fractures and
also of a greater broken-form that engulfs their disintegrations.
Here the figures of the scream-song are *mid-point of no return,
embraces,* and *Speakerly Master.*

The notion of a *mid-point of no return* after which one cannot reach back or harken to an original or true beginning, is another melodic pulse in the Raza texts of being. Yolanda Luera is one of the early Chicana poets to point to a feminist *mid-point of no return* in "Aborto."

> my insides
> howl out to me for a child
> and I deny myself
> my womb pleads
> to burden itself and swell
> and I deny myself
> my lips want
> to sing
> lullabies and I deny myself
> I deny myself
> and I...[4]
>   (my translation)

In the poem, one simply hurdles to a point of boundary--there is a definitive physical and rhetorical struggle that leaves us at the edge of consciousness with a set of contradictions: to release the body inside the body or not, to continue or not to continue the formation of the text. A decade later, in 1983, Margarita Luna Robles directs us to another *mid-point* in her poem "I Am the Chicana You Thought Was a Mexicana."

> I am the Chicana
> you thought was a Mexicana
> when you walked into the room and feasted
> your eyes on
> what you thought was
> an authentic dish
> spicy, flavorful and
> hot
> mujer hermosa with dark round eyes shadowed by dark
> long lashes.

In the opening lines we feel the split between bodies and myths. The poem is declared with the urgency of defilement

211

and violation. Later the poem stalks the myth:

> Chicanas, you have heard
> are loose women with loose values because of their lack
> of identity
> y fácil.

Then, quickly, the poem unveils the myth-maker:

> Mexicano
> your method of scoring is by way of flattery,
> I am confused about the rose petals you throw my way.
> The Chicano does not do this quite like you.[5]

There is no repose for the "Mexicano." He will never find the "Mexicana" of old. And there is no repose for the speaker—she will encounter more "Mexicanos" as she continues walking through the room, a hall of broken mirrors where Chicanos and Mexicanos, Chicanas and Mexicanas, burst out of each other's figures.

In the three hundred years written of by Sor Juana, Frida, Anzaldúa, Luera, and Robles, Mexicanas and Chicanas have crossed over into another body, or perhaps have multiplied into other selves with a clear sense of "no return." Among those thoughts, in that mood, met with that demarcation of cultural and feminist consciousness, their preoccupation with the finality of personal and global transformation takes place.

~~~

An *embrace* is an act of pleasure, a power gesture that can bring about ecstasy. It is a spherical movement of the body going into flight, taking its shape into another form—it is an exchange of temperatures and positions, a new flow of matter and psychic energy; a destructive and a creative act all at once. The *embrace* in Frida's painting *The Love Embrace of the Universe, the Earth (Mexico), Me, Diego and Mr. Xolotl* tosses hair and milk, cactus and universe shards into a new shape. In Robles's work, we see the destruction of the "Mexicano's" feast; an impending extraction of self and/or fetus in Luera's work. All this suggests two separate realizations: pleasure is a malleable source and an end point because Chicana body and being can change radically and find ecstasy—the Chicana has come upon something that is multi-faceted and pleasures?

When Victor Hernández Cruz touches the sources of his ecstasy, he does not go back to a time past with politically linear "smart" poems full of verbs and data, instead chooses to destroy a curious moment of time: the tropicalized urban body shattered by flavor and music:

> Everybody is writing poetry now—I'm going to take painting
> lessons or buy that book which teaches you how to paint
> human emotional landscapes in 5 easy steps—I'll print a book
> in my toilet in my spare time and hit all the readings. Just a
> little bit O money on the set you know—In a country where
> 1% of the populations visits bookstores—It gets tough to
> survive with your poems. Unless you decorate it with music or
> wear a green cape to your readings. What's his or her name
> was here and pulled out a bunch of poems and kept changing
> colors and names and I freaked cause I didn't know who to call
> the ambulance or the place where you report UFO's. Well what
> the hell I play a little bit of koongas maybe I'll start a band and
> turn all the events out ... [6]

Even in his desire for language and structure, there is a pleasure in anti-language itself: the fast phrase, the riff against time, form and space—the juxtaposed play between music and color, reading and writing, what is above and below. Hernández Cruz brings in the velocities of sense and anonymity—the "column" enjoys naming the nameless, decorating things with music more than with science. There is no astonishment or crisis, no center—it is all sound and flow peeking into the unknown; the text does not care to be aware of itself; it changes colors but it does not change its prisms. Hernández Cruz is an early turn towards the pleasure of the anti-text in Raza male writing.

For writers like Alberto Ríos and Jimmy Santiago-Baca, the *embrace* is carved rather than lived. In some instances, there is a sudden finding in the unconscious, in the imagination—in the image: a febrile hand grasping the air, maybe, as in Jimmy Santiago-Baca's long poem "Meditations on the South Valley":

Austere faced hombres
hoeing their jardines
de chili y maiz in the morning,
crush beer cans and stuff them in gunny sacks
and peddle on rusty bicycles
in the afternoon to the recycling scale
and at Coco's shante
at dusk tecatos se juntan
la cocina jammed like the stock exchange lobby,
as los vatos raise their fingers
indicating cuanto quieren.[7]

A chaffing of the text into another realm is where pleasure can begin, as in Gary Soto's title poem, "Who will know us?":

Nostalgia, the cigarette lighter from before the war,
Beauty, tears that flow inward to feed its roots.
The train. Red coal of evil.
We are its passengers, the old and young alike.
Who will know us when we breathe through the grass?[8]

Writers like José Antonio Burciaga in his satire, word and dialect play, in his fusion into visual graphics and art (evident in his new "personal anthology" *Amor Indocumentado/Undocumented Love*), point in a different direction.

And Ray Gonzalez offers the desert, the tiny men touching mud, then turning upon themselves into death and loss:

The nearest hills probe
themselves for men that run
through night canyons,
leave footprints for
the sun in the morning.

Below concrete bridges
of the Río Grande,
a Mexican father lurks
in the mud and searches
for his drowned son.[9]

We are in the hands of a passionate knower—he is inside the earth, tasting lives from that vantage point.

Yet, as a whole, male Raza text retreats, goes back to its scaffolding of places, mechanical actions, childhoods, purified terrains and personas. The male writer keeps the body sealed, the embrace clothed; there are no displacements, there is no bodyless wandering for a body, there are no extractions or disintegrations. This insistence on closing the envelope of language and therefore perception limits the channels for pleasure and transformation. The text without rupture, inwardness or ecstasy has no choice but to end in facile fabrications.

Now, consider the next figure of *Frida's Aria*, the *Speakerly Master*.

In the last three hundred years, if we start with Sor Juana, and then Guillermo Prieto's three volume diary, *Viaje a los Estados Unidos*, the major project of Raza poetics has been to edify, formulate, inform, and shape the figure of a *Speakerly Master*. That is, we have been responding to an overpowering macro-voice and entity that taunts, ridicules and in some instances, titillates us. And in so doing, in many ways, we have invented our own target, our own *Master*. At times the response and invention have been erudite and reflective, as in Sor Juana, decorous and submissive, as in Prieto. At other moments, our call-back has been incendiary, as in Robles and Anzaldúa. Can the exchange become more public and *hilarious?*

As noted earlier, our male poetics took a wrong turn somewhere. It became stolid, it began to fear itself, to cover its ears and scars—it denied the body and didn't let itself die and enter rebirth. Preferring to not talk back, it began to caress its officialdom, its proper fitting in the hierarchies of mainstream literary order. Yet, within the last decade, male poetics has taken up a new challenge—the freedom to embrace. This has been possible largely through *performance*.

The fast-paced Bay Area Chicano Latino Comedy troupe Culture Clash is an example of the knee-slapping response to the *Speakerly Master*. Funny and cagey wordsmiths Herb Siguenza, "Slick" Ric Salinas, and Richard Montoya have gone from local tavern shows on the West Coast in the early 1980s (on occasion along with ex-members José Antonio Burciaga, Marga Gómez, and Mónica Palacios) on to international tours and fiesty encounters with Fox Television in Hollywood in the 1990s. Their most recent work, *A Bowl of Beans*, featured in a PBS special spotlights their multi-media art and pokes fun at the "Quincentennial-Hispanic," punishes "Che Guevara" heroics, autopsies barrio-martyrs, and kicks the liver of Raza-image media makers. They are sexual and sensual—dangerous with their audience and merciless with their own personal histories.

Another male group with a similar aesthetic is the Los Angeles–based group The Chicano Secret Service. There are two exciting things to note: the first is that the comedy-troupe in its own forms of seguey monologues has replaced the old Teatro ensemble made popular decades ago by the Luis Valdez agit-prop street theatre model (even in its newer sheen of contemporary playhouse appeal). The second realization (and perhaps the most significant) is that these new verbal art troupes and performance events are new outlets for an unleashed Latino male poetics.

More about the *Speakerly Master*—using Lorca's famous phrase that he used to refer to his own mouth—*"mi boca es un establo de oro."*

In our poetics of response (to our oppression), we have co-created a fine-featured figure that we imagined as our oppressor. We made Him with words, mostly; our "golden" mouth gave *Him* texture, image, sound and ultimately, being. The dominant feature of the *Speakerly Master* is that He also has only one side. He is, to a large degree, our construction, which means we are free to *disassemble* Him at will.

III. Frida's Bed

We carry something different that up to this point has been undecipherable (even under the most prolonged campaigns of scrutiny). This is good.

There is an idea of sickness attached to the figure of our reassigned body. Our shatterings have been taken into high account (Of course, the Master-surgeon admitted that it was an accident— maybe, there is a sense of guilt, remorse, bad training.) A rush order is in the making—the clinic awaits us. At home, they point to Frida's bed, an art-bed-studio where we can rehearse our limbs, torsos that twitch at midnight. And the left foot, still immobilized in the sack of a pink squid. Everything seems to be at our reach now—

especially paint and canvas. We are left with the choice of re-figuring ourselves—however, mostly in a supine position, laying down in the bed, staring at the canopy with a mirror, once in a while we will look out from our clinic sheets: the syrup colored doorway bends, a staircase reminds us of prolongation and the varying degrees of music that lead upwards (the walls are made of volcanic stone, the kind that has a porous, blackish skin that breathes and hums like Peruvian quenas *with furious winds at the tips). A meticulous aura permeates (as in all clinics). The rain comes down quietly outside, nurturing the small garden that we can no longer reach with our new cast bones.*

Frida's Aria moves on to the figures *sickness, art-bed-studio,* and *supine.* No matter where we turn—toward the song or away from the song—we carry the sense of gravity. There is something uncanny and meticulous in the scream-song, something that feels close to a bed of finely calibrated weights—a structure that only permits us to glance skyward, to toss up our lines, our brush of rage. This is only possible, of course, if we remain stricken, if we remain laying down, looking up—*supine.*

There is a Chicano mural supposed to have been the first painted on a bridge over a barrio-occupied park in the United States. It stands above the toxic waste of naval and industrial residue in the shredded barrio of Logan Heights, in San Diego, California. A crew of local Chicanos banded together as *Toltecas en Aztlán* in 1971, occupied various city-owned buildings and compounds, and by 1973, in the month of March, "attacked the walls" as Salvador "Queso" Torres says in *Chicano Park,* a film about the incident. Almost twenty years later, across California and the Southwest, hundreds of murals cover storefronts, churches, *Galerías,* schools, bookstores, bridges, freeways, hospitals, apartment villas, archways, alleys and transit stations.

Look up and you will see images of *campesinos,* farmworker families, *vatos locos, chucas firmes, abuelitas, vírgenes,* low riders, *pintos, chavalitos, indios, danzantes, calacas, teatros,* pyramids, universities, armies, jaguars, eagles, deer, corn, lettuce, shrapnel, mountains and rivers. Recently, in San Francisco's Mission District, on the corner of 24th Street and Van Ness, the last standing mural by *Las Mujeres Muralistas* was torn down by a new restaurant enterprise. And yet, the Chicana *muralistas* continue tackling buildings and school fronts even if the walls are to be whitewashed or demolished.

There is a *gesture* or drama of *verticality* that permeates all murals and many of our literary works. There seems to be a notion or desire for ascendance—to go up. There is also an ancillary set of feelings and reflections that have to do with affliction—being sick. That is, if you are not sick, if you are well, you can get up and interact with things in a horizontal plane. At one level, verticality in our aesthetics has led to narrow-minded and idolatrous nationalist rhetoric, but it has also brought about a great interest in Pre-conquest histories and theory, a renewed sense of spirituality, a populist and communal art that has to do with ideology, the impact of revitalization movements and with symbols and their subversions.

Can we get up from the Art-Bed? If not, what is keeping us from moving our limbs? Has this paralysis been assigned—how? Are we forever condemned to write, speak, and act from a *supine* position, to always look up from our *art-bed-studio?* Is there an intrinsic "sickness" positioned in the rhetoric of culture, in terms like "ethnic art" and "minority literature"? Can the dispossessed artist break away from the text of sickness unto death?

At an inner-directed level the notions of sickness and, in turn, healing have been explored by various Latina writers and artists, such as Juanalicia, Yolanda M. López and Gloria Anzaldúa. On the West Coast, magical performance work is being done by artists like Margarita Luna Robles and Guadalupe Vásquez. Ritual, pilgrimage, secular shrine-construction and oracle work are a few of the processes that women artists are using to conjure their new texts and senses of spirit and community. Archaic and quotidian wounds are healed; new senses of self, other, and body are identified and released.

In a few cases, male writers and artists have formed their own healing circles. Francisco X. Alarcón accomplishes this through his book *Snake Poems: An Aztec Invocation,* a text realized by reimagining and re-possessing the spirit of Hernando Ruiz de Alarcón in 1629 through his work *Tratado de las supertisiones de los naturales de esta Nueva España.* All this is related to and yet quite different from the "sick" text that is assigned to us by what I will call the *corporate literary system.*

A corporate literary system implies an informally and formally structured network of media interests in the Raza text; specifically, a corporate literary culture that compresses symbolic tellings of "who we are" in its marketeering campaigns across the globe. This is what echos over our words and becomes critical as we approach the twenty-first century and as minorities become 70 percent of the national work-force. The corporate cultural echo is heard as literary products about "minorities" are sold and produced as works of "coming-of-age America," or as "greening oppression," that is, stories of necessary hardships in the midst of impending opportunity. Another corporate-genre has to do with stories of "fossilized folkness," where we engage in our quaint renditions of language and spirit journeys.

The corporate literary process is in the business of imposing a super-text. The writers and artists are not positioned according to their work and status in the world as free agents and/or unknown entities. Rather, a set of symbolic and economic conditions are being maneuvered: a looking up to cultural and material salvation and healing. In short, the minority-body is seen as afflicted; it is immobilized, it lays down. There is nuance and texture in the festive bed and from that rhetorical frame, on occasion, the body looks up with a neck full of hope, prayer, hunger and memory; the paying of tribute to Mega-America.

~~~~~

We go back to Frida's own major figure—*"Yo soy la desintegración."* Is this the deep scream unleashed five hundred years ago? Is this the unending shout that permeates all arenas of destruction and renewal?

Disintegration is *still* here, now. The world and its old "centers" and meanings are being dissassembled. Landless peoples, the dispossessed (the ones assumed to be always in search of themselves) have posited new languages, texts, and social formations. And we are not really left with How? Why? Whom? Once we faced Columbus and his Empire-Europe, now we are left facing Master-America, knowing it has not and will not *discover* us. As we tumble toward the twenty-first century and its various new demarcations, Master-America stands mute—simply stands mute with all its sundry attachments to itself and its failed machinations—without discovery.

Notes

1. Original version by Guillermo Prieto: *Hay en San Francisco, como en todos los Estados Unidos, un tipo altamente repugnante: el mexicano ayankado. Usa bota fuerte, esgrime estupenda navaja, con la que pule y aguza sus uñas, labra palos y se limpia los dientes; habla poco y siempre en inglés, casi se acuesta boca arriba y fija los pies en una mesa, ó un barrote, ó la pared, bebe* wiskey, *masca tabaco, da sendos apretones de mano al primero que le habla y salpica con desvergüenzas desde el saludo, llamándose a los ojos su machucado y desgovernado sombrero.*
2. Gloria Anzaldúa, *Borderlands/La Frontera: The New Mestiza* (San Francisco, Spinsters/Aunt Lute, 1987).
3. Original version by Sor Juana Inés de la Cruz: *Muy ilustre Señora: No mi voluntad, mi poca salud y mi justo temor han suspendido tantos días mi respuesta. ¿Qué mucho si, al primer paso, encontraba para tropezar mi torpe pluma dos imposibles? El primero (y para mi el más riguroso) es saber responder a vuestra doctísima, santísima y amorísima carta.* Translation here by Margaret Sayers Peden. From *A Woman of Genius: The Intellectual Autobiography of Sor Juana Inés de la Cruz* (Lime Rock, 1982).
4. Original version by Yolanda Luera:

   mis entrañas me
   gritan un hijo
   y yo me niego
   mi vientre pide
   abultarse, hincharse
   y yo me niego
   mis labios quieren
   cantar canciones de
   cuna y yo me niego
   yo me niego
   y yo me…

5. Margarita Luna Robles, "I Am the Chicana You Thought Was a Mexicana," *El Tecalote Literario*, Vol 4, No. 2.
6. Victor Hernández Cruz, *Red Beans* (Minneapolis, Minn.: Coffee House, 1991).
7. Jimmy Santiago-Baca, "Meditations on the South Valley," *Martin and Meditations on the South Valley* (New York: New Directions, 1987).
8. Gary Soto, "Who will know us?" *Who Will Know Us?* (San Francisco: Chronicle Books, 1990).
9. Ray Gonzalez, "Twilight and Chants," *Twilights and Chants.* (James Andrews & Co., 1988).

10. The improvisations appearing here are from a larger, unpublished text, *Tell Frida I Love Her.* I thank Margarita Luna Robles, Lesley Link, and Susan Dever for their insights and criticism.

Linda Hogan

Journeys and Other Stories

It is daybreak in the canyon. A horned owl has just become silent. The seepage on canyon walls is in the thin shape of ancient people stepping out from stone as if to witness morning. Clay. Stone. Sand. In the first light of the southwestern land, there is a hint of moisture. Soon there are shadows, then lizard tracks crossing sand, the curling motion of a snake moving into warm sun. These are a language land speaks to travelers in canyons. It is the whisper that draws us to land, a language something like a memory inside us, of wilderness, of an ancient past. It has a beautiful and magnetic longing to it, this mystery of hands on canyon walls, the stories of people who built dwellings of stone so well the walls remain long after the people are gone.

Most of us journey to the land because of that mystery. It is a pilgrimage of sorts. We need, without the saying of it, to see the arrow-shaped deer tracks, fossils, shards of an older civilization, to read the language of an ancient past that is still being spoken in stone, by wind, in petroglyphs. We want to weave together the threads of where we come from with what we are now and where we are going. Our human journey here joins with the stories of snake, owl, lizard, the far-traveling winds and curving waters. We gauge our place by these stories, by our movement, and by our defining the fierce human struggle for survival, for whatever meaning and revelation live in this burning light of day.

We bring to this terrain not only our individual stories, but the larger one that contains them, the one we call history. EuroAmerican history, that is, which has become the main surviving record of what has taken place on this continent.

Most of us think of this history as the accurate record of what has been before us, but we seldom consider how it has been logged and told. Less often do we consider what material is added or re-

223

moved in the telling, but time after time, new information, new stories, rise up through the words and pages of history to assert themselves and shift the story all about. And accounts of the conquest of the American continent are some of the stories still being revised and retold as many contemporary historians are searching not for a story of European arrival on this continent, but for the story of what actually took place.

In considering the new information, it might be best for us to think of those fifteenth-century voyages in their context of time and place, especially since we are finding that we have reached the limits of a way of thinking and living that had its origins in that world where the thinkers and scientists held that the earth was flat and that there was grave danger in traveling toward the ends of the water or land. A man, a ship, they feared, might be carried down into the land of demons, the dangerous, animal-filled wilderness, and fiery hell.

At that time, what is now called "America" was not yet even a seed planted in the mind of its explorers and conquerors. There were no prophecies about this continent; no land mass was even accounted for at that time. A heaven with gold-paved streets lived inside the minds of Europeans, and a far God who didn't live on land but in a distant place with mansions, gold, and winged people, those who had lived well enough to escape the earth. The dominant belief system looked away from land. It was not based, as tribal systems are, on matter, earth, or even the sanctity of life. It did not value the plants or animals that fed the people. The living world was not a sacred, alive thing. The people did not learn to know their own land. They did not know how to maintain a working agriculture that was successful without depleting the soil, and by the time three ships set sail in search of what they came to call "Paradise," the European continent was deforested, the land exhausted. It was a failed belief system even in their own words and biblical terms; by their fruits shall you know them, because the fruits of that society were hunger, plague, and violence. The system, in that time, did not deliver the Europeans. There was no salvation in it. Not only was it lacking in depth and compassion, but it also hadn't established significant values or paid heed to the most plain and common sense that would allow the land to thrive.

In his book *The Conquest of Paradise*, Kirkpatrick Sale writes about European life in the fifteenth century, that "death was so daily, brutality so commonplace, destruction of the animate and inanimate so customary that it is shocking even in our own age of mass destruction."

Out of this wounded, destroyed world, men set sail in search of resources they could take home with them. These were voyages of desperation and necessity. And as much as they did not know or understand the land they were leaving, the one already laid waste, they did not have the capacity to understand, learn, or even describe the ancient and viable world they came, without clear vision, to call "new."

As their own stories note, they wanted what humans could never have, cities of gold, the elixir of youth, eternal life. And just as they were lost in these childlike desires, they were lost physically at sea.

They sailed into a deep fatigue. It was a bitter journey as they searched for land. In the words of Columbus, from his journals, everything became a sign of land: birds that were believed not to live out at sea, rafts of floating vegetation. On September 19, 1492, rain fell and "this was certain indication of land." On the twenty-first, he reports that his men saw a whale, "which is sign that they were near land." On September 26, what they thought was land revealed itself as only a cloud. The sailors were "alarmed and depressed." On October 8, they saw "certain land," but, proceeding in that direction, they found only fresh vegetation and what they thought were land birds. The day of October 10 the men "complained of the long voyage."

Finally, on the eleventh of October they saw a stick, carved by a human hand, floating on the sea and knew they were near land. On landing, they were greeted by people, described by Columbus in a letter to the king. He wrote that "they have no iron or steel or weapons, nor are they fitted to use them…because they are marvellously timorous. They have no other arms than spears made of canes." He also noted their generosity, that "they refuse nothing that they possess, if it be asked of them; on the contrary, they invite anyone to share it and display as much love as if they would give their hearts." These are the same traits that Columbus later said would make the people good "slaves," in the service of the king. That first encounter with the Arawaks proved to be a fatal one that left the entire indigenous population extinct.

The old land, new to the voyagers, bore bountiful fruit, and was green and rich, but it was seen as having no importance because it did not, at first, yield the mythical riches and gold that the Europeans sought and valued. From a contemporary perspective these men's ignorance about the world was a not-knowing that had devastating consequences for people and for the land, as much as it had in their own land, with their own people. Their system of belief, their manner of living, came full force into collision with other systems, ones that had been tried and time-tested and whose key common element was a balanced and healthy relationship with land, wilderness, and other forms of life.

The Indian people had, and in many places still have, considerable knowledge of the land. Survival depended on it, as it does now. Before the Europeans arrived, Peacemaker of the Iroquois Nation had spoken his own vision of a healthy society where human beings whose minds are healthy desire peace. Righteousness, Peacemaker said, occurs when people put their minds and emotions in harmony with the flow of the universe:

> The principles of Righteousness demand that all thoughts of
> prejudice, privilege or superiority be swept away and that
> recognition be given to the reality that the creation is intended
> for the benefit of all equally—even the birds and animals, the
> trees and the insects, as well as the humans.

Centuries of this understanding and working relationship between people and the rest of the natural world went unrecognized by the new arrivals. The life of this American continent, the vision of a balanced system, did not fit into the European world view and categories of thought. What was old, what was time-tested and functional, was changed, broken, and bent to fit the very system that had made the voyages necessary. Natural systems, now called ecology, were simply not understood by those who came from the European cultures and belief systems.

It has become increasingly clear to most historians and thinkers that the conquerers were mentally unbalanced, even delusional men. They were on an impossible journey, fueled by insatiable wants. It could be said that this obsessive search became the

Linda Hogan

center of a madness, one with severe biological and ecological consequences, a madness that destroyed volumes of highly evolved medical information, astronomy, and mathematics as it burned the words and memories of those they believed to be savages. This madness became our joint legacy, of Indians and non-Indians alike, a shared heritage that still defines our lives, is still lived out in the daily ongoing violation of land and human and animal lives. The attempt to shape the world according to what had not worked in Europe, did not work here either.

We are at the end of that way of knowing, that madness. It is as if we have finally reached the limit of that once-flat world, and are falling over. We are almost at the end of ocean, wilderness, and fragile desert. The world is finite, and only now is the intelligence of the natural world, long understood by Native Americans, revealing itself to science as researchers discover that birds find their way to an unknown home by magnetic fields and the sounds of fish beneath the water, that the songs of whales are not only complex and intelligent, but also able to stun squid into stillness. There is even now a newly emerging biology, one not based on the Darwinian model of survival of the fittest and evolution of individual organisms or species, but a biology that recognizes cooperation and relationship, one that allows for the health and survival of all, another concept that tribal people knew at the time of first white contact.

We stand together at the place where the failed European system of belief has led us, at the threshold to the endangered world, at limits stretched to breaking. Too much is moving over the edge, species and lives falling over the end of the earth. We face the possibility of a lifeless earth, a future that will not house us. We have no choice but to face ourselves, history, our fears, and the challenge of change. This time there is no slipping over the horizon to find, magically, that the world will extend itself for us, beyond the horizon, beyond water or land.

If we are going to heal, we have to swallow the bitter tea of memory, to let our stories be remembered And it Is not just us, or the rest of the natural world that needs healing, but meaning, history, and destiny. We need to find a way to join our two kinds of vision, to mend the wounds of a destructive past.

In whatever way we have come to this land, as tourists, resi-

227

dents, or pilgrims, we have come to find what is still unexplored and mysterious, within and without ourselves. We have come for the silence that embraces us, the feel of what's ancient, the safe fold in the universe that feeds our lives.

We are looking for a deepening, expanded, and liberating vision of the world, a different story to live by as we seek to restore the relationships between ourselves and land, between ourselves and others, between then and now.

We have traveled the distance of earth, the depths of water, traveled to the moon, explored the frozen blue-white poles of the planet, journeyed inside the ice and fire of earth, and what we know is that this is home, and that it demands understanding. Until we learn the land, we will not know who we are, it will turn against us, we will remain ignorant and small and helpless.

Hungry for the dimensions of our lives, we think we are not snake, fish, bird, but there is an uncanny knowing that we are part of sand, wind, water, fire, the elemental world millions of years old. We are carbon, hydrogen, oxygen. We are song and possibility, part of THE story, moment by moment holding history in a hand as it unfolds. The land is our elder. It knows and speaks an older history. It has a living memory, a terrestrial intelligence we have betrayed. It holds its own stories and is alive.

It could have been another way, the coming together of all these stories. Think of what it could have been. Think of what it yet may be.

Note

Peacemaker's speech appears in *A Basic Call to Consciousness*, (Mohawk Nation via Rooseveltown, New York: Akwesasne Notes). Other information is from Kirkpatrick Sale, *The Conquest of Paradise* (New York: Alfred Knopf, 1990).

John Nichols is the author of many novels, including *The Milagro Beanfield War*, *The Magic Journey*, and *Nirvana Blues*. He lives in Taos, New Mexico.

Wendy Rose is the author of six books of poetry, including *Builder Kachina: A Home Going Cycle* and *What Happened When the Hope Hit New York*. She is the coordinator of American Indian Studies at Fresno City College in Fresno, California.

Victor Hernández Cruz is the author of six books of poetry, including *Rhythm, Content, and Flavor: Selected Poems* and *Red Beans*. He is a former heavyweight champion of The Taos Poetry Circus and lives in Aguas Buenas, Puerto Rico.

Robert Allen Warrior is a leading Native American activist who has been involved in organizing numerous organizations for the benefit of his people. He lives in Minneapolis, Minnesota.

Rudolfo Anaya is the author of several novels, including the legendary Chicano novel, *Bless Me Ultima*. His other books include *Aztlán* and *A Chicano in China*. He is the editor of *The Blue Mesa Review* and teaches at The University of New Mexico in Albuquerque.

Francisco X. Alarcón is the author of six books of poetry, including *Body in Flames* and *The Snake Poems*. He is a prolific translator and has done extensive research on ancient Nuahtl texts. He teaches at The University of California at Santa Cruz.

Diane Glancy is the author of several books of poetry, short fiction, and essays. Her most recent poetry collections are *Iron Woman* and *Lone Dog's Winter Count*. She received a Fiction Collective Prize for her book of short stories, *Trigger Dance*. She teaches at MacAlister College in St. Paul, Minnesota.

Ed Chávez has written a number of articles for educational publications and is the author of numerous stories for children and young adults. He lives in Albuquerque, New Mexico.

José Barreiro is the editor and publisher of *The Northeast Indian Quarterly*. He is a contributing editor to *Native Nations* magazine, a publication that supports the sovereignty of indigenous peoples. He lives in New York City.

Carlos Muñoz, Jr., teaches Chicano Studies at The University of California at Berkeley and is a contributing editor to *CrossRoads* magazine.

Suzan Shown Harjo is president and director of The Morning Star Foundation in Washington, D.C., an organization formed to provide an indigenous people's response to the Columbus Quincentenary. Her poetry and fiction have appeared in numerous journals in the United States.

Barbara Miner, Suzan Shown Harjo's interviewer, is the editor and publisher of *Rethinking Columbus,* an educational publication that features multicultural writing and alternative views about American education and history.

Gerald Vizenor is the author of numerous novels and nonfiction collections, including *Crossbloods,* a book of essays; *Interior Landscapes,* an autobiography; and *The Heirs of Columbus,* a novel. He teaches Native American Studies at The University of California at Berkeley.

Alicia Gaspar de Alba is the author of a book of short stories, *The Beggar at the Cordoba Bridge,* and one of three Chicana poets featured in the anthology *Three Times a Woman.* She teaches at The University of New Mexico in Albuquerque.

Alberto Alvaro Ríos received The Walt Whitman Prize in Poetry for his first collection, *Whispering to Fool the Wind.* His other books of poetry include *Orchard Woman* and *Teodore Luna's Three Kisses.* His collection of short fiction, *The Iguana Killer,* received a Western States Book Award. He teaches at Arizona State University in Tempe.

Benjamin Alire Sáenz is the author of a book of poetry, *Calendar of Dust,* and a book of short stories, *Flowers for the Broken.* He is a former Wallace Stegner Fellow at Stanford University and will teach in the first bilingual MFA program in the United States, to begin at The University of Texas in El Paso in the fall of 1992.

Ray Young Bear is the author of several books of poetry, including *Winter of the Salamander* and *The Invisible Musician.* He lives in Tama, Iowa.

Inés Hernandez is a poet, essayist, and musician who was a leader in the Chicano movement of the early seventies. Her work has appeared in numerous publications, including *This Bridge Called My Back: Writings by Radical Women of Color.* She teaches in the Ethnic Studies Program at The University of California at Davis.

Victoria Lena Manyarrows has worked extensively with Native American community arts, alcohol/substance abuse, and domestic violence programs in the San Francisco area. She is a visual artist and writer whose paintings and writings have been exhibited and published throughout the United States. She lives in San Francisco.

Ray Gonzalez is the author of two books of poetry and editor of eight anthologies, including *After Aztlán: Latino Poets in the Nineties* and *Mirrors Beneath the Earth: Chicano Short Fiction.* He received a 1988 Colorado Governor's Award for Excellence in the Arts and is the literature director at The Guadalupe Cultural Arts Center in San Antonio, Texas.

Roberta Fernández received a 1991 Book Award from The Multicultural Publishers Exchange for her first collection of fiction, *Intaglio: A Novel in Six Stories.* She is an assistant editor at Arte Publico Press and teaches at The University of Houston.

Juan Felipe Herrera is the author of numerous books of poetry including *Akrilica, Rebozos of Love,* and the Before Columbus Foundation Award winner, *Facegames.* He teaches Chicano Studies at Fresno State University in Fresno, California.

Linda Hogan is the author of several books of poetry and fiction, including *Seeing Through the Sun, Eclipse, Savings,* and the novel *Mean Spirit.* She has received numerous awards for her writing, including a National Endowment for the Arts fellowship. She teaches at The University of Colorado in Boulder.

Design by Nick Gregoric.

Text set in Aster, using
the KI/Composer and Linotron 202N
by Blue Fescue Typography and Design,
Seattle, Washington.

Printed on recycled, acid-free paper
by Maple-Vail, York, Pennsylvania.